The BBC presents the 121st season of Henry Wood Promenade Concerts, broadcasting every Prom live on BBC Radio 3

BBC MUSIC

BBC PROMS 2015 AT A GLANCE

76 PROMS
AT THE ROYAL ALBERT HALL

Performances from leading international orchestras, artists and conductors:

58 MAIN EVENING CONCERTS

12 LATE NIGHT PROMS
After-dark adventures – from sublime solo Bach to swinging Sinatra

6 MATINEE CONCERTS
Proms for all the family, including Life Story, Ten Pieces and Sherlock Holmes

78 PROMS EXTRAS
AT THE ROYAL COLLEGE OF MUSIC

A complementary festival of free workshops, introductions and participation events, as well as Proms Extra Lates (post-concert jazz and poetry at the Royal Albert Hall) – all launched by Daniel Levitin's Proms Lecture

12 PROMS
AT CADOGAN HALL

8 PROMS CHAMBER MUSIC CONCERTS, MONDAYS 1.00PM
From Thomas Tallis to Stephen Sondheim

4 PROMS SATURDAY MATINEES, SATURDAYS 3.00PM
Baroque and new music ensembles

ENGLAND, N. IRELAND SCOTLAND & WALES

The Last Night magic – in the Royal Albert Hall and at Last Night celebrations around the UK – also on BBC Radio, TV and Online

BBC RADIO

Every Prom live on BBC Radio 3; collaborations with BBC Radio 1, 1Xtra, 2, 4, 6 Music and BBC Asian Network

BBC TV

Proms on BBC Four each week; First and Last Nights on BBC Two/ BBC One; weekly *Proms Extra* (BBC Two); Ten Pieces Prom on CBBC

BBC ONLINE

Listen/watch again for 30 days after broadcast – and explore curated clips – at the BBC Proms website

BBC PROMS GUIDE 2015 CONTENTS

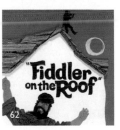

CONCERT LISTINGS

BOOKING

VENUE INFORMATION

INDEXES

FOR THE FIRST TIME, THIS GUIDE IS AVAILABLE AS AN APP!

Fully optimised for iOS and Android on mobile and tablet – download the new Proms Guide app from app stores for £2.99

BBC *Concert* ORCHESTRA

BBC Proms – Live in Concert on BBC Radio 3
– Friday Night is Music Night on BBC Radio 2
BBC Concert Orchestra. Expect the unexpected...

bbc.co.uk/concertorchestra to find out what's on and sign up to our newsletter.
@bbcco or facebook.com/bbcconcertorchestra

ASSOCIATE AT
**SOUTHBANK
CENTRE**

BBC National Orchestra & Chorus of Wales present

THE 2015/16 SEASON

Rachmaninov	Mozart	Poulenc
Handel	Debussy	John Adams
Sibelius	Gershwin	Bernstein
Mahler	Prokofiev	Bartók
Beethoven	Huw Watkins	Dutilleux
Ginastera	Vivaldi	Grieg

15 May — 14 Jun

J.M.BARRIE'S
PETER PAN

by arrangement with Great Ormond Street Hospital Children's Charity
recommended ages 9+

19 Jun — 11 Jul

THE SEAGULL

by **ANTON CHEKHOV**
in a new version by **TORBEN BETTS**

16 Jul — 29 Aug

SEVEN BRIDES FOR SEVEN BROTHERS

Book by **LAWRENCE KASHA** and **DAVID S. LANDAY**
Music by **GENE DE PAUL** Lyrics by **JOHNNY MERCER**
New songs by **AL KASHA** and **JOEL HIRSCHHORN**
Based on the MGM Film and *The Sobbin' Women* by Stephen Vincent Benet

03 Sep — 12 Sep

WILLIAM GOLDING'S
LORD OF THE FLIES

adapted for the stage by **NIGEL WILLIAMS**

**REGENT'S PARK
OPEN AIR THEATRE**

0844 826 4242
openairtheatre.com

CLASSIC *f*M

THE ROYAL PARKS

LOVE
MUSIC
HELP
MUSICIANS UK

"Being a musician is a thrilling career but the constant striving to be the best, combined with an unpredictable lifestyle and earnings, can leave some musicians with nothing to fall back on.

That's why I support Help Musicians UK. If you love and care about music, please support Help Musicians UK too."

Sir Simon Rattle
Help Musicians UK Ambassador

helpmusicians.org.uk
020 7239 9100

BBC Philharmonic

Inspiration with Every Note

Performing at six concerts at this year's BBC Proms.
On air on BBC Radio 3.
At home in MediaCityUK, Salford.
In residence at The Bridgewater Hall, Manchester.
Touring regionally, nationally and internationally.
Connecting with communities where they live.

Find out more, sign up for our e-newsletter, Quay Notes:
bbc.co.uk/philharmonic

Follow us:

BBC RADIO 3

Photograph by Simon Pantling

WELCOME TO THE
2015 BBC PROMS

This year is the year of Nielsen and Sibelius; of Bach and Boulez; of Sinatra, Sondheim and Bernstein; of piano concertos by Mozart, Beethoven and Prokofiev; of choral masterpieces by Verdi, Elgar and Walton; of Ten Pieces and *Life Story*; of family Sunday Matinees and adventurous Late Nights. This is also the year of the Proms Guide app – for the first time you can download this book customised for your mobile devices (see *Contents*).

It's 120 years since Henry Wood raised his baton to conduct the very first Prom on 10 August 1895 at the Queen's Hall in London. 'I can see the packed house now,' he wrote in his autobiography, 'and hear the welcome I received.' Packed houses and welcoming audiences are happily still very much part of every Proms season – thanks to so many of you who are reading this and who continue to make the Proms the joyous celebration of great music that was Sir Henry's original ambition. He cared passionately that the Proms should be accessible and affordable and thanks to the BBC, which took over the running of the Proms in 1927, those ideals continue to be at the forefront of every season. So in a very real way we feel closely connected to Sir Henry in this anniversary year. With 88 concerts at the Royal Albert Hall and Cadogan Hall, plus daily Proms Extra events at the Royal College of Music, there is something for everyone – and Promming (standing) tickets, introduced right from the start in 1895 to make the Proms relaxed and informal, remain at £5.00 for the 10th year running. That all this is possible is, of course, due entirely to the support of the BBC through you, the licence-fee payers.

New this year is a series of Sunday Matinees at the Royal Albert Hall, with programmes designed for all the family, while six of the Late Nights showcase the cutting-edge musical worlds of BBC Radio 1, 1Xtra, 2, 4, 6 Music and the BBC Asian Network. Each of these stations joins forces with Radio 3 – which, as ever, broadcasts every Prom live – plus there's BBC Television and BBC Online to enrich your Proms Summer, wherever you are, and reach the widest possible audiences.

Clockwise from left: Composer Shiori Usui, who receives her first BBC Proms commission; Alina Ibragimova is one of four leading artists to tackle solo Bach in the Royal Albert Hall; *Fiddler on the Roof* comes to the Proms in Grange Park Opera's production, featuring Bryn Terfel as the struggling dairyman Tevye

Central to the Sunday Matinee on 2 August is Beethoven's 'Pastoral' Symphony, performed from memory by the Aurora Orchestra under Nicholas Collon. The sheer brainpower required to achieve this is one of the subjects covered by the distinguished American neuroscientist Daniel Levitin in his Proms Lecture during the opening weekend – just one of over 75 Proms Extra events designed to enhance your appreciation and enjoyment of the huge range of music on offer throughout the season. The Sunday Matinees will also investigate the musical brain of that iconic sleuth Sherlock Holmes; explore Sir David Attenborough's breathtaking television series,

Life Story; celebrate Ten Pieces – the exciting BBC initiative encouraging participation and musical creativity in primary schools – and welcome the European premiere of Eric Whitacre's new choral-orchestral work, *Deep Field*, inspired by the literally other-worldly photographs of distant galaxies sent back to Earth from the Hubble Space Telescope.

The exploration of new musical worlds has always been a vital element of the Proms' DNA. In his first season, Henry Wood introduced audiences to extracts from recent operas by Massenet and Richard Strauss, and some years later he famously added to

his 'novelties', as he called them, the UK premiere of the ultra-modern *Five Orchestral Pieces* by Arnold Schoenberg. This year's world premieres represent the rich gamut of contemporary music and span the generations, from Alissa Firsova, Anna Meredith and Proms newcomers Joanna Lee and Shiori Usui, through Guy Barker, Michael Finnissy, Anders Hillborg and James MacMillan, to HK Gruber and Hugh Wood. There's even a recently discovered late orchestral miniature by Olivier Messiaen – a final glorious four-minute burst of birdsong! Meanwhile, the honours of launching the First and Last Nights go to Gary Carpenter and Eleanor Alberga respectively.

Major new orchestral works by Luca Francesconi and Qigang Chen and a new string quartet by Colin Matthews also come to the Proms for their London, UK or European premieres. Members of Radio 3's New Generation Artists scheme perform the quartet and the BBC's five orchestras, the BBC Singers and two BBC choruses are on hand for many of the array of premieres (32 in total) – vital contributors to the BBC's creative programming, now brought into a wider spotlight by the creation of BBC Music, which unites all aspects of musical offering in the strongest commitment to music for 30 years.

World-class talent from within the BBC has long been matched at the Proms with partner orchestras, ensembles, conductors and soloists from around the UK and visitors from abroad. Each season is a snapshot of the state of the art and a celebration of the best. There are too many highlights to list here – and you will of course find your own as you browse this Guide – but we are particularly delighted to welcome back the Boston and San Francisco Symphony orchestras with their respective music directors Andris Nelsons and Michael Tilson Thomas, and look forward to early music ensemble newcomers Apollo's Fire and B'Rock, which feature in two of the Proms Saturday Matinees at Cadogan Hall. The remaining two matinees celebrate the composer Pierre Boulez in his 90th-birthday year. Some of his most significant ensemble works will be presented by the London Sinfonietta and Birmingham Contemporary Music Group.

Nielsen and Sibelius are the two other major composers whose significant birthdays are being marked at the Proms this season. For Sibelius, the focus is on his symphonies and, for Nielsen, on his concertos, with a range of orchestras, conductors and soloists who are keen advocates for these complementary but very different Nordic composers born in 1865.

The Sultan of Swoon: Frank Sinatra, born 100 years ago, gets a birthday bash from John Wilson and his orchestra

Elsewhere in the season you will find a running thread of piano concertos. We begin with the complete Beethoven concertos as Leif Ove Andsnes concludes his four-year cycle of living, playing and recording these wonderful works. They unfold over three evenings, while the five Prokofiev concertos will be shared by three different pianists in a single Prom and six of Mozart's late great piano concertos will run as a thread throughout the season with a different soloist playing each one. We also hear Mozart's Concerto for two pianos and, at Cadogan Hall, his Quintet for piano and winds, as the weekly lunchtime Proms Chamber Music series continues to elaborate on the themes of the season.

Finally, do check out the operas by Monteverdi, Mozart and Shostakovich; *Fiddler on the Roof* in the production by Grange Park Opera; music for stage and screen highlighting Sinatra and Bernstein; and the many major choral works that will find a thrilling home in the expansive spaces of the Royal Albert Hall. And we're delighted to welcome back Marin Alsop to conduct the Last Night of the Proms in a link-up between the Hall and four Last Night celebrations across the UK to round off the season in festive style. True to the pioneering spirit of Henry Wood, the BBC Proms continues to pursue big ambitions and ever wider horizons. As we travel together on that journey, I do hope you have a glorious musical summer! ●

Edward Blakeman
Director, BBC Proms 2015

ALAN DAVEY
Controller,
BBC Radio 3

A very warm welcome to the 2015 BBC Proms. The Proms is a key part of what BBC Radio 3 is all about: it's the time when we produce and broadcast — on air, in HD Sound online — the biggest and broadest classical music festival in the world. As always, we are broadcasting every Prom live so, even if you can't make it in person to the Royal Albert Hall or Cadogan Hall, you can hear every note throughout the summer from the best seat in the house; and you can see many Proms on BBC Television.

The Proms is also an important part of the mission of BBC Music: to make the best and most interesting music in the world available — live, recorded or on-demand — to the widest audience.

We are proud of the breadth of the Proms and of the number of people who take the festival to their hearts and experience the thrill of great music live or via catch-up for 30 days, at home or wherever they happen to be. All year round, Radio 3 offers an unparalleled mix of live music – classical, jazz, world, contemporary and just plain interesting – as well as informed comment on culture and ideas, and unique drama. It's all placed in context by an unequalled line-up of informed and enthusiastic presenters and guest experts.

It all adds up to a world of discovery and exploration that extends the spirit of the Proms the whole year round. Have a great Proms 2015.

BBC
SCOTTISH SYMPHONY
ORCHESTRA

Chief Conductor Donald Runnicles
Principal Guest Conductor Ilan Volkov
Artist-In-Association Matthias Pintscher
Chief Conductor-Designate Thomas Dausgaard

2015/16 Season includes

MAHLER Symphonies 1 & 10

BRAHMS Piano Concertos
with Denis Kozhukhin

80TH BIRTHDAY CONCERT
conducted by Matthias Pintscher

UNSUK CHIN Concertos for violin,
sheng, and clarinet

As well as appearances at the 2015 Edinburgh
International Festival, and our regular concert
series in Aberdeen, Ayr, Edinburgh, Inverness
and Perth.

BBC SSO at the Proms

Prom 23 VERDI
Requiem with Donald Runnicles

Prom 24 MAHLER
Fifth Symphony with
Donald Runnicles

Prom 40 SIBELIUS
First and Second Symphonies
with Thomas Dausgaard

Prom 42 SIBELIUS
Third and Fourth Symphonies
with Ilan Volkov

bbc.co.uk/bbcsso
facebook.com/bbcsso
twitter.com/bbcsso

BBC
MUSIC

BBC SINGERS

Join the BBC Singers for a thrilling, typically diverse series of concerts in Milton Court Concert Hall as part of their 2015-16 season.

"... renowned pitch-perfect accuracy and radiance."
The Guardian

St Giles' Cripplegate

CONCERTS IN MILTON COURT CONCERT HALL

Tickets £22, £17.50, £10 plus booking fee*

FRIDAY 16 OCTOBER 7.30PM
Monteverdi Vespers

David Hill conductor
BBC Singers
I Fagiolini
St James's Baroque

FRIDAY 18 DECEMBER 7.30PM
A Child's Christmas in Wales

Dylan Thomas's *A Child's Christmas in Wales*, in a magical presentation by the BBC Singers.

David Hill conductor
BBC Singers
Actor to be announced

THURSDAY 11 FEBRUARY 7.30PM
The Somme Remembered

Programme to include:
Music by Judith Bingham, Butterworth, Gurney, Holst, Gabriel Jackson, Ravel and Daniel Saleeh, plus readings from poetry, diaries and letters from the First World War.

Paul Brough conductor
BBC Singers
Reader to be announced

FRIDAY 15 APRIL 7.00PM
Handel's Saul

James O'Donnell conductor
Fflur Wynn soprano
Iestyn Davies counter-tenor
Robert Murray tenor
David Soar bass
BBC Singers
St James's Baroque

SINGERS AT SIX

Short concerts in St Giles' Cripplegate, complementing the BBC Symphony Orchestra's Barbican Hall concert: Mahler's Vienna, American Songs, plus music by Elgar, Judith Bingham and James MacMillan.

ST PAUL'S KNIGHTSBRIDGE

Free concerts in the Victorian splendour of St Paul's Knightsbridge, featuring a wide range of glorious choral music.

bbc.co.uk/singers for full details of all events including our exciting learning projects, and to sign up for our free e-newsletter.

@BBCSingers facebook.com/BBCSingers

BBC RADIO 3: Broadcast on BBC Radio 3 and streamed online

*Booking fees: £3 per transaction for online booking. £4 by phone. No fee when tickets are booked in person. Fees correct at time of going to print.

120 YEARS OF THE PROMS

When the 26-year-old Henry Wood raised his baton at the first Proms concert, on 10 August 1895, no-one could have known whether the festival would take wing. As it happened, Wood presided over the Proms, practically single-handedly, for almost 50 years.

Over the 120 years since the first season, the scale and range of the Proms have changed dramatically – not least in the number of visiting international soloists, conductors and orchestras. However, the original vision of making the best music available to the widest possible audience – and of offering Promming (standing) tickets at an affordable price – still underpins the Proms today. As does Wood's passion for new works – which led him to champion the latest pieces by Tchaikovsky, Rachmaninov, Debussy, Schoenberg and Sibelius, as well as the music of countless British composers.

1895

49 Concerts
18 Pieces per concert *(avg.)*
12 Premieres
0 Visiting ensembles

❙ CONDUCTOR

Henry Wood

❙ ORCHESTRA
Queen's Hall Orchestra

COST OF PROMMING 1s

VENUES

Queen's Hall

1915

61 Concerts
12 Pieces per concert *(avg.)*
10 Premieres
0 Visiting ensembles

❙ CONDUCTOR

Henry Wood

❙ ORCHESTRA
Queen's Hall Orchestra

COST OF PROMMING 1s

VENUES

Queen's Hall

1935

49 Concerts
8 Pieces per concert *(avg.)*
7 Premieres
0 Visiting ensembles

❙ CONDUCTOR

Henry Wood

❙ ORCHESTRA
BBC Symphony Orchestra

COST OF PROMMING 2s

VENUES

Queen's Hall

1895

1902 First appearance at the Proms of Elgar's 'Land of Hope and Glory' (as part of the *Coronation Ode*), with the composer conducting

1912 Wood conducts the UK premiere of Arnold Schoenberg's *Five Orchestral Pieces*

1915

1914–18 National anthems of the Allied countries are played at the beginning of each concert (1914–15); flags of the Allied nations displayed above the organ

1927 BBC takes over running of the Proms

1932 First radio broadcast of a Prom

1935

1939–45 The 1939, 1940 and 1944 seasons are curtailed owing to war; a shortened 1941 season takes place at the Royal Albert Hall after the Queen's Hall is bombed; Wood conducts his final Prom on 28 July 1944 and dies the following month

1940 First televised Prom

1955

49	Concerts
6	Pieces per concert *(avg.)*
13	Premieres
0	Visiting ensembles

6 CONDUCTORS

John Barbirolli   Adrian Boult   Basil Cameron

Charles Groves   John Hollingsworth   Malcolm Sargent

7 ORCHESTRAS

COST OF PROMMING
2/6

VENUES

Royal Albert Hall

1975

57	Concerts
4	Pieces per concert *(avg.)*
3	Premieres *(world)*
2	Visiting ensembles

40 CONDUCTORS

33 ORCHESTRAS

COST OF PROMMING
50p

VENUES

 Royal Albert Hall   St Augustine's, Kilburn

 Westminster Cathedral   Roundhouse, Camden

1995

70	Concerts
4	Pieces per concert *(avg.)*
29	Premieres
16	Visiting ensembles

51 CONDUCTORS

44 ORCHESTRAS

COST OF PROMMING
£2 £3

VENUES

Royal Albert Hall

2015

92	Concerts
4	Pieces per concert *(avg.)*
32	Premieres
16	Visiting ensembles

53 CONDUCTORS

46 ORCHESTRAS

COST OF PROMMING
£5

VENUES

 Royal Albert Hall   Cadogan Hall

 Royal College of Music   Proms in the Park

1955

1961 First complete opera heard at the Proms: Mozart's *Don Giovanni*, performed by Glyndebourne Festival Opera

1966 First non British orchestra at the Proms: the Moscow Radio Orchestra under Gennady Rozhdestvensky

1975

1980 Strike action by the Musicians' Union, following a proposed disbanding of a number of BBC orchestras, results in the cancellation of the first 20 Proms of the season

1984 Odaline de la Martinez is the first female conductor to direct a complete Prom

1995

1996 First Proms Chamber Music series: eight lunchtime recitals at the Royal College of Music (later at the V&A, now at Cadogan Hall)

1997 Pianist Evgeny Kissin gives the first solo Proms recital, performing 'in the round' within the RAH Arena

2015

2003 Proms in the Park reaches out to all four nations in the UK on the Last Night with concerts in London, Belfast, Glasgow and Swansea.

2013 First performance in a single season of Wagner's opera cycle *The Ring of the Nibelung*, conducted by Daniel Barenboim

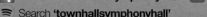 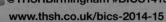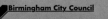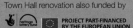

RCM

LONDON

NURTURING YOUR
FUTURE
MUSICIANS

A FORCE OF NATURE

Sibelius may have reconceived the shape of the symphony and responded with passion to national folk themes but, as **HILARY FINCH** unearths, nature was the Finnish composer's single most abiding inspiration

Jean Sibelius was born in 1865 – the year of the first successful transatlantic cable and the publication of *Alice in Wonderland*. He died in 1957 at the age of 91, just two years before the launch of the first spacecraft to reach the moon. So, what are we to make of him, almost 60 years since his death from a sudden cerebral haemorrhage at his beloved lakeside home, Ainola? He died in the evening, as his Fifth Symphony was being conducted in Helsinki, only 25 miles away, by Sir Malcolm Sargent. With each year, the Sibelius mythology deepens, intensifies, occasionally clarifies – but remains as many-layered as the Finnish folklore which meant so much to the composer. As the details of his life and work become clearer, so the quintessence of Sibelius's genius continues to elude the grasp and to resist definition.

In the early years of the 20th century, every critic and composer, throughout Europe and the USA, hailed Sibelius as the greatest living symphonist. Living in a rich cultural milieu which embraced Finnish nationalism as well as Nordic modernism, he was seen as a key player in music's future. Here was the Romantic sublime fractured by a baffling modernism; a sense of structural honing and organic development and synthesis which, as early as the first two symphonies, made listeners ask time and time again, 'But how on earth did we get here?' And, while eschewing 'modern trends' (as he called them), from the Fourth Symphony on Sibelius revealed radical attitudes to form and time which yielded, and demanded, formidable concentration. By 1924, when he composed his stern and majestic Seventh (and last surviving) Symphony, Sibelius's command of symphonic metamorphosis – his uniquely imaginative and assured handling of the form as a single, life-enhancing organism – must have left even the composer wondering exactly where he could go next.

By this time, too, Sibelius had achieved something approaching cult status. Precisely at this point, he lapsed into silence, composing virtually nothing new in the remaining 30 years of his life. Like Prospero – whom he understood well from his study of *The Tempest* – when Sibelius felt that he lacked 'spirits to enforce, art to enchant', he simply broke his staff and buried it 'certain fathoms in the earth'. More specifically, after this cruellest of self-critics had attempted to write an Eighth Symphony, he apparently destroyed the manuscript. As his beloved wife Aino laconically reported, 'There was a big bonfire here.'

By the middle of the 20th century, reverence was turning to rejection, adoration to neglect. The 1960s craved a different language: on the one hand that of the newer gods, Schoenberg and Stravinsky; on the other hand that of Mahler and Bruckner. Yet still Thomas Beecham and Ralph Vaughan Williams championed Sibelius tirelessly. Vaughan Williams once observed that 'only Sibelius could make C major sound completely fresh', so echoing Sibelius's own claim that, while other contemporary composers created 'multicoloured cocktails', he himself offered 'pure spring water'. And then, as the 21st century approached, the wheel turned once again.

For British composer Julian Anderson, Sibelius is 'a key figure in the shaping of current musical thought'. Anderson cites the Finn's music as a catalyst in the development of

A SPIRIT OF WIT AND WISDOM

Violinist Satu Jalas, one of Sibelius's granddaughters, recalls her visits to the composer's home in the Finnish countryside

My mother, Margareta, was the second youngest daughter of Jean Sibelius. As a child, I spent several periods every year with my brother and sister at Sibelius's home, Ainola, near Helsinki.

I remember my grandfather's big, blue eyes and I felt his warmth and spirituality. When we stayed overnight, he would call us every morning and ask what we had dreamt: he wanted a very detailed description. It was his way of knowing us from the inside. There was something heavenly in his way of looking at us children, and this remains in my mind even now. I was 14 years old when he died and it was only after his funeral ceremonies in the presence of thousands of people that I realised his importance as a composer and his recognition among the Finnish people.

Two years before his death, I needed a full-sized violin and he gave his instrument to me with good wishes. I have played this ever since, including – frequently – his compositions. I played to my grandparents several times, including his own compositions, such as the *Romance* and *Religioso* (from the Four Pieces, Op. 78), the *Tanz-Idylle* (from Op. 79) and *Rondino* (from Op. 81). Grandfather listened to my playing in a friendly and encouraging way. Sometimes he corrected my left-hand position a little bit, moving my thumb and my very small little finger.

It is fascinating to explore how Sibelius examined different sound colours on this very instrument, and how he chose different strings for his melodies. The bright and warm colour of the bottom (G) string inspired him in many compositions: the beginning of the slow movement of his Violin Concerto is an especially beautiful example. The top (E) string is very bright and clear, and you can notice this in many compositions, such as in the *Romance*. There are compositions, such as *On the Heath* (from Op. 115) or the second movement of his Sonatina in E major, where you can clearly see how he tries to express the sounds of nature, characterising individually each of the four strings.

When we were sitting in the library room with family members, listening to a symphony or other music on the radio, he was very interested in different kinds of good interpretations of his compositions.

I did not see him play the violin, as his hands already were trembling too much. But very often, when he sat in his chair, he moved the fingers of his left hand on his right arm, playing the violin in his mind. Even after he stropped composing, he was constantly elaborating his musical ideas, right up to the last day of his life.

Sibelius said that you must not waste too many words on compositions, because they are like butterflies: after you touch them, they can still fly, but the slight patina in their wings has gone. Even now I try to preserve this atmosphere and keep this patina in the wings of his compositions …

Sibelius taking breakfast on the veranda of Ainola, his home near Lake Tuusula, where he lived from 1904 until his death

'spectral' music in France (the idea being to explore the acoustical spectra of sound), going on to claim that leading Finnish composer Magnus Lindberg's study of spectral composers such as Gérard Grisey and Tristan Murail led to his own rediscovery of Sibelius. This, in turn, led to an influence on Lindberg's own evolving harmonic language which has elevated his music to that of, arguably, the greatest living Finnish composer since Sibelius.

'There is,' declares Anderson, 'virtually no major composer working today who has not been directly affected by the work of Jean Sibelius.' Danish composer Per Nørgård has been inspired by the Finn's 'metamorphic' qualities of writing to create his own so-called 'infinity row' – a way of developing composition through interacting speeds, metres and frequencies. Nørgård's responses have been set into relief by Sibelius's own declaration that Nørgård had understood his music more deeply than anyone else. Without searching too hard, we can hear echoes of Sibelius, too, in the music of George Benjamin and Oliver Knussen, and in the symphonies of Sir Peter Maxwell Davies.

In recordings, complete Sibelius symphony cycles from John Barbirolli, Paavo Berglund and Leonard Bernstein preceded a glut of new performances as the century turned, and as Colin Davis, Sir Simon Rattle, Mariss Jansons, Sakari Oramo, Petri Sakari and Osmo Vänskä dug deep into the archive of the composer's lesser-known works. Furthermore, life has never been the same since the revelations provided by the Complete Sibelius Edition recordings, to which Vänskä was a key contributor. One of the great discoveries here was the composer's music for the theatre. His

> **"The more we hear, the more we know, the more the image recedes just out of reach, the portrait blurs."**

lifelong involvement with the great playwrights of the day, including Strindberg, led to consummately skilful and imaginative incidental music – including that for *Kuolema* (of which we now know rather more than its ubiquitous *Valse triste*), *The Tempest*, *Pelléas*

Kullervo rides to war: a scene from the Finnish folk epic, the *Kalevala*, the inspiration for many of Sibelius's works, including the symphony *Kullervo* and tone-poem *Tapiola*: painting by Akseli Gallen-Kallela, a friend of the composer

and *Mélisande*, *Swanwhite* and *Belshazzar's Feast*. It's good to see at least a small representation of this part of Sibelius's work in the Proms performance of the composer's haunting four-movement suite drawn from the incidental music he wrote in 1916 for his friend Hjalmar Procopé's play, *Belshazzar's Feast*.

Yet still, the more we hear, the more we know, the more the image recedes just out of reach, the portrait blurs. Like all artists of genius, Sibelius was a man of teasing paradoxes. There was the violin virtuoso who never made it as a performer – and never quite got over it. The forbidding, reticent presence could be transformed into a kindly, genial host, revelling in good food and wine, and smoking

cigars which were, by all accounts, twice as big as Winston Churchill's. The man who loved to indulge in earthy joviality and excess would also seek 'spiritual ablution'. The recluse, so desperate for solitude that he would take himself off to an island in the Finnish archipelago and work there for eight weeks at a time, could also speak of 'the terrifying creatures of eternal silence'. And the composer who was able and willing to write any number of salon and occasional pieces to order would also agonise throughout his life over how 'to write what is ultimately and forever right'.

What was right for Sibelius can be distilled down to two central preoccupations of his life and music. First, there was the language and folklore of Finland – in particular the eastern

STEINWAY & SONS

"The Steinway is not only an instrument, it is a work of art of the first rank." *Christoph Eschenbach*

borderland of Karelia – as handed down orally by rune-singers (whom Sibelius sought out), and as collected in the compendium of tales which forms Finland's national epic, the *Kalevala*. Sibelius was raised in an exclusively Swedish-speaking, middle-class family; but he had access to this literature in its original language thanks to the fact that his parents chose to send him to a Finnish-speaking school. He grew to love the vowel-rich inflections of the Finno-Ugric language, and the pentatonic melodies of its rune-songs. The tales from Elias Lönnrot's great 1835 anthology inspired works such as *Luonnotar* and the orchestral *Lemminkäinen Suite*, which focuses on the exploits of the *Kalevala*'s wide-boy. And the *Kalevala* metre (imitated in Longfellow's *Hiawatha*) pulses through so much of what Sibelius wrote, just as the five notes of Finland's ancient pentatonic zither, the *kantele*, permeated his melodic thinking.

Nowhere is this more evident than in his remarkable symphony *Kullervo*, the work which kick-started his entire symphonic production. *Kullervo*, with its chorus and soloists, focuses on four crucial episodes in the life of the cursed and cursing delinquent anti-hero of the *Kalevala*. And it forces us to recognise and remember that Sibelius's 'Finnishness' goes way beyond a sense of national celebration and identity to an exploration into the heart of darkness and the transcendent human insights to be found in all the world's great storytelling. 'The more I immerse myself in the fate of Kullervo,' wrote Sibelius, 'the smaller I feel.' *Kullervo* has been described as 'a mountain Sibelius had to climb in order to see the opportunities beyond'.

Transcending even the verbal and musical language of his homeland, there were the horizontals of its wide lakes, the verticals of its pines and birches, and the ubiquitous mighty outcrops of granite which, Sibelius declared, made Finnish composers able to treat the orchestra as they did. *Tapiola* takes us far beyond the forests of the North, but is born in them. *En saga* has been described as a profound expression of the Nordic mind. Nothing, it's safe to say, meant more to Sibelius than the relationship between the human soul and the natural world. His first composition, at the age of 10, was a work for pizzicato violin and cello called *Water Drops*. While writing his Fifth Symphony, Sibelius famously noted, 'I saw 16 swans – their call like that of cranes, but without the tremolo'. Rosa Newmarch, the composer's close friend (and, for some 20 years, chief programme note-writer for the Proms), wrote of his 'passion for trying to catch the pedal notes of natural forces' and of seeing him trying to 'catch' the vibrations of Lake Saimaa. Per Nørgård has commented, significantly, that Sibelius's music isn't simply *about* nature: it *behaves* like nature. For Nørgård, Sibelius is a prophet, transcribing nature's eternal patterns into organic and timeless musical form. Throughout the Proms celebration of Sibelius this summer, keep the composer's own words in mind:

I come closer and closer to Heaven. My heart is full of sadness and adoration for nature. It is strange to think that nothing in the whole world, neither in art nor in music, affects me like the cranes and the swans and the wild geese: their cries and their very being. I have seen them flying south, calling their music to the winds, and relived the spontaneity of the sound. This is the thread running through my life. ●

Hilary Finch is a music critic for *The Times* and a regular broadcaster on BBC Radio 3. As a freelance writer, she specialises in the field of song, and in the music and literature of the Nordic countries.

The folk poet Larin Paraske, celebrated for her rune-singing from the *Kalevala*; Sibelius heard her while working on his *Kullervo* (painting, 1893, by Albert Edelfelt)

JEAN SIBELIUS AT THE PROMS

Belshazzar's Feast – suite
PROM 1 • 17 JULY

Finlandia; Symphony No. 1 in E minor; Symphony No. 2 in D major
PROM 40 • 15 AUGUST

Symphony No. 3 in C major; Symphony No. 4 in A minor; Violin Concerto in D minor
PROM 42 • 16 AUGUST

Symphony No. 5 in E flat major; Symphony No. 6 in D minor; Symphony No. 7 in C major
PROM 43 • 17 AUGUST

Tapiola
PROM 47 • 21 AUGUST

En saga; Kullervo
PROM 58 • 29 AUGUST

BBC Symphony Orchestra & Chorus

Concerts 2015–16

Sakari Oramo, Chief Conductor of the BBC Symphony Orchestra, conducts six concerts at the heart of the BBC SO's new Barbican season.

barbican
Associate Orchestra

Comments from the press on Sakari Oramo and the BBC Symphony Orchestra's 2014-15 Nielsen symphony cycle.

"Orchestral concert of the year? It would need to be outstanding to better this one…the BBC Symphony Orchestra were on blazing form all evening"
The Guardian

"The Dane's Fourth Symphony… is a fireball of life-force and Oramo's direction ensured that this was celebrated to the full." *The Times*

Great symphonies by Mahler, Elgar and Strauss, new music by Anna Clyne, Jospeh Phibbs and Brett Dean and English music by Bax and Vaughan Williams, with the BBC Symphony Chorus.

See us at the Barbican, Royal Albert Hall, Maida Vale Studios and beyond. Hear us on BBC Radio 3.
For full details and to sign up to our free e-newsletter.
bbc.co.uk/symphonyorchestra

GET IN TOUCH
@bbcso or facebook.com/bbcso

BBC Symphony Chorus

The BBC Symphony Chorus is one of the country's finest and most distinctive amateur choirs, enjoying the highest broadcast profile of any non-professional choir in the UK. It performs a wide range of exciting and challenging works alongside the BBC Symphony Orchestra at the Barbican and at the BBC Proms.

Appearances in the 2015 BBC Proms include performances of Walton's *Belshazzar's Feast* and Sibelius's *Kullervo* with the BBC SO and Sakari Oramo, and concerts conducted by Marin Alsop and Eric Whitacre. Performances during the BBC SO's Barbican season include Tippett's *A Child of our Time* with Edward Gardner, Stravinsky's *Symphony of Psalms* with Ryan Wigglesworth and Berlioz's *Romeo and Juliet* with Sir Andrew Davis.

Join us!

If you are an experienced choral singer who would like to sing new and challenging music, as well as key choral works, then the BBC Symphony Chorus could be for you!

Membership is free, and auditions for new members are held throughout the year. To find out more about auditions, or about our Open Rehearsal on Friday 26 June, visit the chorus website or contact the Chorus Administrator by email at **bbcsc@bbc.co.uk** or telephone on **020 7765 4715**.

bbc.co.uk/symphonychorus

NIELSEN AND THE IDEA
OF DANISHNESS

A composer of remarkable breadth and striking originality, Carl Nielsen is acclaimed as a central figure in Danish musical culture, but has been slow to gain an international reputation. As the BBC Proms celebrates 150 years since the composer's birth, **DANIEL M. GRIMLEY** places the life-affirming spirit of Nielsen's vision in a more cosmopolitan light

Reflecting upon the startling range and richness of Carl Nielsen's work showcased at this year's BBC Proms, marking the 150th anniversary of the Danish composer's birth, it is easy to wonder why he has not been recognised more widely as one of the most creative and original figures in 20th-century music. Despite his music's very obvious melodic appeal, Nielsen has never enjoyed quite the same international acclaim as that accorded to his great Nordic contemporary Sibelius. The reasons for such historical imbalance are complex: Nielsen's symphonies were championed during his lifetime by musical celebrities such as the composer-pianist Ferruccio Busoni and superstar conductor Wilhelm Furtwängler, yet he never benefited from the kind of sustained patronage that Arturo Toscanini, Henry Wood and Thomas Beecham lent to Sibelius's music. The two composers' respective national contexts also reveal significant differences. Sibelius became the musical emblem for a nation struggling heroically (and brutally) to achieve political and cultural independence in the early 1900s.

Nielsen, in contrast, was a more ambivalent figurehead for a once-influential European power whose reach had gradually diminished during the 19th century, not least following its ill-fated border war with Prussia in 1864, and which seemed increasingly peripheral as the 20th century progressed.

It is Denmark's passive 'bystander' mentality, as Nielsen's biographer Jørgen I.

reception is the peculiarly Danish modesty and reserve known as 'the Law of Jante' (*Janteloven*), a term coined by novelist Aksel Sandemose in 1933 which decrees that 'one should never believe that one is anything': a considerable barrier to any form of self-promotion or advancement. Yet Denmark is also the country that has produced a striking range of great writers, from Hans Christian

> Among the most engaging aspects of Nielsen's musical development is the way in which he both resisted and embraced the idea of 'Danishness' as an integral element of his aesthetic outlook.

Jensen has argued, that may inadvertently have limited the wider international dissemination of Nielsen's work, and that fostered a degree of artistic insularity against which the composer himself evidently struggled. 'I am, or rather was, a bone of contention,' Nielsen once recalled, 'because I wanted to protest against this soft Danish smoothness: I wanted stronger rhythms, more advanced harmony.' No less pervasive in his

Andersen and Jens Peter Jacobsen to Karen Blixen, philosophers such as Søren Kierkegaard, scientists such as Niels Bohr and Inge Lehmann, and artists such as Vilhelm Hammershøi and the sculptor Anne Marie Carl-Nielsen, the composer's wife. Among the most engaging aspects of Nielsen's musical development, therefore, is the way in which he both resisted and embraced the idea of 'Danishness' as an integral element of his

Cello by
Matthew Hardie
Edinburgh c.1800

F.N. Voirin, Paris, c.1875-78

Cello by
Joseph Hill, London
c.1770-1780

Tom Woods

LONDON'S CELLO SPECIALIST
www.tomwoodscellos.com
+44 (0)20 7362 1812

Eugene Sartory
Paris, c.1930

Nicolas Leonard Tourte
Paris, c.1785-80

Cello by
Albert Caressa
Paris, c.1926

Victor Fetique, Paris, c.1925

Cello by
Louis Guersan
Paris, c.1760

> Nielsen's music never entirely let go of its rural roots, even in its most seemingly transcendental and cosmic passages.

Carl Nielsen (*centre*) with his family outside Fuglsang Manor, an artist's retreat on the Danish island of Lolland

aesthetic outlook and the extent to which he should properly be regarded as a more cosmopolitan, internationally oriented figure than the image of 'den lille-store dansker' (the little-great Dane) suggests: a musician whose friends and colleagues included contemporaries as diverse as Schoenberg, Hindemith and Stravinsky.

The eventual breadth and scope of Nielsen's musical achievement could hardly have been foreseen, given the modest circumstances of his upbringing. Although Nielsen later wrote evocatively about his early life in his autobiography *Min fynske barndom* ('My Childhood on Funen', published in 1927) and claimed that 'even the trees dream and talk in their sleep in a Funen dialect', the actual reality is more difficult to imagine. Born into a working-class family in central Denmark (on the same island as Hans Christian Andersen), Nielsen was the seventh of 12 children and his music never entirely let go of its rural roots, even in its most seemingly transcendental and cosmic passages. Writing in 1905 about his childhood memories playing alongside farmers, school teachers and his father in the local music society, he recalled, 'I still remember how on the way home after these musical evenings through the beautiful landscape I used to dream and fantasise in music, and I am certain that it had an important influence on my musical development.'

Landscape, place and tradition were formative parts of Nielsen's musical make-up, just as he sought to explore the most cutting-edge advances in European compositional technique in many of his large-scale works, such as the Second Symphony. As late as 1929, for example, the music critic Gunnar Heerup could write with pride that 'Carl Nielsen has retained the farmer's basic ability to approach his material from an entirely objective and practical standpoint', and in the memorial issue of the *Danish Musical Times* after Nielsen's sudden death following a heart attack in 1931, Otto Mortensen claimed that 'with Carl Nielsen we had the beginnings of an independent Danish musical culture. For too long we have made do with a ready-made, Germanicised musical life which, when it came down to it, did not really suit us.'

The selection of pieces at this year's Proms gives an excellent sense of the scope and depth of Nielsen's output, from the mystic Nordic-Hellenism of his *Helios* overture, whose breathtaking opening was formerly played at midnight every 1 January on Danish radio to herald the start of the new year, to the fairy-tale exoticism of his *Aladdin* suite, taken from music written for a lavish production at the Royal Theatre in Copenhagen of a play by Nielsen's great early 19th-century Romantic precursor Adam Oehlenschläger. Among his most popular works, especially for his domestic Danish audience, is the overture to his second opera, *Maskarade* ('Masquerade'), based on an 18th-century text by the renowned Danish-Norwegian playwright Ludvig Holberg, although it is perhaps the mischievous spirit of Andersen who hovers most prominently in the mind for listeners overseas. The vernal cantata *Springtime on Funen*, written in praise of Nielsen's native island, is typical of the style of his popular

NIELSEN AND BRITAIN

Is it time for our enthusiasm for all things Nordic to extend to the music of Carl Nielsen? Andrew Mellor investigates

Audiences in Britain have never taken as readily to the music of Carl Nielsen as they have to that of his Nordic contemporary Jean Sibelius. But, just as curious minds on these isles grew so surprisingly attached to the TV series *Borgen* and *The Killing* – broadcast on the BBC in their original Danish, an almost unfathomable language, whose rapid rattle can appear worryingly devoid of vowels – so Nielsen's breathless, irascible and very 'Danish-sounding' music can prove utterly absorbing once you've attuned your ears to it.

Nielsen came to Britain twice. Firstly, in 1910, with his wife and daughter; the family investigated the new series of Promenade Concerts and met its co-founder Henry Wood, who knew enough about Nielsen to tentatively propose Proms performances of his works. But it wasn't until Nielsen's second visit here, in 1923, that his music was heard in Britain, with the composer conducting the London Symphony Orchestra. Nielsen made quite an impression during that visit; his sense of humour wasn't lost on the LSO players and he had tea at Marlborough House with Denmark's Queen Alexandra (then Queen Mother) with the top button of his (borrowed) suit trousers undone – a neat representation of the composer's gentle disdain for authority, both political and musical.

Back then, Nielsen's music was met with the mixture of mild intrigue, aesthetic confusion and casual Nordic stereotyping that he was

becoming so used to in Europe. It wasn't until the 1950s, two decades after his death, that British ears were turned to Nielsen's music once more: the Danish Radio Symphony Orchestra visited the Edinburgh Festival and the English composer Robert Simpson published his landmark book *Carl Nielsen: Symphonist*.

While some of Simpson's analyses have since been superseded (not least by Daniel M. Grimley, *see main article*), he revealed much about Nielsen that other commentators had missed. But Simpson was also passionate about finding an audience in Britain for the Dane's music, writing: 'Nielsen's cast of mind … full-blooded yet utterly free from exaggeration, has all the qualities that appeal to Englishmen.'

However right Simpson was in that assertion – the 1950s and 1960s did see a flurry of Nielsen performances in Britain, mostly of the Fourth and Fifth Symphonies – Nielsen's early symphonies, cantatas, songs, operas and wonderfully idiosyncratic chamber works have effectively remained strangers to these shores. But perhaps not for long. The composer's 150th anniversary has arrived right on cue, at the height of Britain's cultural awakening to all things Nordic. Will Nielsen prove to be the next unmissable Danish thriller?

Andrew Mellor is a journalist with a particular interest in the culture of the Nordic countries. He writes for *Klassisk* magazine, *Finnish Music Quarterly*, *Gramophone*, *The Strad*, *Opera* and *Moose Report* (which he founded).

Sculptor Anne Marie Carl-Nielsen with her 1939 monument to her husband, *The Young Man Playing Pan Pipes on a Wingless Pegasus*, which now stands in Copenhagen

songs, many of which were composed in collaboration with the educationalist Thomas Laub. Like the tunes that Vaughan Williams composed for the *English Hymnal*, Nielsen's stirringly diatonic melodies are still sung every day by schoolchildren in Denmark, who remain blissfully unaware of the identity of their composer.

Perhaps the most remarkable works to be heard this summer, however, are the two wind concertos, for flute and for clarinet, which belong to the final phase of Nielsen's compositional career. In 1922, Nielsen had written a chamber work for the Copenhagen Wind Quintet, inspired by a performance of Mozart's Quintet for piano and winds, K452, and he subsequently promised to write a concerto for each of the players individually. In the event, Nielsen lived to complete only the first two of the set, but they are among the most characterful and demanding works of their kind in the repertoire. Nielsen once described how he wanted to 'depict the instruments as independent individuals … I think out from the instruments themselves – almost like creeping inside them', and wrote that the clarinet could sound 'simultaneously warm-hearted and completely hysterical, as mild as balm, and screaming like a tramcar on poorly greased rails': a diagnosis that is amply borne out by the solo writing in these two concertos.

A similar concern with psychological intensity and extremes of emotion motivates the Second Symphony, which Nielsen subtitled 'The Four Temperaments'. Inspired, he claimed, by a painting of the basic personality types that Classical theorists believed determine human behaviour, the four movements of the symphony correspond to each individual temperament in turn, starting with the choleric. This concern with the essential vitality and robustness of human life, despite its emotional vulnerability, remained a recurrent thread throughout Nielsen's work, crystallised most vividly perhaps in his Fourth Symphony, the 'Inextinguishable', written during the carnage of the First World War, and it is among the most compelling qualities of his musical outlook.

Nielsen's enduring legacy for more recent Danish composers, from Per Nørgård and Pelle Gudmundsen-Holmgreen to Hans Abrahamsen, is his sense of playfulness: the adventurous approach to new sounds and instrumental combinations alongside his commitment to the individual textures and gestures of the musical characters – vagrant

A scene from David Pountney's 2005 production of Nielsen's *Maskarade* for the Royal Opera, Covent Garden

percussion, volatile winds, mercurial strings – which became a defining feature of his work. In this sense, among others, he resists the diminutive image of the cosy national patriarch that his reception has sometimes inadvertently suggested. But it is perhaps his music's life-affirming optimism, in the face of some of the 20th century's most violent and unforeseen ruptures and conflicts, which is its more lasting contribution and that makes him such a pivotal figure. There can be few more eloquent testaments to music's transformative agency than the story of Nielsen's career, from his working-class country origins to the whirling strains of the contemporary avant-garde. Above all, however, it is in its open-mindedness, its willingness to embrace the most complex and demanding musical ideas alongside the simplest singing tune, that Nielsen's work has its most irresistible and delightful pull. ●

Daniel M. Grimley is a Lecturer in Music at the University of Oxford and a tutorial fellow at Merton College. His books include *Carl Nielsen and the Idea of Modernism* (Boydell, 2011) and (as editor) *Jean Sibelius and his World* (Princeton University Press, 2011).

CARL NIELSEN AT THE PROMS

Maskarade – overture
PROM 1 • 17 JULY

Clarinet Concerto
PROM 7 • 22 JULY

Wind Quintet
PROMS CHAMBER MUSIC 2
27 JULY

Overture 'Helios'; Three Motets;
Hymnus amoris; Symphony No. 2,
'The Four Temperaments'
PROM 46 • 20 AUGUST

Flute Concerto
PROM 54 • 25 AUGUST

Aladdin – excerpts
PROM 64 • 3 SEPTEMBER

Springtime on Funen; Violin Concerto
PROM 72 • 9 SEPTEMBER

Mark Ellidge/ArenaPAL

LEARNING BY
HEART

How – and why – do musicians memorise?
As the Aurora Orchestra prepares to
perform Beethoven's 'Pastoral' Symphony
without printed scores, neuroscientist
JESSICA GRAHN explores the nature
of musical memory

The extraordinary ability of musicians to recall millions of
musical notes over a lifetime is undoubtedly one of the most
impressive feats of human memory. For scientists, memory feats
provide an opportunity to understand how human memory works
– but, for musicians, having to achieve this on a regular basis can
be terrifying. Most musicians will have to perform from memory
at some time in their career. Some, especially singers or soloists,
have to perform from memory most of the time. Feelings about the
practice are divided. Some musicians feel that performing without
a score allows them to be freer and more expressive. Others feel
that memorisation is time-consuming and less reliable than using
a written score. Moreover, the fear of memory 'slips' can hamper
expressive performance, or worse: debilitating stage fright may
cause a musician to withdraw from the profession entirely. Most
ensembles escape the burden of memorisation – with notable
exceptions being the Kolisch Quartet in the 1930s and the Chiara
and Zehetmair Quartets today – and an entire orchestra playing

from memory, as the Aurora Orchestra does this summer at the Proms, is all but unheard of.

Musicians with a hatred of memorisation may bemoan Clara Schumann and Franz Liszt, who were among the first 19th-century musicians to spark this trend. The image of a piano virtuoso was beginning to form at this time, with Liszt declaring that 'virtuosity is not an outgrowth, but an indispensable element of music'. Before this time, it was considered arrogant to perform without the score. Beethoven explicitly disapproved of one of his pupils, who could play the composer's entire set of works from memory, as he was concerned that important details in the score could be missed. Chopin was angered when he heard that one of his pupils wanted to play him a Nocturne from memory. Mendelssohn had an amazing musical memory, but would not let on – before one performance when his score was

> Simple repetition, the most common practice strategy, does not necessarily prevent memory slips.

unavailable, he had a page-turner place a random book in front of him and pretend it was the score. However, prior to the Renaissance, playing from memory was a necessity, as little or no musical notation was available.

Memorised music performance has interested scientists since as far back as the 1800s. One type of memory that musicians use is commonly called 'muscle memory', but the memories are not actually stored in the muscles. Muscle memory instead refers to a type of 'procedural' memory called motor learning, in which memories for movement patterns are acquired through repetition. Procedural memory is separate from other types of memory, such as our memory for events (autobiographical memory) or general knowledge about the world (semantic memory). We use procedural memory for actions such as driving, typing on a keyboard or riding a bike. This is the type of memory for which 'practice makes perfect', and it allows us to perform complex actions, such as driving a car, with little attention. However, when we are stressed or anxious, procedural memory may fail, and we 'choke'. Choking is often seen in athletes in high-pressure situations. Musicians also experience choking, for example when performance anxiety disrupts a procedural memory that is normally second nature, resulting in mistakes or memory slips.

Many of the practice strategies that musicians use are aimed at preventing and recovering from slips. Simple repetition, the most common practice strategy, does not necessarily prevent slips. A more useful set of strategies for performers is to vary the interactions with the music, providing different sources of memory in case one source fails. For example, musicians may write out the score to rehearse their visual memory, or conduct harmonic analyses to strengthen their memory of the music's structures. Another strategy is to practise the piece starting from multiple points within it. Procedural memories often form as chains of actions, with each action triggering the memory for the next action, and starting anywhere but the beginning of the chain is difficult. If musicians only practise from the beginning, then any momentary distraction (like an audience cough or ringing phone) can break the action chain, and the memory for the next action won't be triggered. Simply knowing that various starting points are

Franz Liszt (1811–86), one of the earliest piano virtuosos, and one of the first to perform from memory

available may reduce anxiety enough that memory slips are less likely to occur.

The demands placed on musicians' memories may physically alter their brains. When hearing familiar music, both musicians and non-musicians activate a key brain area called the hippocampus, but in musicians the activity is higher. Moreover, musicians have more 'grey matter' in their hippocampi, as do others in memory-demanding professions, such as London taxi drivers who have completed 'the Knowledge'.

Neuroscientists have found that musical memories can be preserved in the brain even when most other memories are lost. Memory loss, such as that experienced by amnesiacs, provides a window for neuroscientists to study how memory works. One amnesiac patient, a German professional cellist, had such profound memory loss that he could not remember well-known facts about Germany, nor important details from his youth or adulthood. He had no memory of relatives and friends, except for his brother and his full-time care-giver. However, he could still play the cello and sight-read music. Moreover, his memory for

SECRETS REVEALED

Discover the top-secret Codebreaking world of WW2 Bletchley Park, where pencils and brains helped win the war.

Open daily, except 24-26 Dec and 1 Jan

Quote JG2015 for 10% off regular admission to the Bletchley Park heritage site.*

*Not valid with any other offer; terms and conditions apply

Use Jct 13 off the M1 or 45 mins from London Euston to Bletchley train station; located opposite the train station, MK3 6DZ, on Sherwood Dr.

www.bletchleypark.org.uk

BLETCHLEYPARK

COLLECTIVE FREEDOM

Nicholas Collon explains why he and the Aurora Orchestra – having performed Mozart's Symphony No. 40 from memory last year – decided to play another symphony from memory at this year's Proms

For many members of the Aurora Orchestra, performing Mozart's Symphony No. 40 from memory at last year's BBC Proms ranked as one of our most intense and rewarding musical experiences. In every way it deepened and enriched our relationship with this extraordinary piece of music, forcing us to internalise nuances that can be easily glossed over when reading from the page. Gone, in rehearsal, were the traditional footholds – bar numbers, bowings, articulations. Suddenly we were let loose in a world of endless possibilities, where the tiniest variation in a semiquaver run could seem so rich with significance!

Performing from memory takes communication to a new level. While it feels naked to be on stage without stand and music to hide behind, it intensifies the levels of trust between players. My hope and belief is that it also communicates in a new way with the audience: not that it should feel surprising or dangerous to watch, but more that we are all – conductor, players and audience – unshackled from the printed notes.

We expect it of concerto soloists and opera singers, we've seen it with string quartets and choirs: an orchestra performing from memory is not an impossibility, nor a gimmick, even if limitations on rehearsal time mean it's not often practical. I am thrilled to undertake this journey again with Beethoven's 'Pastoral' Symphony, a piece that is so close to me, and look forward to walking out with the Aurora players onto a Royal Albert Hall stage devoid of music stands.

Beyond the score: the Zehetmair Quartet, one of the few chamber ensembles to perform from memory

music from his past was just as good as that of his non-amnesiac colleagues. He could even learn to recognise new music (but not new faces or objects). Somehow, his musical memory system was intact, even though most of his other memories were gone.

Neuroscientists are still trying to discover why music can be resistant to memory

> Music, like smell, taps into primitive emotional centres in the brain.

problems. One possibility is that music, like smell, taps into primitive emotional centres in the brain that have widespread connections to other brain areas. These connections across the brain are what make the memories robust. This wide distribution could also explain why music conjures up rich memories, as for example with a song that hasn't been heard for decades.

Even if expectations of memorisation change, there will no doubt continue to be musicians who feel that memorisation is indispensable to performance. And scientists will be glad, as music provides a rich avenue to study the limits of human memory. ●

Jessica Grahn is a cognitive neuroscientist and an Assistant Professor at the Brain and Mind Institute at Western University, London, Ontario. She investigates how music affects the brain and behaviour.

MUSICAL MEMORY AT THE PROMS

Beethoven Symphony No. 6, 'Pastoral'
Anna Meredith Smatter Hauler
Played from memory
by the Aurora Orchestra

PROM 22 • 2 AUGUST

See also Proms Lecture (18 July): neuroscientist Daniel Levitin on 'Unlocking the Mysteries of Music in Your Brain'

Benjamin Eclovega (Collon); Christopher Tribble (Zehetmair Quartet)

PEREGRINE'S PIANOS

Quality instruments for the professional pianist.

Spacious rehearsal rooms for the working musician.

Peregrine's Pianos, 137A Grays Inn Road, London WC1X 8TU   Tel: 020 7242 9865

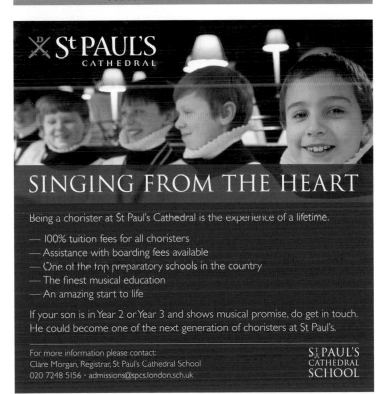

Hölger Talinski

BACK TO
BEETHOVEN

LEIF OVE ANDSNES looks back over his four-year Beethoven journey, which culminates at this year's Proms, when he both plays and directs all five of Beethoven's piano concertos, plus the rarely heard 'Choral Fantasy'

Four years ago, celebrated Norwegian pianist Leif Ove Andsnes embarked on an epic musical journey that has seen him perform Beethoven's five piano concertos and 'Choral Fantasy' with the Mahler Chamber Orchestra in 55 cities and 22 countries, to great critical acclaim. The main focus of the final year has been a series of residencies in Hamburg, Bonn, Lucerne, Vienna, Paris, New York, Shanghai and Tokyo, climaxing in three final concerts at this year's Proms. As the Beethoven Journey nears its end, Leif Ove Andsnes looks back over a momentous project that has taken the musical world by storm and seen him become the proud father of twins.

Beethoven's music has an indomitable presence – it is impossible to ignore. Yet, for me, it was not love at first sight. As a student I felt drawn to its energy and the revolutionary nature of his writing, but it wasn't until I organised a series of chamber concerts in Norway between 1996 and 1998, exploring the three main periods of his creative life, that I fully appreciated his colossal expressive range. Since then his music has formed an increasingly important part of my life. He speaks with an unvarnished directness and sincerity – free of theatrical rhetoric and sensuality – that goes straight from the heart to the heart. I think that is why I struggled initially to get on the wavelength of his slow movements, which are not emotional confessionals in the manner of Chopin or Schumann, but more an expression of lofty ideals that achieve an extraordinary level of spiritual intensity.

I had been contemplating for some time how I might channel my vision of this supremely great composer when, about seven years ago, things crystallised in, of all places,

> Beethoven speaks with an unvarnished directness and sincerity that goes straight from the heart to the heart. The slow movements achieve an extraordinary level of spiritual intensity.

a hotel lift in São Paulo! The background music turned out to be a continuous loop of Beethoven's first two piano concertos and every time I used the lift I found myself

arriving at a different point. At first I thought this might become rather irritating, yet the opposite proved true, as I was struck time and again by the sheer originality and exuberance of Beethoven's invention. There and then I decided the time was right to commit myself to an extensive exploration of the concertos and 'Choral Fantasy', and came up with the idea of undertaking a four-year 'journey' with the Mahler Chamber Orchestra, climaxing in a three-concert series at the Proms in 2015.

Perhaps the most challenging decision was to direct the entire cycle from the keyboard. The first three concertos and even the 'Choral Fantasy' did not pose any insurmountable problems, but the revelation came with the 'Emperor' Concerto (No. 5), about which I was initially apprehensive, as there are so many notes to play. How would I fit in any conducting around that? That was when working with the remarkable musicians of the Mahler Chamber Orchestra really came into its own, because I had to put my complete faith and trust in their ability to pick up on the slightest musical or physical gesture. All my concerns about playing entirely together – about 'vertical' precision – simply melted away as we achieved an amazing symbiosis: a collective sense of knowing and feeling exactly what was required at any given moment. Even the notoriously tricky tempo transition in this concerto between the dreamy slow movement and exultant finale actually became easier to negotiate without a conductor.

As a natural result of having lived so intensely with this music over such a long period, I now find that I give fewer conducting gestures, because an immense trust has developed between myself and the musicians, allowing for more vitality and spontaneity.

Apollo, leader of the Muses: Carlos Acosta in the title-role of Stravinsky's *Apollon musagète* (Royal Ballet, 2007); each programme of Leif Ove Andsnes's Beethoven cycle pairs Beethoven with Stravinsky – another composer to 'set the musical agenda'

One thing I was particularly keen to avoid was a sense of cosy chamber music-making. From the start we were determined to convey something of the 'shock of the new', relishing those moments where soloist and orchestra appear almost to be pulling in opposite directions. It can feel a bit like a musical battleground at times, which makes those passages where soloist and orchestra are in complete accord feel especially poignant.

One of the joys of sitting among the musicians is that you relate more directly to what is going on around you, so that, for example, co-ordinating the piano's bustling octave scales towards the end of the rondo finale of the First Concerto becomes much easier and allows me to enjoy the orchestral interaction more readily.

Performing Beethoven's music in so many important musical centres has been an incredibly uplifting experience, although there is no denying the special atmosphere generated by his adopted city, Vienna. To play in the very place where this music was originally conceived and premiered just over 200 years ago, was truly humbling. Yet the most memorable performance for me occurred in my home town of Bergen. I had recently cancelled part of the Beethoven Journey as my partner Ragnhild had given birth to twins: they arrived 12 weeks early and I naturally wanted to see them safely through those challenging first few weeks. (They are doing absolutely fine now, thankfully.) The German pianist and conductor Alexander Lonquich kindly stood in for me but couldn't make the Bergen performance, so I directed that concert and all the emotion that had been building up over the previous few weeks overwhelmed me at the end of the Fourth Concerto, whose bracing affirmation of life inspired tears of joy.

Now we have the final stage of our Journey to look forward to at the Proms, where in the past I have enjoyed some of the most memorable concerts of my career. We hit upon the idea of programming Beethoven with Stravinsky, as both composers went through similar phases of stylistic development and also they might be said to have set the musical agendas, respectively, for

The 16-year-old Beethoven playing for Mozart in 1787 (anonymous painting, c1870): Beethoven's First Piano Concerto arrived eight years later

the 19th and 20th centuries. I adore the special atmosphere generated by Proms audiences and I imagine there will be quite a celebration afterwards to mark the end of what has been an extraordinary musical pilgrimage for me and the orchestra.

When we launched our series and I looked at the large number of concerts ahead of us, I was initially a little concerned about sustaining high levels of inspiration and intensity. However, this has proved one of the great revelations of the Journey. In fact, Beethoven's unquenchable vitality and inventiveness have continually struck me as increasingly astounding. There is always something new to discover in music of this supreme quality, so that every performance feels like a fresh voyage of discovery. ●

LEIF OVE ANDSNES PLAYS BEETHOVEN'S PIANO CONCERTOS AT THE PROMS

Piano Concerto No. 1 in C major;
Piano Concerto No. 4 in G major

PROM 9 • 23 JULY

Piano Concerto No. 3 in C minor;
Fantasy in C minor for piano, chorus and orchestra, 'Choral Fantasy'

PROM 10 • 24 JULY

Piano Concerto No. 2 in B flat major;
Piano Concerto No. 5
in E flat major, 'Emperor'

PROM 12 • 26 JULY

INTERNATIONAL ORCHESTRA
SERIES

2015/16

Great orchestras from around the
world at Southbank Centre

Barenboim 60th anniversary
concert with **Dudamel**

Wozzeck performed by
Zurich Opera

The Magic Flute with
Budapest Festival Orchestra

Jenůfa featuring **Karita Mattila**
& **Czech Philharmonic**

**Simón Bolívar Symphony
Orchestra** & **Dudamel** return
for three concerts

southbankcentre.co.uk/orchestra
0844 847 9934

Media partner
THE TIMES

Supported using public funding by
ARTS COUNCIL
ENGLAND

LOTTERY FUNDED

**SOUTHBANK
CENTRE**

JOLOMO

2015 EXHIBITIONS

Gallery Q, Dundee opens 27th March
Gallery 8, Mayfair, London opens 17th May
The Sage, Gateshead opens 13th June
The Archway, Lochgilphead opens 7th August
Clydebank Museum & Art Gallery opens 21st August
Strathearn Gallery, Crieff opens 12th September
Gullane Art Gallery, Gullane opens 9th October
The Mitchell Library, Glasgow opens 19th November

Jolomo
www.jolomo.com

Strings

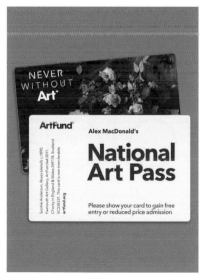

No strings

The National Art Pass. Free entry to over 200 galleries and museums across the UK and half-price entry to the major exhibitions.

Buy yours today at artfund.org

ArtFund

WITH
ONE VOICE

Few experiences are as stirring as hearing a large-scale choral work at the Proms in the vast Royal Albert Hall. BBC Radio 3 presenter (and choir-member) **SARA MOHR-PIETSCH** sings the praises of the UK's buoyant choral tradition and looks forward to some of this summer's choral offerings

A while ago, on BBC Radio 3's *The Choir*, I asked listeners to send in their choral epiphanies. These were pieces of choral music they had either sung or heard which had had a profound effect on their lives, or got them hooked on singing. To get the ball rolling, I offered one of my own: Verdi's *Requiem*. I remember going to my first choral society rehearsal at a nearby school when I was about 14. I'd been in my school choir for a few years already but had only ever sung with girls. This was a full chorus of mixed voices, and the sound of so many people around me singing the hushed opening 'Requiem aeternam' sent shivers up my spine.

And then, in 2001, I heard it again. This time, I was in the audience – standing in the Arena of the Royal Albert Hall on the penultimate night of the Proms season. It was less than a week since 9/11 and the world still seemed raw and unknown. The atmosphere in the hall was electric and, as the final notes of the 'Libera me' faded away, the air felt thick with silence. I remember holding my breath until someone clapped.

It's no coincidence that some of the most striking moments in Proms memory have involved choirs – such is the power of the human voice. In 1997 Verdi's *Requiem* became a double memorial, to Princess Diana and to Georg Solti, who had been due to conduct it but died suddenly one week before the Prom. A few years later, in 2001, the finale of Beethoven's 'Choral' Symphony (No. 9) was added into the Last Night of the Proms as a

response to the 9/11 attacks a few days earlier, directed by an American: Leonard Slatkin, the BBC Symphony Orchestra's then Chief Conductor. Anyone who was there will remember a strikingly sombre event, far from the flag-waving of the traditional concert, and will recall the power of Schiller's words as much as Beethoven's setting of this ode to human fellowship. The Royal Albert Hall always seems a suitably grand space for utterances on a large scale and this was key to the atmosphere, its circular arrangement also drawing the audience together.

Choral singing has never been more popular. Over the past decade there has been a massive resurgence in singing together across the UK, one which rivals even our renewed obsession with baking. Choral animateur and TV presenter Gareth Malone is a national hero, choirs compete on national television,

and Eric Whitacre (who conducts his new work, *Deep Field*, in Prom 32) has made headlines with his Virtual Choir. Working on Radio 3's *The Choir*, I'm constantly amazed by how rich the choral scene is in the UK, and how sophisticated it's becoming. Organisers and choral directors are taking particular care to nurture the young generation of singers, which is why the BBC Proms Youth Choir,

BBC Symphony
Chorus Soprano
ANNE TAYLOR
on the choral bug

Singing in any choir is a joy and a life-affirming experience. Singing with the BBC Symphony Chorus is, in addition, a wonderful privilege. My favourite concert every year is the First Night of the Proms: the atmosphere is electric, with a palpable sense of anticipation for the season to come from both the performers and the incomparable Proms audience.

I remember my first rehearsal for the First Night back in 2002, on Walton's *Belshazzar's Feast* – also my first ever rehearsal of that piece. We launched straight into it, taking no prisoners, and I was completely in awe of – and not a little daunted by – what I thought was the amazing sight-reading of my BBC Symphony Chorus colleagues. I soon realised that a large proportion of the Chorus knew the piece well already, meaning that novices like me learnt it very quickly. That speed of learning is typical of this chorus, both for well-loved pieces and for the considerable number of premieres in which we perform.

And there's nothing like being one of hundreds of performers producing a wall of sound and feeling the power of the magnificent Royal Albert Hall organ literally shaking the building. So I can't wait to sing *Belshazzar's Feast* again at this year's First Night!

A vision of Purgatory from *The Coronation of the Virgin* (altarpiece by Enguerrand Quarton, c1410–c1466); Verdi's depiction of the Day of Judgement in the 'Dies irae' of his *Requiem* is no less visceral

The BBC Proms Youth Choir and City of Birmingham Symphony Orchestra performing Britten's *War Requiem* at the 2014 BBC Proms, marking 100 years since the outbreak of the 'war to end all wars'

now in its fourth year, is such a fantastic initiative (*see panel, right*).

Involving young people in choral singing is a great way of ensuring it's not a passing fashion. Then again, it's not in much danger of disappearing. Although it might feel like a new movement, this choral obsession of ours points to a musical heritage that dates back as far as the early 18th century, when Handel arrived in London and when what is now the Three Choirs Festival held its first concerts. For more than two straight centuries, choral music was the lifeblood of amateur music-making in the UK, which is why this latest renaissance has such a strong foundation on which to build.

It has also taken hold because singing is good for us. It gets air into our lungs, promotes physical and mental wellbeing and is great for our social life. But, for me, the greatest joy of singing in a choir is getting to know fantastic

music from the inside out. Week after week you work in rehearsals on getting to know each vocal line intimately. It's rather like reading and re-reading a favourite poem or novel: Elgar's magical and moving *The Dream of Gerontius*, Walton's dazzling picture of *Belshazzar's Feast*, Haydn's concise, exultant *Te Deum* and Orff's colourful *Carmina burana* – all favourites you can encounter during this Proms season.

Then there are the traditional moments in the Proms season which wouldn't be the same without singing – most of all, the singalong at the Last Night, which this year marks the 50th anniversary of the film version of *The Sound of Music*. And there are wonderful discoveries that can only happen in the context of such a vast festival. Scroll through the list of choral works (*see opposite*) and you can curate your own journey. Here's one, for example – the 'wordless chorus', where a composer uses a choir but no text. The wordless chorus can be

Choral director
SIMON HALSEY
on directing the
BBC Proms Youth Choir

The BBC Proms Youth Choir grew out of a one-off project: a youthful performance of Handel's *Messiah* in 2009. What would it sound like with hundreds of teenaged voices? In the event, it gave a whole new lustre to the work and made us all listen to it afresh. And the singers? They are still talking about it six years later!

The BBC Proms Youth Choir has performed at the Proms every year since 2012. It comprises young members from all over the country, different singers every year from a variety of backgrounds. We meet for a week of intensive preparation at the University of Birmingham just prior to the concert and rehearse in the greatest depth with a marvellous staff of coaches and conductors. We encourage all the singers to approach the score as if they were detectives (or conductors), to discover what the composer was trying to achieve and to imagine themselves as part of the creative process.

Each year some 300 young singers are inspired to understand and love the Proms and our great oratorio repertoire, singing with leading conductors and orchestras. This year it's Sir Simon Rattle and the Vienna Philharmonic!

Our encounter this year with Elgar's *The Dream of Gerontius* (Prom 75) is a voyage of discovery. Our rehearsals are being held at Birmingham University, where Elgar was the founding professor of music, and only five minutes from where Cardinal Newman (whose text Elgar set) established his magnificent Oratory. We'll be studying the background and context as well as the music itself.

And the orchestra, having itself 'discovered' *Gerontius* recently, will be joining us, wide-eyed in wonder at the score that has evaded them for so many years. One thing's for certain – it will be no run-of-the-mill outing.

other-worldy, as in the celestial women's voices hidden from sight at the end of Holst's atmospheric portrait of Neptune from *The Planets*, and the invocation of cosmic bliss in the second of John Foulds's *Three Mantras*. Or it can be strangely comforting and grounding, as in the case of Charles Ives's Symphony No. 4, where, in the closing moments of the final movement, the choir intones the much-loved American hymn tune 'Bethany' (best-known to the words 'Nearer my God to thee'). It's a tune Ives used several times in his work, and the one that the string quartet on the *Titanic* reportedly played as the liner sank.

And here's another theme you could go for: 'Choral works I've never heard live before'. I guarantee there's at least one of the following

> Singing is good for us. It gets air into our lungs, promotes physical wellbeing and is great for our social life.

you've never heard in a concert performance: Schoenberg's *Friede auf Erden*, Vaughan Williams's *Sancta civitas*, Nielsen's *Hymnus amoris* and Brahms's *Triumphlied*. Really? You've heard them all? OK, then: Hugh Wood's *Epithalamium* (receiving its world premiere this summer). Go on – take a punt on something new! It's what the Proms are all about, and you never know – it may be the epiphany you've been waiting for. ●

Broadcaster Sara Mohr-Pietsch presents *The Choir* on BBC Radio 3 (Sundays, 4.00pm). She also presents *Composers' Rooms*, *Hear and Now* and *Live in Concert*, and can be heard most Mondays at the Radio 3 Lunchtime Concert, live from London's Wigmore Hall (1.00pm).

CHORAL MUSIC AT THE PROMS

Walton Belshazzar's Feast
PROM 1 • 17 JULY

Handel Zadok the Priest
PROMS 2 & 3 • 18 & 19 JULY

Beethoven Symphony No. 9 in D minor, 'Choral'
PROM 4 • 19 JULY

Tallis Church music and English motets
PROMS CHAMBER MUSIC 1 • 20 JULY

Haydn Te Deum;
Stravinsky Symphony of Psalms
PROM 6 • 21 JULY

Hugh Wood Epithalamium
BBC commission: world premiere,
Ravel Daphnis and Chloe – Suite No. 2
PROM 7 • 22 JULY

Beethoven Fantasia in C minor for piano, chorus and orchestra, 'Choral Fantasy';
Schoenberg Friede auf Erden
PROM 10 • 24 JULY

Holst The Planets
PROM 13 • 27 JULY

Vaughan Williams Sancta civitas
PROM 17 • 30 JULY

Bruckner Mass No. 3 in F minor
PROM 20 • 1 AUGUST

Verdi Requiem
PROM 23 • 2 AUGUST

Eric Whitacre The River Cam; Cloudburst; Equus; Deep Field *BBC co-commission: European premiere*
PROM 32 • 9 AUGUST

Foulds Three Mantras
PROM 38 • 13 AUGUST

Nielsen Hymnus amoris; Three Motets
PROM 46 • 20 AUGUST

Bach Mass in G minor, BWV 235; Magnificat in D major, BWV 243
PROM 48 • 21 AUGUST

Sibelius Kullervo
PROM 58 • 29 AUGUST

Brahms Alto Rhapsody; Triumphlied
PROM 62 • 1 SEPTEMBER

Orff Carmina burana
PROM 69 • 6 SEPTEMBER

Ives Symphony No. 4
PROM 72 • 9 SEPTEMBER

Elgar The Dream of Gerontius
PROM 75 • 11 SEPTEMBER

Pärt Credo; **Rodgers** The Sound of Music – medley; Last Night of the Proms favourites
PROM 76 • 12 SEPTEMBER

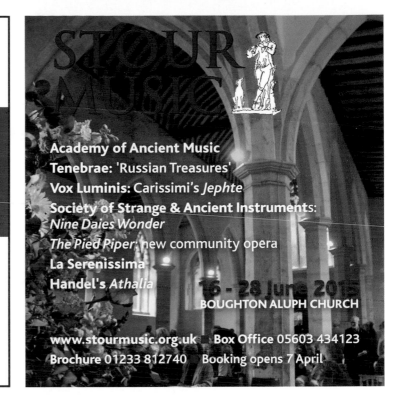

BEAUTIFUL
LOGIC

Born 90 years ago, composer, conductor and polemicist Pierre Boulez has left an indelible mark on the landscape of modern music. **PAUL GRIFFITHS** traces the ideas of a polymath whose keen structural rigour does not preclude his works from standing enigmatically open-ended

No-one alive today has changed the musical world more than Pierre Boulez – not just through his compositional work (though certainly that) but also by communicating a radical vision to his contemporaries, to performing musicians, to administrators, and ultimately to us, the audience: a vision of where we are musically at the present time, and where we might go.

Boulez had sorted out his core repertoire long before he began conducting, but it was his performances that revealed his thinking. Debussy's *La mer* was not just about the sea but about waves of exultation and anger, anxiety and unrest, delivered with keen clarity. Webern's music was not dry stabs and silences but glistening filaments, weightless. These composers and others – Stravinsky, Schoenberg, Bartók, Berg, Mahler, Ravel – he performed again and again, stamping them as the 20th century's classics. And, in programming them with later music, he showed them as foundation stones, not end points.

His influence in this respect goes on, to be found, for example, in the two concerts François-Xavier Roth conducts at the BBC Proms this season, each of which places a Boulez piece in an appropriate context of music that marked him – music by Ravel and Stravinsky, Bartók and Ligeti. Boulez himself became a conductor in 1956 in order to present his *Le marteau sans maître* under the best possible conditions, but he remained a conductor so that he could continue that work, maximising the potential of new music.

For his own works, the sources have always been clear: Debussy's perpetual reinvention, Webern's precision, the clang and the quick excitement of Messiaen (his teacher), the scintillating irony of Ravel, the fierceness of Bartók or Schoenberg and, if only at rare moments, the emotional abundance of Berg. When he was starting out as a composer, these chosen forefathers fuelled his rapid acquisition of a strong voice and a sure technique. By the time he was 20 he was already writing fully characteristic music – at once tough and seductive, tense with rhythmic energy and expressive force – as in the 1945 set of 12 short piano pieces, *Notations*, on which he has been reflecting for the past 30 years and more, expanding them into sumptuous and exuberant orchestral fantasies (five so far, with more awaiting completion). The violent passion of his youthful music still burns in these orchestral revisitings, but now wielded by a master.

In a way, the orchestrated *Notations* tell the story of Boulez's life. In Paris in 1945, newly encountering music that had been banned during the Nazi occupation, he was excited by challenge and eager to make it his own mode of expression. By the 1970s, when he was principal conductor of orchestras on both sides of the Atlantic – the BBC Symphony Orchestra and the New York Philharmonic – there was no longer any need to be caustic

and disputatious, as he had been in his youth, both in his music and in his actions in support of it. He was not fighting the musical world now, for he had helped reshape it.

This was a fulfilment, but it may have left him with a sense that the big endeavour of creating a thoroughly new musical language was over. What he wrote in his twenties and early thirties had been motivated largely by that effort. Hence, for example, his reconstitution of the orchestra, in seating and sonority, in a piece he originally, in 1957, called *Doubles*. But, as this grew into *Figures–Doubles–Prismes* through the 1960s, it became something more. An essay in sound turned into an adventure in expression – expression, in particular of frustration, solitariness and lament, in terms of rampage, sudden questioning stillness and unending song.

Like the orchestral *Notations*, *Figures–Doubles–Prismes* remains open, with the possibility that more could be added. The same is true of another work Boulez started at the same time, immediately following the climactic achievement of *Le marteau*: his Third Piano Sonata (1955–7). And it is true, too, of an orchestral score he began a few years later: *Éclat/Multiples* (1970), a kind of snowball piece that, initiated by a dazzling group of tuned percussion instruments in the original *Éclat* (1965), was to gather in its ensuing 'multiples' other orchestral groups around these, starting with a whole

Paul Klee's *Fugue in Red* (1921), a work Boulez selected for an exhibition of Klee's work he curated in Brussels in 2008

viola section. Since that fascinating and poignant first accretion, though, the score has been waiting more than 40 years for any further development.

There was a practical reason for so many stalled projects, in that conducting, which Boulez needed to do – and from which he learnt so much, with shadows of Berg, Mahler and Debussy all hovering around *Figures–Doubles–Prismes* – left him with little time or energy for composition. There were also aesthetic justifications he put forward: the impossibility of closure in music that no longer had tonality's clear pull towards cadence and resolution, and the wish also to create works that would engage with the infinite, opening more avenues than they could ever explore.

Yet another reason for Boulez to hesitate was his feeling that music needed new material and new tools in order for its potential to be realised. Dissatisfied by his experiences with electronic music at radio studios in Paris and south-west Germany, where he settled for

BOULEZ AT THE BBC

Pierre Boulez's association with the BBC – by far the longest in his professional career – began on 6 May 1957, when he arrived at the Concert Hall of London's Broadcasting House with his Domaine Musical ensemble from Paris to conduct a programme including his *Le marteau sans maître*. He gave his first concerts with the BBC Symphony Orchestra in February/March 1964, and made his Proms debut the following year, again with the BBC SO – though his music had got there three years ahead – a partial performance of *Le marteau* under John Carewe.

With a keen supporter in William Glock heading both the Proms and the BBC music department, Boulez was a regular visitor from this point on, bringing his cherished 20th-century repertoire to the Proms and the Royal Festival Hall, often with studio sessions following for CBS records. In 1967 he made the first of several films for BBC Two television, introducing a wider audience to his own music and to that of Berg, Stravinsky, Varèse and others.

In the concert hall he was able, with Glock, to devise unusual programmes: the Brandenburg Concerto No. 6 (in which he played harpsichord), Berg's *Lulu* suite, his own *Éclat* and Debussy's *Images* at a 1966 Prom, for instance. It was also at the Proms that he conducted Mahler for the first time: the Fifth Symphony in 1968. The following year he brought his *Pli selon pli* to the Proms, with the BBC SO, to which he then entrusted the world premieres of his *Éclat/Multiples* (1970) and *Rituel* (1975).

During his time as chief conductor of the orchestra, between 1971 and 1975, his Proms commitments increased (though never to include the Last Night), as did his repertoire, to embrace such unlikely

works for him as Beethoven's *Missa solemnis* (opening the 1972 Proms). He also added a series of concerts at the Roundhouse, in Camden, focusing on new and recent music.

His visits became much less frequent after 1975, though there was a Boulez Prom with the BBC SO most years through the next three decades, often involving a work of his own. In 1982 he brought the Ensemble Intercontemporain from Paris to present his first IRCAM project, *Répons*, at the Proms, and in 1989 he conducted the BBC SO in a retrospective of his music at the Barbican. He has not appeared again with the orchestra since their all-Janáček concert at the 2008 Proms, but of course his music goes on: as in Daniel Barenboim's Beethoven/Boulez series at the 2012 Proms and, most recently, at the BBC SO's Total Immersion day in March at the Barbican in London.

> In asking him to become the next Chief Conductor of the BBC Symphony Orchestra, I was influenced by … my admiration for him as a composer, as a man of brilliance and imagination, and as a human being. Someone wrote of him that he is a clairvoyant observer of everything around him, and his judgements can certainly be violent at times. But there is nothing small in his behaviour, any more than in his conducting.

William Glock, the BBC's Controller of Music, 1959–72, on why he appointed Pierre Boulez to lead the BBC Symphony Orchestra

Top: Boulez with his predecessor Adrian Boult (Chief Conductor of the BBC Symphony Orchestra, 1931–50) at rehearsals for a BBC SO concert in 1972
Bottom: At the Roundhouse, Camden, where he gave groundbreaking concerts as part of the BBC Proms

20 years in the late 1950s, he was invited by Georges Pompidou, the French president, to establish the organisation that opened in 1977 as the Institut de Recherche et Coordination Acoustique/Musique (IRCAM). His hope was to find new tools – redesigned instruments, extended performance techniques, interpenetrations of live music and electronics – for which purpose he invited to Paris fellow composers, performers, computer experts and instrument builders. This was, however, just the moment when digital means were rapidly being developed for the analysis, synthesis and transformation of sounds, and the computer department of IRCAM quickly engulfed the whole enterprise.

That may not have been what Boulez intended, but he took note and, in his fifties and sixties, learnt how to be a different sort of composer. He drastically reduced his conducting schedule and worked with assistants on very precise ways to have instrumental sounds electronically treated and projected in real time. A work he had always planned as mediating between instrumental and electronic domains, '... explosante-fixe ...', imagined in 1971 as a memorial to Stravinsky, he was at last able to realise more than 20 years later as a concerto for electronically modulated flute and chamber orchestra, a labyrinth of gleaming sound in which we keep coming back to the same place from different directions.

Boulez was, however, far too practised – and far too skilled – an orchestral composer to feel he must always have some technological adjunct on hand. Since '... explosante-fixe ...' he has gone back to purely instrumental media, notably in Dérive 2, for 11 players, a continuous 45-minute stream, typically

20th-century titans: Boulez (*centre*) with Luigi Nono (*left*) and Karlheinz Stockhausen (*right*)

alternating calm with furious activity. Begun in 1988 and left to stand in 2009 – again, with the possibility that the brilliant flow could continue indefinitely – this work shows how far Boulez had come in rivalling the symphonic sweep of the old tonality but within a style where motifs can proliferate freely and at different speeds simultaneously. Listening to it, or to any other of Boulez's major pieces, we may feel our situation to be precarious, trying to catch ideas that vanish like sparks in the night – though not before they have conveyed excitement and wonder.

That so many of these pieces remain unfinished is not just the result of their composer's busy life as a conductor and institution leader. Rather their message is that renewal can never be over. ●

A critic for over 30 years, including for *The Times* and *The New Yorker*, Paul Griffiths is an authority on 20th- and 21st-century music. Among his books are studies of Boulez, Cage and Stravinsky as well as *A Concise History of Western Music* and the *New Penguin Dictionary of Music*; he also writes novels and librettos.

PIERRE BOULEZ AT THE PROMS

Notations 2, 12 & 10; La treizième (arr. J. Schöllhorn); Dérive 2
PROMS SATURDAY MATINEE 1 25 JULY

Notations 1–4 & 7
PROM 13 • 27 JULY

Figures – Doubles – Prismes; Frontispice (Ravel, arr. Boulez)
PROM 36 • 12 AUGUST

'... explosante-fixe ...'
PROM 55 • 26 AUGUST

Mémoriale ('... explosante-fixe ...' Originel); Domaines; Éclat/Multiples
PROMS SATURDAY MATINEE 4 29 AUGUST

THE NINTH

ENGLISH MUSIC FESTIVAL

Join us for the Ninth English Music Festival, in the heart of the Oxfordshire countryside. Highlights for 2015 include the World Première of George Butterworth's *Fantasia for Orchestra*, performed by the BBC Concert Orchestra in a concert also featuring Finzi's haunting Cello Concerto with Raphael Wallfisch; Roderick Williams starring in a concert of Butterworth, Holst and Boughton, and choral music by Howells, Vaughan Williams and Walton from the Elysian Singers. From British folk-songs and chamber recitals to early music and a 1930s dance band, this Festival offers a wealth of music to discover and explore.

Book at **www.englishmusicfestival.org.uk/boxoffice.html** or contact Festival Director **Em Marshall-Luck** at **em.marshall-luck@englishmusicfestival.org.uk** or on **07808 473889** to receive a full programme brochure.

DORCHESTER-ON-THAMES, OXFORDSHIRE
22-25 MAY 2015
www.englishmusicfestival.org.uk

WIGMORE HALL

Wigmore Series
2015–2016

Iestyn Davies   Jean-Guihen Queyras   Christian Gerhaher   Igor Levit   Jordi Savall
Magdalena Kožená   Sir Simon Rattle   Mitsuko Uchida   L'Arpeggiata   Waltraud Meier
Stephen Kovacevich   Martha Argerich   Elīna Garanca   Michael Collins   James Baillieu
Nash Ensemble   Sarah Connolly   Bertrand Chamayou   The Sixteen   Borodin Quartet
Christian Zacharias   Florian Boesch   Alina Ibragimova   Cédric Tiberghien   Heath Quartet
Franco Fagioli   James Ehnes   Stile Antico   Patricia Petibon   Brad Mehldau
EXAUDI   Ensemble Correspondances   Eggner Trio   Thomas Hampson   Jan Lisiecki
The English Concert   Christiane Karg   Vox Luminis   Llŷr Williams   Christoph Prégardien
Nikolaj Znaider   ATOS Trio   Birmingham Contemporary Music Group

Booking opens 29 May 2015
Online Booking www.wigmore-hall.org.uk   Box Office 020 7935 2141

Director: John Gilhooly OBE   Wigmore Hall, 36 Wigmore Street, London W1U 2BP   Registered Charity Number: 1024838

Department for Culture Media & Sport   LOTTERY FUNDED   Supported using public funding by ARTS COUNCIL ENGLAND

PLAYING
PROKOFIEV

Spanning two decades, Prokofiev's piano concertos embody the composer-pianist's innovative and provocative style in microcosm. **DANIEL JAFFÉ** reveals the striking personality that Prokofiev brought to the genre

Probably no other composer has combined prankish fun with such a serious and innovative approach to the piano concerto, creating works that influenced generations of composers, particularly in his native Russia but also in the West (notably Roussel, Ireland and Britten). Prokofiev was, of course, not the first to bring a sense of humour to the genre: more than a century earlier, Beethoven's First Concerto had included several moments of sly wit. Yet even that work does not quite match the cheek of Prokofiev's own First Concerto (1911–12), composed when he was a student at the St Petersburg Conservatory. After its pompous opening, the soloist launches in not with some heroic theme, but instead with a helter-skelter *étude*-like passage at breakneck speed – a fair impression of the young Prokofiev when performing his self-consciously 'devilish' works (whether the *Suggestion diabolique*, or his fiendishly demanding *Toccata*), only here playing a mock conservatory-style exercise with devil-may-care panache and insouciance.

In the First Concerto, one can sense Prokofiev kicking over the traces of his rigorous piano training under the legendary Anna Yesipova, as he subverts and pokes fun at the conventions and form of the concerto. This, of course, would not have been possible without an in-depth knowledge of the standard concerto repertoire. Prokofiev had himself conquered one of its great masterpieces, Tchaikovsky's First Piano Concerto, and studied, performed or conducted the works of Beethoven, Liszt and Saint-Saëns (whose orchestration Prokofiev found 'simply astounding!'), as well as concertos by the prolific and much-celebrated founder of the St Petersburg Conservatory, Anton Rubinstein. On the other hand, Prokofiev had developed a withering contempt for works by the Conservatory's then director, Alexander Glazunov, noting in his diary that Glazunov's *Jubilee Cantata* made 'inept and stupid' use of a theme borrowed from Rubinstein's Fourth Piano Concerto. Composers who borrowed clumsily or obviously from others never impressed Prokofiev – he didn't even spare Stravinsky for this practice – since he prized original and authentic expression above all other qualities.

No work exemplifies this better than his Second Concerto (1912–13, revised 1923). Dark and acerbic, it was not simply Prokofiev 'pushing the envelope' after his First Concerto's light, diverting style: much of its character was inspired by his friendship with a sardonic and intelligent fellow student, Maximilian Schmidthof. Its finale – both beguiling and ferocious – appears to be effectively a memorial to his friend, who committed suicide before Prokofiev completed the work. Furthermore, the concerto's powerfully expressive character determined its unorthodox structure: four movements (instead of the usual three), of

Prokofiev at the piano c1924, by which time he had completed the first three piano concertos and left the USA (where he had moved in 1918) for Europe

DANIIL TRIFONOV ON PIANO CONCERTOS NOS. 1 & 3

Prokofiev's rebellious and sarcastic nature is evident from the first bars of his First Piano Concerto, – he takes the key, D flat major, which one immediately associates with Tchaikovsky's Piano Concerto No. 1, and even starts with the same theme – only it's played backwards! The Third Concerto combines the rhythmical choreography of his ballets, the characters and atmospheric scenes of his vocal music and a variety of truly symphonic orchestral episodes.

SERGEI BABAYAN ON PIANO CONCERTOS NOS. 2 & 5

When I think of Prokofiev's music, I feel time's ability to transform something that was perceived as barbarian and avant-garde into something that represents Romanticism, especially the Second Piano Concerto, one of the brightest examples of that age. The Fifth Concerto is a kaleidoscope of ideas found in Prokofiev's piano writing, where real feelings and hidden messages interact like a game, expressed under Prokofiev's mischievous, mysterious smile.

ALEXEI VOLODIN ON PIANO CONCERTO NO. 4

Prokofiev's Fourth Piano Concerto is an athletic, virtuosic piece, which requires at the same time a certain power and subtlety from the pianist. Being a brilliant pianist himself, Prokofiev knew how to challenge the soloist with a variety of moods, rhythms, passage-work and nuances. The transparency of his piano writing is also a challenge – you are never covered by the orchestra and your left hand has to work perfectly!

which the first includes an astonishing cadenza of tumultuous passion, followed by two different forms of scherzo – one a propulsive toccata, the other a grotesque procession.

Although he began his Third Concerto (1917–21) while still living in Russia, Prokofiev completed it after he had left post-Revolutionary Russia to seek his fortunes in the USA and Europe. The need to improve his chances of success with a non-Russian audience may, to an extent, explain why he chose in that work to follow the concerto's most conventional form of three movements: first a sonata-allegro, then a theme and variations for the second and a finale that begins and ends in lively style, yet frames one of Prokofiev's most nostalgic and wistful themes (reflecting his seldom acknowledged admiration for Rachmaninov's concertos). But this was not a cynical or even merely a pragmatic move: Prokofiev, while studying conducting under

Nikolay Tcherepnin at the Conservatory, developed a genuine affection for the Classical 18th-century composers Mozart and Haydn, both of whom helped to establish the concerto's standard three-movement form. Indeed, Prokofiev had already written his First Symphony, which he named 'Classical', in conscious tribute to Haydn.

The Fourth Concerto (1931) was written not for Prokofiev's own use, but for the Austrian pianist Paul Wittgenstein, who had lost his right arm during the First World War. Wittgenstein commissioned several composers – including Britten, Strauss, Ravel and Schmidt as well as Prokofiev – to write left-hand concertos for him to perform. Facing this limit on what could be demanded of his soloist, Prokofiev effectively reflected this by using a smaller orchestra than in his other concertos and a more subdued instrumental palette. Wittgenstein ultimately chose not to perform Prokofiev's work, so this modest yet attractive concerto lay neglected until its first performance in 1956, three years after the composer's death. That it is still little known is a pity, since it includes one of Prokofiev's most beautiful slow movements, written according to the 'new simplicity' he was then creating, which ultimately came into full blossom with his ballet *Romeo and Juliet*.

With the Fifth Concerto (1932), Prokofiev returned to the very visual virtuosity (these concertos are very much to be seen as well as heard) of his first three concertos. He later recalled that, in composing the work, he collated ideas such as 'a passage running across the entire keyboard, with the left hand overtaking the right', or 'chords in the piano and orchestra interrupting one another'. The Fifth Concerto was launched in style, with the composer as soloist performing with

Pianist Paul Wittgenstein in 1927 – Prokofiev was one of a number of composers commissioned by Wittgenstein to write left-hand concertos for him, following the loss of his right arm in the First World War

the Berlin Philharmonic conducted by Wilhelm Furtwängler. It was to be Prokofiev's final bow as a concerto soloist, since he increasingly resented the amount of time spent touring as virtuoso composer-pianist rather than actually composing. Yet he did not skimp in creating this final work in the series. On the contrary, it has one of the most unusual structures – being in no fewer than five movements – and provides, as a perfect balm to its generally pugnacious style, an oasis of pastoral calm in its slow fourth movement: this opens with soothing flute and strings, then reaches one of Prokofiev's most enticing inventions with trickling piano figuration through which woodwind play the movement's principal opening melody.

In his autobiography, Prokofiev complained that his lyrical gifts were not widely recognised. Listeners today, familiar with such works as *Romeo and Juliet* and *Alexander Nevsky*, may now readily recognise that lyricism and hear it ripen and develop, even through the sometimes flinty invention of those five brilliant showpieces. •

Daniel Jaffé is the author of *Sergey Prokofiev*, published as part of Phaidon's 20th-Century Composers series, and in 2012 published a *Historical Dictionary of Russian Music*. He has lectured and broadcast extensively on Russian music, including on BBC Radio 3 and BBC Four.

PROKOFIEV PIANO CONCERTOS AT THE PROMS

Piano Concertos Nos. 1–5
Daniil Trifonov (Nos. 1 & 3), Sergei Babayan (Nos. 2 & 5), Alexei Volodin (No. 4)

PROM 14 • 28 JULY

EDINBURGH INTERNATIONAL FESTIVAL

7–31 AUGUST 2015

EXCEPTIONAL MUSIC-MAKING THIS AUGUST IN EDINBURGH, THE WORLD'S FESTIVAL CITY

2015 highlights include Komische Oper Berlin, San Francisco Symphony, Oslo Philharmonic Orchestra, Iván Fischer and the Budapest Festival Orchestra, Lang Lang, Anne-Sophie Mutter, Esa-Pekka Salonen and the Philharmonia Orchestra, Diana Damrau and many more.

EIF.CO.UK

Watch videos, hear the music and enjoy insights into our artists

 Follow us @EdintFest

 Like us

 Subscribe to our channel

 Follow us @EdintFest

The Magic Flute | Komische Oper Berlin
Photo **Iko Freese** / drama-berlin.de
Charity No SC004694

 ·EDINBVRGH·
THE CITY OF EDINBURGH COUNCIL

 CREATIVE SCOTLAND
ALBA | CHRUTHACHAIL

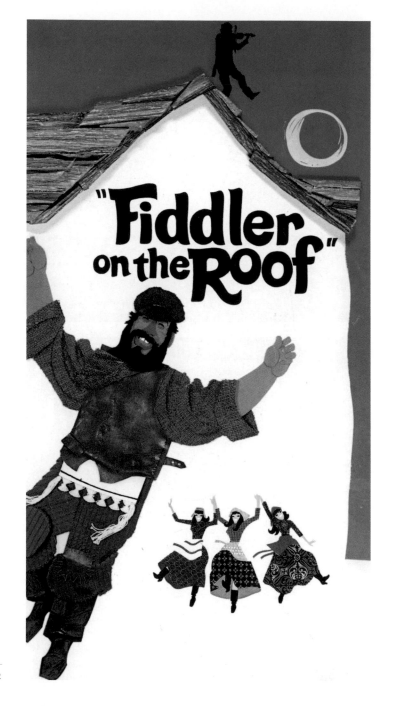

MIRACLE OF MIRACLES!

As Bryn Terfel takes on the role of Tevye in *Fiddler on the Roof*, **DOMINIC McHUGH** discovers how the show took the Broadway musical back to its Jewish roots, and became an enduring hit

Some of the most important contributors to the early development of the Broadway musical were of Jewish ethnicity, and had either emigrated to America themselves or been born there as the children of immigrants. In the process, many changed their names in order to assimilate into a new society: Israel Baline became Irving Berlin, Frederick Austerlitz transformed into Fred Astaire and George Gershwin's family name was originally Gershovitz. One of Berlin's earliest memories was of sitting at the side of the road as a child in Russia, watching his house burn to the ground in one of Tsar Nicholas II's vicious pogroms. His family moved to New York City, where Berlin would eventually write a string of hit songs, including 'White Christmas', 'Easter Parade' and 'God Bless America'. Ironically, in light of his Russian background, he and his fellow Jews came to represent the new American culture.

This American identity was consistently reinforced on Broadway until 1964, when an intense collaboration between Jerry Bock (composer), Sheldon Harnick (lyrics) and Joseph Stein (book) resulted in the revolutionary *Fiddler on the Roof*. Bock and Harnick's theatrical partnership was already well established: they were responsible for four previous musicals together, including *Fiorello!*

(1959), which won the Pulitzer Prize for Drama, and the popular *She Loves Me* (1963). But these were comparatively standard Broadway fare and the team was ready for a different approach.

They found inspiration from Sholem Aleichem's *Tevye and His Daughters*, a series of short stories about a poor milkman and his family living in the fictional Jewish settlement of Anatevka around the turn of the 20th century. The tales had appeared between 1894 and 1914, and their depiction of the romantic exploits of Tevye's daughters, as well as Tevye's struggle to come to terms with their choices, seemed the perfect vehicle for a charming musical. Yet the show also provided an unexpected reflection of the experiences of the families of many in the Broadway audience. Like Irving Berlin and his family, Tevye and his friends are forced to move from

Russia to New York at the end of the show, leaving behind the life and traditions they had striven hard to maintain. For the musical's early audiences, this must have been especially poignant after the devastation of the Holocaust.

Reflecting the theme of the plot, Bock and Harnick also played with tradition in their score for the show. They discarded more than 30 songs along the way, indicating the complexity of the challenge they faced. In spite of a few familiar Broadway gestures such as the waltz in the song 'Matchmaker, Matchmaker', most of the numbers are crafted to incorporate melodic and harmonic features that reference the ethnicity of the story. Yet their approach reaped its rewards: *Fiddler* gave birth to a hit song in 'If I were a rich man', which is more reminiscent of Jewish klezmer music than the classic

32-bar Broadway ballad. Indeed, in many ways the show as a whole is the complete antithesis of the other successful musical of the year, Jerry Herman's *Hello, Dolly!*. Nevertheless, with its lively opening number and dazzling ensembles, *Fiddler* still features an exuberance that confirms its affinity to Broadway.

When *Fiddler on the Roof* opened at the Imperial Theatre on Broadway on 22 September 1964, it was met with critical acclaim. Indeed, the *Daily News* called it 'one of the great works of the American musical theater'. It went on to run for a record-breaking 3,242 performances, won nine Tony Awards, and has been revived for stars ranging from Topol to Alfred Molina.

Now in 2015 it provides the perfect material for the dream team of Bryn Terfel, whose humour and musicianship promise to breathe new life into the role of Tevye, and David Charles Abell, an ideal musical theatre conductor. Last year's sensational *Kiss Me, Kate* Prom was heard in Abell's new critical edition of Cole Porter's score, and in his hands the opportunity to return to *Fiddler*'s full original orchestration has the potential to be no less revelatory. ●

Dominic McHugh is a lecturer in Musicology at the University of Sheffield. His books include *Loverly: The Life and Times of 'My Fair Lady'* (OUP, 2012) and *Alan Jay Lerner: A Lyricist's Letters* (OUP, 2014).

FIDDLER'S GLOBAL CONQUEST
How the Jewish-themed, all-American musical took to the world's stages

Many musicals remain associated with the performers from their original productions: Rex Harrison in *My Fair Lady*, Barbra Streisand in *Funny Girl*, and so on. But, although the role of Tevye in *Fiddler on the Roof* was written for the beloved Zero Mostel, the show is associated more with Chaim Topol. The actor had played the role briefly in Tel Aviv and was a young unknown when he was invited to star as Tevye in the first London production in 1967. Topol's success in the part led to his being offered the role in the 1971 movie version, as well as revivals on Broadway (1990) and in London (1983 and 1994), plus a 'farewell tour' in 2009.

Yet *Fiddler*'s greatest achievement might be its journey across the globe: the show quickly transcended its original context and was seen in cities as disparate as Tokyo (1967), Hamburg (1968), Prague (1968) and Paris (1969). It finally reached

Chaim Topol in London, 1983, while appearing as Tevye at the Apollo Victoria Theatre

Moscow in 1983 – a natural destination, since one of the show's key inspirations was the Russian folk-inspired work of artist Marc Chagall, several of whose paintings depict a fiddler to show that music is a vital part of the Jewish spirit. *Fiddler*'s universal themes of tradition and the family have resonated with audiences from Rhodesia to Norway, from Argentina to Spain: a global conquest for a Broadway classic.

FIDDLER ON THE ROOF AT THE PROMS

David Charles Abell conducts Grange Park Opera's production, with a cast led by Bryn Terfel
PROM 11 • 25 JULY

LONDON.
IN HIGH DEFINITION.

SEE ALL OF LONDON IN ONE BREATHTAKING EXPERIENCE.

theviewfromtheshard.com

THE VIEW
FROM THE SHARD

POPULAR
IDOLS

This year John Wilson and his orchestra return for not one but two Proms – celebrating anniversaries for Frank Sinatra and Leonard Bernstein – two figures, as **DAVID BENEDICT** discovers, close to Wilson's heart

The moment the audience for the spectacular Proms performance last year of *Kiss Me, Kate* finally stopped applauding, the cry went up: what are John Wilson and his virtuoso orchestra going to do next? The answer? Leonard Bernstein and Frank Sinatra. No, not together: this year, Wilson's top-flight players are letting rip not once, but twice. On 5 September they're delivering the symphonic glories of Bernstein's scores for stage and screen. First up, however, is their Late Night Prom on 7 August devoted to Frank Sinatra, born 100 years ago.

The John Wilson Orchestra has always been an inspired cross between a plush symphony orchestra and a dance band. Its leap into the limelight at the 2009 MGM Prom seemed like an overnight sensation but was actually the result of playing together for over 15 years. And, during that time, the material Sinatra sang – in the scintillating big-band arrangements by Nelson Riddle, Gordon Jenkins and Billy May – had been at the core of its repertoire. But Wilson's appreciation of Sinatra goes back even further.

'He was my introduction to popular music. When I was 11, my school music teacher suggested I listen to Sinatra, but I didn't like it because for me, at that age, it was too jazzy. But, when I was 16, a friend of my father's had lots of his records, so I tried again. Second time around, I was knocked out by the astonishingly high level of Sinatra's musicianship.'

For Wilson, Sinatra's unique approach goes beyond beauty of tone and technical accomplishment, both of which are givens. 'The words always come first. He gets to the heart of the text, the story of the song. And he's a master of the lost art of weaving in and out of an orchestration.'

Sinatra had acquired many of these qualities on the job, working as a band singer. 'He noticed the way bandleader and trombonist Tommy Dorsey snatched discreet breaths in unobvious places. He used that in his own breath control. He used to practise swimming underwater to extend his lung capacity.'

He also noticed the way violinist Jascha Heifetz's bow changes were seamless and wanted to emulate that in his singing. Indeed, it was Sinatra's all-round musicianship, forever evident in the demands he made of his composers, lyricists, arrangers, conductors and players, that created his sound-world. Unusually for a singer, he's less of a soloist, more of a collaborator – and he only worked with the best.

'Many of these arrangements, drawn mostly from the classic LPs he released with Capitol records from 1954 to 1962, have become benchmarks of popular music and are widely considered to be the definitive settings of these songs. That's the key to why we're doing this. And, by featuring other singers alongside Seth MacFarlane, we're

> Sinatra gets to the heart of the text … And he's a master of the lost art of weaving in and out of an orchestration.

making it clear that it's not an evening of imitation: they'll all give this music their own slant.'

Sadly, Sinatra sang barely any songs by Leonard Bernstein. He famously starred opposite Gene Kelly in 1949's three-sailors-on-shore-leave picture *On the Town*, based on Bernstein's 1944 Broadway musical, but producer Arthur Freed only retained four of Bernstein's original songs. Freed's reason for decimating Bernstein's score was that he considered his music 'too avant-garde'. That description now seems bizarre for the music of the man who wrote the extravagant operetta-spoof 'Glitter and Be Gay' for *Candide* and the beloved score of *West Side Story*, the 1961 film version of which nabbed a record-breaking 10 Oscars and whose original soundtrack album sat at the No. 1 spot of the *Billboard* charts for a staggering, and still unrivalled, 54 weeks.

Once again, there happens to be an anniversary – it's 25 years since Bernstein's death – but Wilson's passion for his music goes way back.

'I've revelled in every element of Bernstein's output all through my musical life. I was riveted by him as a conductor before I even knew he was a composer. I had recordings of his performances of so much of the standard repertoire.' Immersion in Bernstein's compositions swiftly followed.

There's plenty to choose from in Bernstein's output, which includes the musical *Wonderful Town*, an adaptation of *Peter Pan* that starred Jean Arthur and Boris Karloff and his short-lived White House musical *1600 Pennsylvania Avenue*, which ran for only seven performances. But, as soon as Wilson decided he wanted to conduct an all-Bernstein programme, he knew he would include the composer's own suite from his sole film score, *On the Waterfront*. This epic crime-and-conscience drama about mob corruption and the unions won eight Oscars – though, sadly, none for Bernstein's score. Symphonic in both scale and structure, it's driven by passion, one of the hallmarks of this orchestra's playing.

'Shooting sparks into space': star-crossed lovers Tony and Maria in their furtive balcony scene from the film of *West Side Story* (1961), which won 10 Oscars

The piece closest to Wilson's heart, however, is *West Side Story*. 'It was the first conducting I did. It was at Newcastle College when I was 16. Twenty-five years later, I conducted it again at Sage Gateshead. Every single dynamic indication, every accent, every marking in the score has a clear dramatic implication.' Who better to conduct it? ●

David Benedict is a broadcaster and critic specialising in musical theatre. He is currently writing the authorised biography of Stephen Sondheim.

JOHN WILSON AND HIS ORCHESTRA AT THE PROMS

Late Night Sinatra
PROM 30 • 7 AUGUST

Bernstein – Stage and Screen
PROM 67 • 5 SEPTEMBER

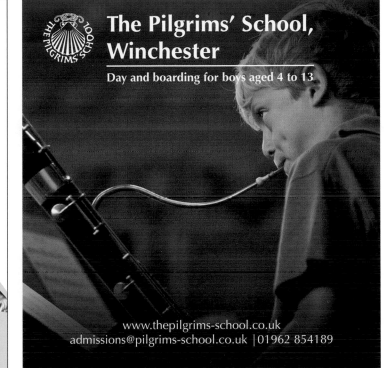

NATURAL
SOUNDS

Composer **MURRAY GOLD** on writing the score for *Life Story*, BBC One's recent landmark natural history series narrated by Sir David Attenborough

B ack in 2011, I got an email from Series Producer Rupert Barrington asking if I was available to write music for an as-yet-untitled natural history series by BBC Earth scheduled to air in 2014. I wrote back saying I would write music for just about *anything* BBC Earth was making. It wasn't just that my copy of *Life on Earth* still sits on my bookshelf. It wasn't even that *Life on Earth*, *Blue Planet* and *Frozen Planet* and all those other wonderful shows had for years been my refuge from the grim, depressing stories in the news. It was, above all, that this programme would be a chance to write music for great characters in great stories, because that's what the 'stars' of these shows are – the puffer fish, the octopus, the turtles, the meerkats, the whole carnival of life captured by the remarkable directors and cameramen who film them. Those animals demand that music is written for them. Their adventures and misadventures, their romances and strategies for survival are the most truthful of dramas and are the perfect inspiration for music.

One of the first conversations Mike Gunton (Executive Producer), Rupert and I had was about 'anthropomorphism', a word that is usually used pejoratively to describe the false attribution of human values, feelings and motives to animals. The argument that there is a more 'objective' way of seeing animals, which involves looking at them coldly and scientifically, as specimens, leaves out everything the camera catches. It is an argument that wilfully denies what the eye sees. If a puffer fish creates a complex, decorated structure on the bed of the ocean and sits inside it waiting for a female puffer fish to find him impressive, how can we think of that as anything other than courtship? If a monogamous albatross waits for its partner of 20 years to return and be reunited on a beach, how can we not think of that as love?

So I wrote the music to *Life Story* as if human protagonists were caught up in hundreds of life-and-death plot lines. Each plot played out as a tiny ballet, silent and full of movement. Usually, the film of these 'ballets' had been edited so that each story consisted of a number of musical movements. Most of the music was written before the narration was recorded – in other words, to silent film. Preparing to present it in the Royal Albert Hall at this year's Proms has been a relatively simple process of stripping back everything except the music, which on television is balanced by the natural sounds and the commentary.

When Sir David Attenborough's narration was later recorded and added to the final film, *Life Story* suddenly and instantly became the most recent in that series of landmark television programmes I have loved since I was a child. So many years after first reading and watching *Life on Earth*, I was making a contribution to one of the great man's shows. His voice led me and millions of others to the wonder and magic of living creatures. He opened up countless worlds. ●

Executive Producer
MIKE GUNTON
on *Life Story's*
natural soundscape

The use of music in documentaries is not without controversy and wildlife films are no exception – some people like nature films to be purely observed and accompanied only by the sounds of nature. But *Life Story* was different – in the sense that the series didn't simply report the wonders of the natural world, but tried to give the audience an experience of what life is like for an animal and of the world in which it lives.

We did this visually by showing both the scale and power of the landscape and framing the survival stories through the eyes of individual animals. But the images are only half the story. The soundscape does perhaps even more to give a sense of the drama of nature. Animal sounds and the sounds of their habitats create atmosphere, but the full drama – the beauty, danger, pathos, humour and even the cruelty of life and landscape – can be further and wonderfully evoked by a skilful, artistically composed score.

There are pitfalls: the combination of intense images, natural sounds and music can be overwhelming, but in the hands of a sensitive, sympathetic musician the score can take the viewing experience to a level of immersion that is hard to imagine being possible without music. Who cannot have felt empathy for the obsessive, industrious puffer fish or have forgotten the almost unbearable tension as the goslings prepared to jump from the cliff top. We were fortunate on *Life Story* to have such a musician and composer as Murray Gold.

A wildlife camera operator underwater in Japan, filming new behaviours for BBC's *Life Story* – here a puffer fish building a nest in the sand – using equipment specially designed and built for the purpose

Tom Crowley/BBC

LIFE STORY PROM

Music by Murray Gold and footage from the 2014 BBC One series, presented by Sir David Attenborough
PROM 59 · 30 AUGUST

LIFE STORY

Talented Dancer or Musician?

Yes, TALENT is ALL you need for a place at a Music and Dance School.

All our schools are dedicated to encouraging talented young people from all financial and cultural backgrounds... we can offer up to 100% Government funding for places.

Music and Dance Schools are committed to the highest teaching standards in music and dance, as well as an excellent academic education.

If you are interested in one of the Music and Dance Schools just visit our website for contact details.

www.musicanddanceschools.com

There are nine Music and Dance Schools throughout the UK

- Chetham's School of Music, Manchester
- Elmhurst School for Dance, Birmingham
- St Mary's Music School, Edinburgh
- The Hammond, Chester
- The Purcell School for Young Musicians, Herts
- The Royal Ballet School, London
- Tring Park School for the Performing Arts, Herts
- Wells Cathedral School, Somerset
- Yehudi Menuhin School, Surrey

MUSIC
& DANCE
SCHOOLS
ACCESS TO EXCELLENCE

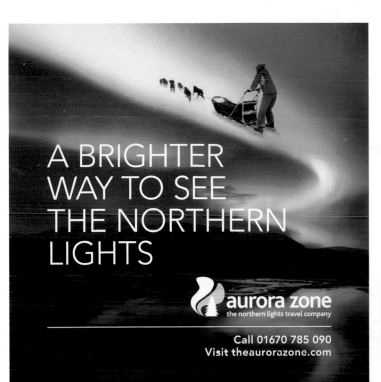

TEN
PIECES

SUZY KLEIN, an ambassador for the BBC's scheme to get classical music into every UK primary school, outlines the project's ambitions ahead of the two Ten Pieces Proms

As you're reading this Proms Guide, it's likely you're already a fan of classical music. Where that journey begins is different for each of us, but there's one common factor: that moment when we feel for the first time the visceral jolt, the emotional and imaginative thrill that a great piece of music unleashes in us. For me, it was hearing the operas of Mozart on a well-worn, scratchy old cassette that started a lifelong journey into classical music, that place which explains to us our deepest feelings and desires, a language that bypasses the rational, teaching us instead what it means to be human and to embrace fully all that life throws at us. What would it be like if we could introduce every primary-school child in the country to that magical world?

That was the ambitious challenge the BBC set itself when it launched Ten Pieces – a project which aims to bring the joy and richness of orchestral music to young children and, in doing so, reveals their potential to listen, share and create work of their own. Led by BBC Learning and the BBC's world-beating six professional Performing Groups, the scale of the initiative is unprecedented, with more than 230 arts and music organisations across the UK teaming up with the BBC to put classical music right at the heart of the creative life of Britain's children.

The 10 pieces chosen for the scheme cover a dizzying variety of musical styles and they span the centuries: from Handel, Mozart, Beethoven and Grieg to Britten, Holst, Mussorgsky, Stravinsky and John Adams. There's also new music in there, with a specially commissioned piece for body percussion written by the brilliant young composer Anna Meredith: *Connect It* showcases the possibilities of communal sound and movement produced only by the human body – no instruments allowed!

Officially launched in October last year, Ten Pieces all began – as so many people's first interaction with classical music does – with a trip to the cinema. More than 120,000 children from schools around the country tripped along to their local multiplex, thousands of others were posted a free DVD to their classrooms. What they were shown was a visually spectacular Hollywood-style short film, bringing the chosen works to life with a host of famous faces joined by the BBC National Orchestra of Wales. In just one week, in every corner of the UK, thousands of children got to know those 10 pieces at the same time.

Next was the invitation to the children to get creative back in their classrooms – making up their own pieces of dance, digital art or composition inspired by the film. Not only did teachers have access to a wealth of resources produced by the BBC, but a huge range of Ten Pieces 'champions' organisations came to schools around the country, sharing their passion and expertise. Together, they have created puppet shows, gym lessons, science experiments, playground games – even synchronised swimming! There seems to be no limit to what you can do with just 10 pieces of classical music.

I was delighted to be asked to join some illustrious musicians as a group of 'ambassadors' for the project, charged with spreading the word across the country. Alongside Nicola Benedetti, Julian Joseph, Cerys Matthews, Alison Balsom, Catrin Finch and Laura Mvula, I have seen up-close how children have reacted to the music and it has been a deeply joyful thing to behold.

Now we are nearing the end of the first Ten Pieces journey, where the focus shifts to performance, with children showcasing their creative work in a series of local and regional concerts. And it all culminates at the Royal Albert Hall with the two special Ten Pieces Proms, putting the children themselves in the spotlight, performing and presenting their own work, alongside the original 10 pieces.

Starting from the initial notion that every child should have access to the world's greatest music, the Ten Pieces scheme has, I think, achieved something rather spectacular since its launch. It has welcomed the nation's children into the joyous world of orchestral music, igniting their creative potential, getting them truly excited by the possibilities that classical music has to offer. And that initial moment of realisation, the shock and joy at hearing what an orchestra can do when its power is fully unleashed by a great composer, is something classical music fans like us share with them. ●

Singer-songwriter, BBC Radio 6 Music presenter and Ten Pieces ambassador Cerys Matthews at a Ten Pieces primary-school workshop last October

Suzy Klein is a presenter of BBC Radio 3's *In Tune*, *Music Matters* and *Live in Concert*, among other programmes. She can also be heard on BBC Radio 4's *Saturday Live*. A Silver prize-winner at the Radio Academy Awards in 2013, she has also written for *The New Statesman*, *The Guardian* and *BBC Music Magazine*.

CERIAN ROLLS
a teacher at Gaer Primary School in Newport, Wales, describes the effect of Ten Pieces at her school

When you are gifted the opportunity of a new door to learning through music that you can offer to the minds of the future, you simply smile, take it with both hands and work out the details later. That's what we did in our primary school when we first came into contact with Ten Pieces, even though my pupils had had almost no previous contact with classical music!

We were definitely inspired following a visit from the super-talented harpist Catrin Finch, but when it came to the next step of creating our own pieces in response, we were starting from scratch. The Ten Pieces were a world away from our pupils' experience to date, but they were nevertheless inspired. Challenged, too!

From Handel to Anna Meredith – across 10 classes of pupils aged 5 to 11 – we enjoyed as we listened. We had very little in the way of conventional musical skills, but we had other strengths and experiences that allowed us to access this musical world. We used art and story-boarding to interpret hidden depths and meanings. We brought in dance and movement to articulate expression. We made kazoos. Performances and workshops whirled in at a dizzying rate, giving the pupils hands-on experience – and now I can proudly boast that we have gone from 0 to 157 instrumentalists in four months, all inspired by Ten Pieces.

TEN PIECES PROM

Featuring all Ten Pieces, plus creative responses from primary-school children
PROMS 2 & 3
SATURDAY 18 JULY • 6.30pm
& SUNDAY 19 JULY • 11.00am

ME, MYSELF AND
BACH

As four leading artists come face-to-face with the solo instrumental works of J. S. Bach, **LINDSAY KEMP** explores this hallowed realm of the repertoire, which even today tests the greatest of performers

For many Proms-goers it is a familiar scene. The finale of some lush Romantic concerto for violin or cello – Tchaikovsky or Dvořák, perhaps – has just come to an exhilarating close and soloist and conductor are all smiles as they acknowledge the applause. After both have made their returns to the stage, the soloist reappears alone and, taking position in front of the orchestra, prepares to play an encore. In a moment the mood changes. Suddenly there is solemnity in the air; some listeners may even bow their heads. For, in the few seconds before the music starts, we know that we are about to hear solo Bach.

It is a dramatic coup that seldom fails to hit home. Perhaps the drama of that single performer inhabiting the giant space of the Royal Albert Hall heightens the effect. But how do we know that it will be solo Bach? Well, partly because, for violinists and cellists, it is by far the finest unaccompanied music for their instruments; but surely also because, after a rich and extrovert orchestral feast,

> For violinists and cellists, solo Bach is by far the finest unaccompanied music … This, it feels, is the purest form of music, direct from the source.

where else can you go but inward – there to contemplate the meticulous details of line, harmony, structure and rhythm set before us by perhaps the greatest of all musical minds? This, it feels, is pure music, direct from the source.

Of course, it was not conceived that way. Bach was a pragmatic musician and his solo music – whether for violin, cello, harpsichord or organ – generally came into being for practical reasons. Although later in life Bach pursued an almost encyclopedic interest in the arcana of composition, in his thirties, when he wrote the solo violin and solo cello works, he was composing for performance. Yet the lack of explanation from him of their purpose, the absence of any indication of who might have played them, their technical and intellectual difficulty and the sheer symbolism of their unaccompanied state adds to the aura of these pieces as a kind of primal music. Later composers, and good ones too, have written for solo violin or cello, but none –

Ysaÿe, Hindemith, Bartók, Kodály and Britten included – has escaped their shadow.

Given that, in common with much of Bach's music, a lot of this solo repertoire was scarcely performed for at least a century after his death, it is the six unaccompanied violin works – three Sonatas and three Partitas (or suites), completed in 1720 – that resonate most strongly through history. Unusually, they were relatively widely known in Bach's lifetime: in an obituary of his father, Carl Philipp Emanuel Bach reported, 'one of the greatest violinists once told me that he had seen nothing more perfect for learning to be a good violinist' – and they continued to be performed in the second half of the 18th century. Ferdinand David performed them in Leipzig during the 1840s (though only after he had persuaded his friend Mendelssohn to provide what he felt was a necessary piano accompaniment). Busoni made his famous piano transcription of the Chaconne from the Partita No. 2 in D minor in the 1890s.

And one of the earliest classical violin recordings, by Joseph Joachim in 1903, was of two solo Bach movements. There has been no shortage of successors, either.

Bach was not the first to compose for unaccompanied violin, and nor were the formal frameworks of Bach's solo violin pieces without standard models. Yet in his hands the technique of using double- and multiple-stopped chords and skilfully written 'broken-chord' melodies – to provide harmony and counterpoint, both real and implied (he was even able to wrestle fugal textures out of it) – touched a new technical and artistic level. At the same time his treatments of the sonata and partita forms were greatly extended and deepened. For a supreme example, one need look no further than the Partita No. 2, for which he wrote a final movement almost as long as the other four put together, a mighty Chaconne in which 64 elaborate variations on a four-bar chord sequence run into each other with epic

A view of Cöthen (engraving, 1650): it was probably while working here as Kapellmeister at the court of Prince Leopold that Bach composed his Sonatas and Partitas for solo violin and his Suites for solo cello

Pablo Casals (1876–1973), the first modern champion of Bach's six Cello Suites; he regarded his discovery of them as 'the great revelation of my life'

structural inevitability. It is an astounding achievement of sustained invention, even by Bach's standards, yet also the one movement for solo violin where we have an inkling of a personal expressive significance: there is a theory that Bach thought of it as an elegy on the death of his first wife, Maria Barbara, with one diligent German musicologist even identifying in it a network of fragments from chorale (or hymn) melodies associated with death and mourning.

Such, indeed, is the intellectual stature of Bach's solo violin music that it can be easy to lose sight of the fact that much of it is based on dance forms – the various allemandes, courantes, sarabandes, minuets, bourrées, gavottes and gigues that were standard components of the Baroque suite. The spirit of the dance is harder to miss in his six Suites for solo cello, however, for here it is nearer the core, somehow more elemental to the music's being, perhaps because the sequence of dances

– five in each, introduced by a prelude – is more settled and focused than in the Sonatas and Partitas. But there is another important way in which the Cello Suites differ. They too are thought to date from around 1720, when Bach was engaged at the court of Cöthen, but although we do not know if they were composed before, after or at the same time as the violin pieces, they come across as a refinement of their vocabulary. The cello is less able to play chords than the violin but Bach meets this challenge with such genius, making wide leaps across the strings to pick out the essential notes of music conceived in two or more parts – that the effect is of a distillation of the complex language of melody and harmony into one fluid thread. This is a paring-down executed with the grace and skill of an artist rendering a human arm or face with no more than the line of a pencil.

Bach's Cello Suites do not have the unbroken performance history of his Sonatas and Partitas; long considered as mere exercises, their reintroduction to the regular repertoire is generally credited to the great Catalan cellist Pablo Casals, who – in 1889, aged 13 – discovered an old copy of them in a second-hand shop in Barcelona. 'I did not even know of their existence,' he later recalled. 'It was the great revelation of my life.' Casals did not attempt to play them in public for 12 years, however, and it was not until 1936 that he embarked on his famous recording of the complete set, the first ever made. Since then the Suites have grown ever more central to the repertoire of cellists – many have recorded them, some more than once – yet still their difficulty and scale can present an intimidating prospect to even the best of players; no less a figure than Mstislav Rostropovich felt he had to wait until his sixties to record them.

Bach was not himself a cellist and, although he did play the violin, it seems unlikely that he could have mastered the difficulties of the Sonatas and Partitas. He was, however, an organist, and one of the finest of his day at that. As a young man it was how he made his name in the towns and cities of northern Germany, and in the preludes, fugues, fantasias and toccatas he

SIR ANDRÁS SCHIFF
on Bach's 'Goldberg' Variations

My first encounter with Bach's 'Goldberg' Variations was in the mid-1960s, through recordings by Wanda Landowska and Glenn Gould. It was immediately clear to me that Bach was the greatest composer who ever lived and that this work was among the pinnacles of his art, indeed of all music.

To study and to learn this piece became my innermost wish; my first public performance took place in Budapest in 1973, after several years of intense work. Since then I've had the honour and the privilege to play it on countless occasions and to record it several times. One can never get tired of it: Bach's freshness, spirituality, virtuosity, his variety of characters never fail to amaze me. The great minor-key variations (especially No. 25) bring us into the world of the Passions, while others invite us to dance.

No-one combines the sacred and the secular like Bach does. To perform this work in the vast space of the Royal Albert Hall – and on the 'wrong' instrument (it was written for a harpsichord with two manuals) – is a major challenge, but the Proms is very special indeed and Bach's universal message surpasses all times and limitations.

wrote at this time the flamboyance of youth is seldom far from the surface. We must remember that in one of his early church jobs he was chastised for introducing 'strange harmonies' into the music of the service, echoes of which can be heard in his many organ chorale-settings. And, as with the solo violin, perhaps the single greatest piece he wrote for organ was firmly rooted in the variation ideal: the Passacaglia and Fugue in C minor, composed in his mid-twenties, maintains a steady tread through 20 variations on an eight-bar bass-pattern, before opening up into an imposing, brilliantly composed fugue.

The harpsichord music, too, is something we can think of as more directly personal to Bach. At its heart lie three more 'sets of six' (the English Suites, French Suites and Partitas), *The Well-Tempered Clavier* (a double set of wide-ranging preludes and fugues in all the keys, also known as the '48'), and the monumental 'Goldberg' Variations – an hour-long set of 30 variations on a simple but beautiful 'Aria' theme, in which virtuoso brilliance and contrapuntal ingenuity, especially in imitation (or canon) are present in equal measure. Were there any doubt about how far Bach's fearless approach to difficulty – for body *and* mind – was a vital part of his musical personality, we need only consider the reaction of one determined amateur, who wrote of the Partitas in a letter to her husband: 'the pieces that arrived for harpsichord by Bach are as hard as they are beautiful. If I play them 10 times, I still feel myself a beginner with them.' Nearly 300 years later, nothing much has changed. Next to Bach, we all feel like beginners. ●

Lindsay Kemp is a producer for BBC Radio 3, Artistic Director of the London Festival of Baroque Music and a regular contributor to *Gramophone*.

The Allemande Dance: copper engraving after a painting by Michel Vincent Brandoin (1733–1807); the instrumental form of the Allemande features in each of Bach's six Suites for solo cello and in Nos. 1 & 2 of the three Partitas for solo violin

SOLO BACH AT THE PROMS

Sonatas and Partitas Nos. 1–3
Alina Ibragimova (violin)

PROM 19 • 31 JULY
PROM 21 • 1 AUGUST

'Goldberg' Variations *Sir András Schiff (piano)*

PROM 50 • 22 AUGUST

Passacaglia and Fugue in C minor, BWV 582; Chorale Preludes 'In dir ist Freunde', BWV 615, 'Aus tiefer Not schrei ich zu dir', BWV 686, (attrib.) 'Christ ist erstanden', BWV 746 *Thierry Escaich (organ)*

PROM 52 • 23 AUGUST

Cello Suites Nos. 1–6 *Yo-Yo Ma (cello)*

PROM 68 • 5 SEPTEMBER

MORE BACH AT THE PROMS

Violin Concerto in E major, BWV 1042; Brandenburg Concerto No. 5 in D major, BWV 1050

PROMS SATURDAY MATINEE 3
15 AUGUST

Mass in G minor, BWV 235; Brandenburg Concerto No. 2 in F major, BWV 1047; Magnificat in D major, BWV 243

PROM 48 • 21 AUGUST

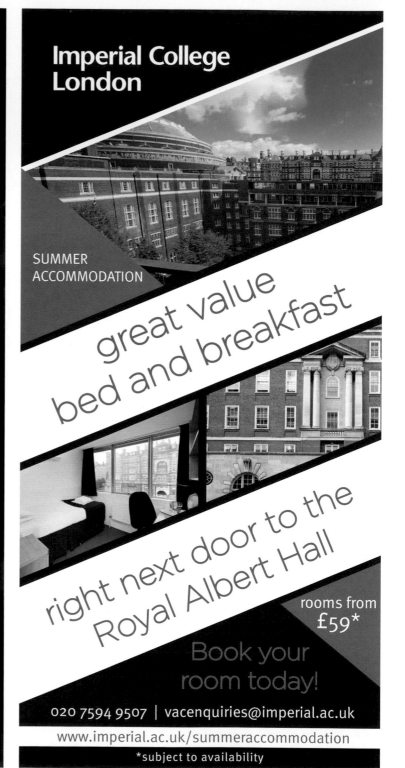

Erich Lessing/akg-images ('Orpheus and Eurydice' by Jacopo Vignali, 1592–1664)

A GRAND
ARRIVAL

TIM CARTER introduces Monteverdi's 'play in music' on the story of Orpheus and Eurydice, the lavish entertainment for the Mantuan court that heralded the beginning of opera

O n 23 February 1607, Carlo Magno wrote from Mantua to his brother in Rome:

> Tomorrow evening the Most Serene Lord the Prince [Francesco Gonzaga] is to sponsor a play in a room in the apartments used by the Most Serene Lady [Margherita] of Ferrara. It should be most unusual, as all the actors are to sing their parts; it is said on all sides that it will be a great success. No doubt I shall be driven to attend out of sheer curiosity, unless I am prevented from getting in by the lack of space.

He was referring to *Orfeo*, Claudio Monteverdi's first 'play in music' (*favola in musica*), his curiosity aroused by the fact that all the actors would sing, rather than speak, their parts. And the new musical style of 'recitative', midway between speech and song, was clearly 'most unusual'. Magno might also have wondered just how plausibly it could play out on the stage, given the rule that drama should somehow be true to life.

What we now call opera had emerged in Florence only recently. The first example to survive complete, Jacopo Peri's *Euridice*, celebrated the wedding of Maria de' Medici to King Henri IV of France in Florence in 1600. The Duke of Mantua, Vincenzo Gonzaga, attended those festivities, and his retinue included his secretary Alessandro Striggio, the librettist of *Orfeo*. Monteverdi may or may not have been there, but clearly he knew Peri's opera (it was published in early 1601). By creating another version of the Orpheus story, the Mantuans were now setting themselves up in competition with the Florentines.

The plot is simple enough: Orpheus and Eurydice are to be married (Acts 1–2); Eurydice dies of a snake bite (Act 2); Orpheus descends to Hades to recover his bride, moving the gods with the power of his song (Act 3), although (in Act 4) he fails Pluto's test and loses Eurydice a second time. Orpheus is left in despair, but – in a late addition to the opera – he is taken up into the heavens by Apollo (Act 5). However, the subject matter is significant. The mythological heroes of early opera served courtly propaganda by extolling the virtue and power of the ruling elite. Dealing with the most renowned musician of classical antiquity also mitigated the problem of how to justify singing on the stage. But there is a

> **In the 16th and early 17th centuries, arguments ran rife over music's power to arouse the emotions.**

further point to be made. In the 16th and early 17th centuries, arguments ran rife over music's power to arouse the emotions. *Orfeo* makes a forceful statement about the nature of the art.

After joining the Mantuan court musicians in 1590 or 1591 as a player of stringed instruments, Monteverdi moved up the ranks to become Duke Vincenzo's *maestro della musica*. As a result, he took an increasingly active role in writing music for court entertainments, be it *Orfeo* or a wide range of music for the wedding festivities of Prince Francesco Gonzaga and Margherita of Savoy in 1608, including the (now lost) opera *Arianna*. It was exhaustion caused by these festivities that prompted Monteverdi to start looking for employment elsewhere: he moved to Venice in 1613 to take up the prestigious position of *maestro di cappella* of St Mark's Basilica.

But Monteverdi never lost sight of his roots as a performer: *Orfeo* showcased not just a Mantuan patron, poet and composer, but also the Mantuan court musicians. It requires a substantial number of wind, brass and stringed instruments, plus a large continuo group. However, it was originally intended to be performed by a small cast of just nine or 10 singers (all male) – doubling up the solo roles and singing the choruses – which matches the number employed at the Gonzaga court. Monteverdi also wrote the title-role with the virtuoso tenor Francesco Rasi in mind, whose abilities come to the fore in the Act 3 showpiece, 'Possente spirto, e formidabil' nume'. This is a formal song, an aria, in which Orpheus seeks to move the powers of Hades, with instrumental echo effects to increase the sense of divine enchantment.

Orfeo may have been a 'new' opera, but it also drew on earlier theatrical genres typical of late Renaissance Italy, including the pastoral and also the Florentine *intermedi*, with their marvellous stage effects and large-scale vocal and instrumental pieces. Similarly, while the recitative was newly invented by Jacopo Peri, Monteverdi enriched it by way of the expressive dissonances and chromaticism he had developed in his 'old-style' polyphonic madrigals.

We are on the cusp between the Renaissance and Baroque periods. As with his Orpheus, Monteverdi leads us into uncharted terrain with a palpable sense of excitement at musical and dramatic possibilities hitherto unimagined. The echoes would resound through operatic history. ●

Tim Carter is David G. Frey Distinguished Professor of Music at the University of North Carolina at Chapel Hill. He is the author of *Monteverdi and His Contemporaries* (Ashgate, 2000) and *Monteverdi's Musical Theatre* (Yale University Press, 2002).

Claudio Monteverdi, whose innovations in marrying music and drama gave rise to the birth of opera as we now know it: portrait by Bernardo Strozzi (1581–1644)

MONTEVERDI'S ORFEO AT THE PROMS

Sir John Eliot Gardiner conducts the Monteverdi Choir and English Baroque Soloists
PROM 25 · 4 AUGUST

NEW MUSIC

With themes ranging from gods and demons to poetry and science, this year's world, European, UK and London premieres are an eclectic mix.
IGOR TORONYI-LALIC finds out more

Igor Toronyi-Lalic is arts editor at *The Spectator*, author of *Benjamin Britten* (Penguin, 2013) and co-director of the London Contemporary Music Festival.

ELEANOR ALBERGA

(BORN 1949)

Arise, Athena! (2015)
BBC commission: world premiere

PROM 76 • 12 SEPTEMBER

There is much about the Last Night that could intimidate. But Eleanor Alberga doesn't seem to do fear. She's relishing having such a large orchestra at her disposal. 'The larger the better,' she says. If she has a calling card, it is colour. 'I love dealing with a big palette.'

Although educated in the European classical tradition – Alban Berg's influence shines through much of her music – Alberga's sense of colour, energy and rhythm has Jamaican roots. 'Even in my least West Indian-sounding pieces the influence is still there,' she admits. 'The timbres I go for might actually come from a visual intake, from the exciting, bright colours of Jamaica and the West Indies in general, the bright sunlight, the vivid hues of the landscape, the clothes, the energy. There's a lot in that that influences my music. Even if it still sounds European.'

This is her first Proms commission – and her first experience of the Last Night. Composers haven't always responded to the gaiety of the event with complete solidarity. Some have chosen to go against its merry mood. 'I won't be doing that,' she insists. 'It's very important to go with that feeling of elation.'

That optimism is there in the name of her work, too: *Arise, Athena!* 'Athena is the goddess of the arts and of wisdom – among other things – and I think we need her at the moment.'

B TOMMY ANDERSSON

(BORN 1964)

Pan (2015)
BBC commission: world premiere

PROM 64 • 3 SEPTEMBER

Pan and pipe. They go together like jam and bread. It would have been churlish, then, for B Tommy Andersson, in his new orchestral work *Pan*, not to make use of the most famous and majestic pipes of them all.

But don't get too excited: an organ concerto this is not. He's done one of those already. This is a new challenge. More of a tone-poem with a prominent part for organ: 'The instrument is a kind of avatar for Pan,' he explains. Think of the violin part in Strauss's *Ein Heldenleben*.

He likes the organ, does Andersson. He's written nearly a dozen works for the instrument. And he is particularly happy to be working with the Royal Albert Hall beast. 'It's such a splendid instrument because, although it is a monster, it also displays great beauty. It has fantastic pipes and stops. And being as loud as it is, the instrument can work in dialogue with the orchestra in a very effective way.'

A kaleidoscope of gestures, moods and volumes is the aim: 'The intention is to create a Bacchanalian topography.'

But how to evoke the frisky, elfin Pan on such a mighty thing? 'Pan might have been small in size but he was very powerful,' Andersson reminds us. 'The word "panic" comes from the feeling that spread in forests when people and animals sensed his presence.'

GUY BARKER

(BORN 1957)

The Lanterne of Light (2015)
BBC commission: world premiere

PROM 69 • 6 SEPTEMBER

It's a makeover not everyone would be brave enough to attempt. Turning the angelic trumpet of Alison Balsom into something demonic. But that's what trumpeter-composer Guy Barker chose to do when Balsom and he agreed to work together on a new trumpet concerto for the Proms.

'Whenever I see reviews of your playing,' he explained to her, 'people always talk about the purity of your tone. So why don't we go completely the other way?' They hit on the story of the seven deadly sins and their corresponding demons.

They lined up the demons in an order and gave them each a section within a 30-minute framework. Lucifer opens the work with a passage titled 'Before the Fall'. 'Remember, he was once the beautiful one, the morning star.' The work ends with a part called 'Rant and Rave', dedicated to the most unhinged of the demons, Aamon.

Improvisation turns to ugliness. The tritone (the devil's chord – but also the chord that Dizzy Gillespie championed) starts to rear its head. With a virtuoso trumpeter at his disposal, some would be tempted to push Balsom to her limits. Not Barker. 'I know when it's time to take the trumpet off your face,' he explains. 'There are still bits when she'll look at me and say, "Guy, you should know better." But mostly I will back off. The most important thing is for the soloist to shine.'

LUKE BEDFORD

(BORN 1978)

Instability (2015)
BBC commission: world premiere

PROM 20 • 1 AUGUST

Instability gets a bad rap, says Luke Bedford. Yet we need it to develop. 'Planets and galaxies wouldn't be able to form if matter was very stable.'

Constructive chaos is at the core of Bedford's new orchestral work, which, at 25 minutes, is his most substantial to date. 'Originally the piece was going to contain five well-behaved separate movements. But, as I was about halfway through sketching the piece, it didn't feel like it was working in the way I wanted it to.' So Bedford started to scramble the sections. 'In a playful way I broke the movements up and cut between them. Suddenly everything seemed much more exciting and dramatic and made more sense.'

Instability is now part of the work's DNA. 'There's a constant battle between different ideas and the whole thing almost collapses.' Even the pitches are unstable. 'Some wind instruments are tuned down a quarter-tone so there's a sense of a struggle between music that sometimes sounds quite diatonic and sometimes the opposite.'

There is also the threat of the organ, an instrument that 'can obliterate the whole orchestra – if it wants to. That's quite fun.' Only the outer octaves of the instrument are sounded. 'It's quite perverse,' admits Bedford. 'But by expanding the range of the orchestra, using the very low pipes and the very high ones, you get to the limits of human hearing.' Sound you feel rather than hear.

PIERRE BOULEZ
arr. J. SCHÖLLHORN

(BORN 1925)

Notations 2, 12 & 10; La treizième
(1945, arr. 2011) *UK premiere*

PSM 1 • 25 JULY

1945. By day the 20-year-old Pierre Boulez is studying with Messiaen at the Paris Conservatoire. By night he's at the Folies Bergère (where he's the house pianist) or at the Théâtre des Champs-Élysées booing the latest bit of subpar Stravinsky. Amid all this youthful high jinks, he's also polishing off his opus 1, his 12 *Notations* for solo piano. Explosive, inventive, buzzy little insects of piano sound, the *Notations* are a year zero for post-war music.

Although Boulez has made several huge orchestral expansions of some of the *Notations* himself, the only real arrangements – that is, faithful translations of the piano score to an orchestra – are by Johannes Schöllhorn. For Boulez's 90th-birthday year we get the UK premiere.

Keeping the dimensions of the piano original, Schöllhorn simply coloured them in. 'The energy of the piano version remains, but it now has a chamber-music intensity and reveals links to Bartók and Schoenberg.'

The orchestration is not how Boulez would have done it, admits Schöllhorn. 'It's softer and string-based. Boulez wasn't much interested in strings.'

One important addition is the inclusion of a 13th movement, which is a cut-up made up of the first bar of the first piece, the second bar of the second piece and so on, and, Schöllhorn says, works surprisingly well. Even Boulez approved. 'We signed the original score together.'

GARY CARPENTER

(BORN 1951)

Dadaville (2015)
BBC commission: world premiere

PROM 1 • 17 JULY

Gary Carpenter likes titles. He collects them. Wandering around Tate Liverpool recently, he came across one he particularly enjoyed: *Dadaville*, a painted relief by Max Ernst. 'I actually thought it was a painting. It looks incredibly solid,' he says. What was behind the work's muddy front, Carpenter wondered. 'I found that question rather exciting.'

The other big advantage of a title like *Dadaville*, Carpenter explains, is that it gives you your first four notes. 'On the crudest level *Dadaville* is literally the place where the notes D and A live.'

Artworks are often the trigger for his compositions. But the resultant music 'is very seldom descriptive', he says. 'It's always to do with structure or a number of questions that arise in my own thinking about the artwork.'

Don't expect Dadaist absurdity, then. This won't be any kind of musical urinal. 'I didn't want to go down the whacky route.' The work is instead about what the dark barrier that dominates it is covering up and how 'the darkness itself is somewhat illusory because of its fragility'.

The work is on the same programme as Walton's *Belshazzar's Feast* and so 'there are a lot of extra players hanging around, which I'm not going to exploit. In our dreams composers like to think our pieces might be done at least once more. And that's not going to happen if it's got 32 brass in it.'

Benjamin Ealovega (Bedford); J. Henry Fair (Boulez); Daniel Kidane (Carpenter)

QIGANG CHEN

(BORN 1951)

Iris dévoilée (2001)
London premiere

PROM 15 • 29 JULY

'Messiaen woke me up,' Qigang Chen once said. If any composer needed revitalising, it was Chen. For three years, he was incarcerated and forced to endure 're-education' as part of China's Cultural Revolution. It sent many of his classmates mad.

In 1983 he was given the chance to study abroad. He went to France, where Messiaen coaxed him out of his creative coma and left a huge mark on his musical language. Colour, textural clarity, harmonic richness: Chen's compositional traits betray the influence of his adopted country of France, where he has lived ever since.

One of his most celebrated works, *Iris dévoilée*, receives its London premiere at the Proms this year. And it's probably the work that most clearly shows off what Messiaen noticed as Chen's 'total assimilation of Chinese thinking to European musical concepts'. In it, a Beijing Opera singer and three traditional Chinese instruments – the lute-like pipa, the two-string erhu and the zither-like zheng – ride gentle Ravel-like waters, full of swells and swoops.

Sensuous and dreamy, the work unfolds in a series of reveals. 'Nine aspects, nine frames of mind, nine facets of the same woman, changeable, elusive.' Moving from the chaste to the hysterical, the eponymous Iris is unveiled. And, with her, a major Chinese talent.

TANSY DAVIES

(BORN 1973)

Re-greening (2015)
world premiere

PROM 31 • 8 AUGUST

It almost didn't happen, this commission. 'I initially said no. I don't like to rush things,' explains Tansy Davies. 'But I thought about it and realised that it would be totally different to what I normally do.'

The brief – which included the stipulation that part of the work would have to be memorised and that there could be no conductor – meant that a detailed notated score wouldn't be necessary.

As a counterpoint to Mahler's Ninth Symphony, which follows the work, the idea was to devise a piece that celebrated the National Youth Orchestra. 'Nothing too fully formed or regimented,' says Davies. 'The work would be about freedom, growth and springtime.' Davies sees the musicians walking on stage, waiting for the conductor, and, before the Mahler starts, something bubbles up from within them, something that is simultaneously an expression of themselves and also a celebration of spring.

There is a medieval subtext to the title *Re-greening*, the Middle English name for spring, and to the thematic material, which mines some of the earliest counterpoint to have survived.

Having written a number of orchestral works recently, Davies is feeling confident about taking this different approach. The energy will be 'spontaneously light but also spontaneously forceful in places because it's about new shoots.'

MICHAEL FINNISSY

(BORN 1946)

Janne (2015)
BBC commission: world premiere

PROM 42 • 16 AUGUST

In his 1934 musical survey *Music Ho!*, composer Constant Lambert proclaimed that the future of English symphonic writing lay with Sibelius. It didn't quite turn out that way. But what if he'd been right?

That's Michael Finnissy's starting point. 'I also thought it might be fun to do an imaginary portrait of the child Sibelius, violin in hand, wondering what he was going to be when he grew up,' he explains. (Janne was Sibelius's family name as a child.) 'But what I really wanted to do was to wrestle with the Sibelian way of writing,' he adds.

Finnissy found some recordings of the *Kalevala*, the ancient Karelian saga that Sibelius started to mine 'when he eventually got around to being a Finnish composer as opposed to a rather bad German-trained one. And I thought, yeah, this is quite something,' says Finnissy. 'I started from here, as if I was making the same journey as Sibelius.'

We're encouraged to imagine the work and its component parts as a piece of abstract expressionism. 'Think of it as a Barnett Newman canvas turned sideways. It's a series of panels, with each panel containing one basic type of texture and music, which continues throughout that panel.'

Programmed with two Sibelius symphonies, the orchestration was a challenge. 'No doubling, a certain number of horns, trombones and timpani and strings. And a glockenspiel! What do you do with a glockenspiel?'

What *do* you do with a glockenspiel? 'Wait and see.'

ALISSA FIRSOVA

(BORN 1986)

Bergen's Bonfire (2015)
world premiere

PROM 56 • 27 AUGUST

'A couple of years ago, I had a dream about the end of the world,' explains Alissa Firsova. 'It was the most realistic dream I ever had. I was shaking for days.'

One moment she was admiring the tranquillity and beauty of the world, the next it was in flames. Somewhere in the back of her mind Firsova was trying to think about how to make a piece out of it, when the Bergen Philharmonic asked her to write an orchestral piece. When she suggested the subject of the dream to its music director Andrew Litton, he didn't think she was serious. They wanted a celebratory work for the orchestra's 250th anniversary and Firsova was offering an apocalyptic tone-poem. 'But I was totally serious,' she says. 'Maybe they still don't know that.'

Then by a miracle she figured out how to make it work. 'At the end of the world, a new one would begin, a brilliant, naive paradise, the start of something fresh and innocent.' She was also reading about Ragnarök, the Norse myth on which Wagner based *Götterdämmerung*. She began to weave this into the piece. The result is a three-part colossus.

It's a tonal language Firsova uses. 'My music definitely looks back.' So does her writing regime. Like her hero Mahler, she escapes to the countryside to compose. 'I was in Toblach this summer, where Mahler wrote his final three works. And I listened to the Ninth Symphony in his hut. It was a life-changing experience.'

CHERYL FRANCES-HOAD

(BORN 1980)

Homage to Tallis (2015)
world premiere

PCM 1 • 20 JULY

Cheryl Frances-Hoad's choral output is small in size but big in impact. Her setting of Psalm 1, which won a 2010 British Composer Award, piles chromatic surprise upon terrifying chromatic surprise, until we're sitting in a nihilistic wasteland. Elsewhere, she's mastered the art of ventriloquism, with homages to Beethoven, Mendelssohn, Grieg, Schubert and Janáček.

For her first Prom commission, more impersonation. This time, of Thomas Tallis, whose work is being celebrated by Andrew Carwood's vocal ensemble The Cardinall's Musick. The homage will be clear, she says.

'There are so many ways to do a homage but I'd like it to be audible,' she explains, especially as it's going to sit within an otherwise all-Tallis programme. 'It won't be knowing. If one gets too academic or serious or deliberate about it, one just cripples oneself. I try to immerse myself and forget everything and hope that what remains will have some of myself in it as well as some of Tallis.'

Polyphony will be the key, of course. 'I went to Cambridge, so I did all that tonal comp till I was blue in the face,' she says. But the voice-setting will be determined by practicalities as much as by style.

'My writing is harmonically more traditional because that's the only way you can actually hear everything you write and the only way that people can sing everything accurately. I want people to sound their best.'

LUCA FRANCESCONI

(BORN 1956)

Duende – The Dark Notes (2014)
BBC co-commission with the Swedish Radio Symphony Orchestra and RAI National Symphony Orchestra: UK premiere

PROM 13 • 27 JULY

Duende: a state of excitement, alteration, magic. Federico García Lorca defined it as the feeling that 'surges up, inside, from the soles of the feet'. *Duende* is also the name of Luca Francesconi's second violin concerto and, he believes, the key to all music.

'If you don't feel overexcited, if you don't feel in another state when you compose a piece of music, you won't be able to make the audience feel the same state of alteration,' explains Francesconi. 'It's why composing is so hard. No-one wants to have a 42-degree fever every single day. It's a huge effort psychologically.'

At the heart of his new work, there is a duality: the feeling of something that has lost its body; and the feeling of something that is only body. Both are on display in the opening movement, 'where Leila Josefowicz goes down to the lowest string and simulates a kind of Jimmy Hendrix distortion'.

The third movement, a Gypsy-like maelstrom, is dedicated to the memory of Nicolae Neacşu, a member of the famous Romani band Taraf de Haïdouks.

The last movement enters into the 'atom of sound' using spectral techniques. 'We break apart the note, go inside the note and find another dimension,' Francesconi explains. This happens in the cadenza, which daydreams on natural harmonics. The end is a funeral, he says, a 'bye-bye to the human dimension'.

HK GRUBER

(BORN 1943)

into the open … (2010)
world premiere

PROM 5 • 20 JULY

HK Gruber is one of the great musical chameleons. His stylistic shimmying is reminiscent of Stravinsky. Stravinsky is partly to blame, in fact. 'I do not have a main god,' Gruber explains, 'I have a few gods. One of them is Stravinsky. Another is Alban Berg. And from time to time you'll hear some Webern ideas too.'

His recent work, *into the open …*, a symphony for solo percussion and large orchestra, is very Second Viennese School and 'you will probably hear some ideas of Hanns Eisler in there too'.

It is his second work for percussion and orchestra. 'After the first, I realised that, if the orchestra is too small, the percussion dominates too much,' he says, 'so this time the orchestra will double each of Colin Currie's notes.' Each pitch is, therefore, smudged. The soloist becomes 'the top of an ice mountain'.

Currie's percussion section is 'huge', says Gruber. 'It looks like a sculpture.' And his sound-world is 'rather hardcore', he laughs. 'It doesn't go back to any models of the past – it's not light music; it's not entertaining.'

The work is dedicated to the late new music director at Boosey & Hawkes, David Drew, who taught Gruber about Kurt Weill. 'On the day I was told that David was no more, I began to edit into the work material from Weill's song, "Oh moon of Alabama". The music attempts to find the tune of the song but, ultimately, fails.'

ANDERS HILLBORG

(BORN 1954)

Beast Sampler (2014)
UK premiere

PROM 47 • 21 AUGUST

The score radiates terror. Bullying exclamation marks, aggressive pitchless chevrons, quadruple *fortes* on virtually every page. Beast by name, beast by nature. 'I often refer to the orchestra as a sound-animal,' Anders Hillborg explains. 'And I love to create sounds that are not immediately discernible in the sense that you don't know what instruments are making which sound.'

Another element was that 'there should be absolutely no melody. From the start there would only be sound bordering on noise. And no harmony. A bit like Xenakis.' But he failed. 'I couldn't resist writing some harmony.'

At times the work is terrifying, 'That's my hope. But it depends on the players. The strings may have some resistance in going as far as I want them to go. I have told them that I don't mind if they miss some notes, just as long as they get some very rough expression out of their instruments.'

His stipulations to be as loud as possible and not get quieter crop up again and again. 'I write that every second bar. Psychologically, when that happens, when they reach the bar with *ffff*, after two bars they've lost it. So I usually tell them that, when they've reached that point, they should mentally start a crescendo.'

We pass through aviaries of woodwind noise and a quieter but giddy string section before encountering the tumultuous end. 'My image there was of something boiling over like a volcano,' says Hillborg. 'It works pretty well.'

BETSY JOLAS

(BORN 1926)

Wanderlied (2003)
UK premiere

PSM 1 • 25 JULY

'Did you know I'm going to be 90 next year?' asks Betsy Jolas. 'I'm a pre-war person. I've been through a lot. I have quite a bit to say.'

Daughter of Eugene Jolas – founder of the literary magazine that first published fragments of Joyce's *Finnegans Wake* – assistant to Olivier Messiaen, pupil of Darius Milhaud, friend to Nadia Boulanger, Jolas is a composer worth listening to.

Storytelling is at the heart of her 2003 work *Wanderlied*. In it she imagines the cello that takes centre stage as an ageless fabulist. 'It's the tradition you see round the world. Old people always have lots to say and people gather round them,' she explains. 'In my piece some of the people who gather like the cellist – some don't.' The cor anglais, for example, clearly doesn't like her.

'The cello tries to force a dialogue but can't go beyond the F above middle C, which is quite high for the cello. It's dramatic. She's trying to say something that she can't say and then she gets over that.'

'I say "she",' Jolas adds, 'because the cellist is a "she" and actually "she" is probably me.'

The drama ratchets up, as the dialogue between the cello and the chamber orchestra begins to flow. Listen closely to the end. There is a surprise, inspired by a Goethe performance Jolas once saw. Exactly what happens she wants to remain a secret. But she will say this: it's not easy to conduct. 'It's an act of theatre. And I've heard it done properly only once.'

JOANNA LEE

(BORN 1982)

Hammer of Solitude (2015)
BBC commission: world premiere

PSM 1 • 25 JULY

You couldn't find two composers more different than the experimental young East Anglian Joanna Lee and the no-nonsense French nonagenarian Pierre Boulez. He chisels crystalline gems from mathematical abstractions; she spins wrong-footing yarns from wild vocal safaris. His is the music of set theory; hers the music of the laugh-out-loud. 'I don't do dour,' she admits.

Surprising and intriguing then to see her lined up to provide a birthday tribute to the post-war giant. 'We're two composers who don't necessarily align. But I relate to him through his *Le marteau sans maître*,' she explains. It is the instrumental and conceptual basis for her work *Hammer of Solitude*. 'Although on the orchestration front I'm not as smart as Boulez. He has no bass instruments. So I've expanded the orchestra.'

The beauty of Boulez's work lies as much in its title, 'The Hammer Without a Master', as in his working-out of the idea of the clockwork machine. Using the same René Char text, she'll deconstruct the voice, like Boulez, but 'pulling apart the words a lot more into their phonetic components'. And then she'll match them up to colours in the BCMG ensemble.

'I'm looking to the text and finding colours within each word, playing around with rolled Rs or stopped consonants like Ps and Ds. Plosives are linked to wooden sounds. It's the strange way my brain thinks.'

JAMES MACMILLAN

(BORN 1959)

Symphony No. 4 (2014–15)
BBC commission: world premiere

PROM 24 • 3 AUGUST

James MacMillan's musical language, characterised by a clear, thematically rich idiom that's lavishly ornamented and coloured, is well suited to long spans of music-making. This is his second go at a fourth symphony. 'I had thought about a fourth symphony before but it didn't materialise – there was nothing there. I had to pull back from that commission.' The word was a problem, he admits. 'You have to have a justification for using the word "symphony".' As ideas began to settle, he realised he could use the term again with some validity.

The result is an abstract work and one infused by ritual. 'I can't help but have my liturgical music feed back into my instrumental work.' Listen out for allusions to the pre-Reformation music of 'Scotland's greatest composer' Robert Carver. 'I've always wanted to do something with his music,' MacMillan says. Fragments of Carver's 10-part Mass *Dum sacrum mysterium* creep into the scores of the back-desk string players. 'It feels quite distant. It's like a subliminal message.'

As a regular collaborator with the BBC Scottish Symphony Orchestra and Donald Runnicles, MacMillan can be even more personal than usual. 'I've begun to see faces when I'm writing certain parts.'

The example of the great symphonists of the past hovers in the air – it's inescapable, he says. But there are no explicit nods backwards. What's on the rest of the programme? He chuckles. 'Mahler 5.'

CHRISTIAN MASON

(BORN 1984)

Open to Infinity: a Grain of Sand
(2015) *BBC co-commission with the Lucerne Festival: UK premiere*

PSM 4 • 29 AUGUST

Composing a musical birthday card for Pierre Boulez must be a bit like painting a portrait for Titian. A headache at best. But Christian Mason, who was mentored by Boulez at the Lucerne Festival Academy and has already written a work for him, is in a better situation than most.

The title explores what Boulez as a figure means to Mason, as 'an archetype and a master of fine details'.

'Someone once told me that "time doesn't exist for Boulez any more." I liked that idea.' He also liked and remembered the Blake poem, 'To see a World in a Grain of Sand'. 'It connected the Boulezian ideas of detail, precision and eternity.'

Mason's orchestration echoes the piano, harp, percussion trio in Boulez's *Sur Incises*, with each instrumental family from the chamber orchestra providing a background colour. 'Usually I add lots of unusual instruments. With this one I wanted purity and primary colours.'

Still working out the details of the piece, Mason offers a few possibilities. 'I might go down the chord multiplication route. That would be interesting as an experiment, as I haven't used that technique. I will probably put in a few technical homages. The structural backbone will be serial.' And there's the chance to get in touch with the inner Boulez. 'He is so known for abstraction and rigour rather than emotional exuberance that it makes me want to get in touch with that side.'

ØRJAN MATRE

(BORN 1979)

preSage (2013, rev. 2015)
world premiere of this version

PROM 56 • 27 AUGUST

Like many composers, Bergen-born Ørjan Matre wasn't keen to write a concert-opener. 'Quite often I turn those down because I don't like to be placed at the start of a programme,' he admits. 'Orchestras tend to do this, though – play the short contemporary piece at the start and then go on to do "the real stuff".'

But he had worked very closely with the Oslo Philharmonic, so he thought maybe he could do this. The work would lay the ground for the rest of the concert, he decided. This included Stravinsky's *The Rite of Spring*. An important piece for Matre. 'It was the first piece I really got into as a young composer.'

He created a decipherable link to the piece. 'I used the material from a tiny part of *The Rite*. A very short movement called "The Sage",' he explains. 'It's a section that's over before it's started. It's extremely simple: the sage comes onto the stage and kisses the ground.' Beyond this there are two musical elements: a simple rhythm for contra-bassoon and 'a very strange string chord with lots of harmonics'.

'Those two things – the rhythm and that string chord – are the start of my piece.'

Each time some Stravinskyan sound emerges, it appears misshapen, as if caught in a hall of mirrors. The material works its way up to a climax and, there, loses all strength.

COLIN MATTHEWS

(BORN 1946)

String Quartet No. 5 (2015)
European premiere

PCM 3 • 3 AUGUST

'The Isambard Kingdom Brunel of contemporary music' is how one critic has described Colin Matthews. And you can see why. Finely engineered, sturdily structured, bustling with energy, his music is the embodiment of Brunelian qualities. To an extent, his life is too. As an industrious arts administrator, an amanuensis to Benjamin Britten in his final years, Matthews has been an important musical bridge himself.

For many critics, his string quartets are a valuable bridge too, furthering the 19th- and 20th-century tradition in interesting ways. The First was hailed as 'superb' at its premiere, the Third a 'masterpiece'. Each has ploughed its own distinct furrow.

All, however, have been aware of the past – in every one you can hear the quartet whistling a snatch of Beethoven or Bartók before getting back to business.

All have also been intensely focused, united in their forward momentum. Not the latest. Don't expect steam or energy in the Fifth Quartet; instead, prepare for space and contemplation.

'My Fifth Quartet differs from the previous four in being in a single movement, with a duration of around 12 minutes,' Matthews writes, 'and is more restrained and detached than its predecessors, initially concentrating on the silence between the notes as much as on the notes themselves.'

ANNA MEREDITH

(BORN 1978)

Smatter Hauler (2015)
BBC commission: world premiere

PROM 22 • 2 AUGUST

What happens when you take away an orchestral player's score? Fear? Possibly. But also greater understanding. That's the hope with this composition, which follows the London premiere of her body percussion work *Connect It* in the Ten Pieces Prom. The BBC has now commissioned Scottish composer Anna Meredith to compose a work for the Aurora Orchestra that the players will have to commit to memory.

'I've got to be sensitive to the situation,' she explains, 'but I don't want to patronise them. I'd like to challenge the musicians and allow them to get something out of it.'

'Normally I like doing stuff where I have a little pattern that glitches or tumbles over itself. That kind of stuff is incredibly difficult to play. I've thought about that and am keeping the processes simple.' The easy way out would be to make it a composition that was open to chance. 'I'm too much of a control freak. One of the things I'm better at, and love doing most, is thinking about big shapes and builds.'

That said, Meredith isn't the kind of composer who likes to make life deliberately difficult for audience or performer. She likes legible structures, transparency, clarity. 'I'm not embarrassed about being explicit about what I'm trying to do,' she admits. 'I like to hear a process. If everyone can hear what you're doing, then hopefully there's an emotional connection because people aren't just baffled by the whole thing.'

OLIVIER MESSIAEN
orch. C. DINGLE

(1908–92)

Un oiseau des arbres de Vie (Oiseau tui) (1987–88, orch. 2013–14) *world premiere*

PROM 29 • 7 AUGUST

A Messiaen premiere? More than 20 years after his death? You're right to be confused. Just before the French composer died, however, he wrote one final bird-inspired epic, *Éclairs sur l'au-delà …* ('Illuminations of the Beyond …'). During its four-year gestation, one of its movement was completed but rejected and, unusually, left unorchestrated.

'Knowing his music as well as I do, it occurred to me that, as I'd been saying for a while that somebody ought to complete this work, I was in the best position to do it, so I did,' Messiaen scholar Christopher Dingle explains.

The evidence for how the work should sound was limited. So Dingle sought precedents for the spacing and voicing by finding music that had been composed to portray birds similar to the New Zealander tui from the same period of writing. He doesn't pretend that the final result is anything but a 'realisation' – 'but it is a very close approximation'.

Messiaen doesn't make things easy for Dingle. Commissioned by the New York Philharmonic for its 150th anniversary, *Éclairs* is scored for the largest orchestra Messiaen would write for – including 10 flutes, 10 clarinets and three sets of tubular bells. It's a lot of work for four minutes of music. Is it worth the effort? Without doubt, says Dingle. 'It's not often you unearth a top-drawer four-minute movement from a composer at the height of his powers.'

NEW MUSIC

JONATHAN NEWMAN

(BORN 1972)

Blow It Up, Start Again (2011)
European premiere

PROM 32 • 9 AUGUST

The work began life as an encore. A commission from the Chicago Youth Symphony Orchestras, *Blow It Up, Start Again* was programmed to come after a warhorse, whose language and manner Jonathan Newman's piece would, metaphorically, 'blow up'. It was 'a cheeky wink using contemporary styles,' he explains.

The programme note the composer wrote to accompany the work is as punchy as its title: 'If the system isn't working anymore, then do what Guy Fawkes tried and go anarchist: blow it all up and start again.' But it's not a political statement. 'It's actually supposed to be kind of funny,' says Newman. 'I'm not an anarchist,' he adds. 'I was just concerned that the programme note would take longer to read than to listen to the piece.'

The anarchism, Newman insists, is more musical than political. The inclusion of dubstep, of funk, of various vernacular idioms suggests a thorough-going upturning of the rules of the game. But, even so, tongue is 'firmly esconced in cheek'.

There'll be those who get the references – to Sigur Rós and Skrillex and to the dubstep-like wub-wub-wub in the bass – and those who won't. Ultimately, it doesn't matter.

'Don't overthink the work,' he stresses, just enjoy it. 'It wasn't made to win any Pulitzers. It's a four-minute piece that is supposed to be exciting and loud and fun.'

JOHN PSATHAS

(BORN 1966)

View from Olympus
(2000, rev. 2015)
world premiere of this version

PCM 4 • 10 AUGUST

For John Psathas, Mount Olympus isn't just a mythological stage set. The mountain was his neighbour for a while. His parents' home overlooks it and in 2000 that's where this New Zealand-born son of Greek immigrants was living. 'I drank a lot of ouzo, ate a lot of food, went for a lot of swims and wrote the basic ideas for *View from Olympus* there,' he says.

The work, a highly energetic double concerto for piano and percussion, was commissioned for the Manchester Commonwealth Games by Dame Evelyn Glennie. The first movement is called 'The Furies', 'who were the ones you couldn't hide from'. The second, 'Smiling Child', is a 'clear expression of the love of a young father'. The third tackles the wild, drunken antics of Dionysus's followers, the Maenads: 'it's about the need for ecstatic release'.

Shot through with Greek scales, a jazzy drive and a rock-like punch, Psathas's work also has a personal subtext. The concerto dynamic – the mass versus the individual – has always fascinated him. 'I'm an exile in New Zealand but also a complete foreigner in Greece,' he explains. 'So there's no place for me in the world. I'm an outsider everywhere. Which is awesome for a composer. It's an amazing liberation. And combine that with being in New Zealand where we don't have a musical tradition – I really don't have any peers – I'm an island on an island. That comes out in the concerto.'

SHIORI USUI

(BORN 1981)

Ophiocordyceps unilateralis s.l.
(2015) *BBC commission: world premiere*

PSM 1 • 25 JULY

The obsessive clawings of an eczema sufferer. The burbling churn of an upset stomach. Bodily functions are to Shiori Usui what sonata form was to Haydn. The result is intense – a music of the hospital ward.

Recently she's turned her attention to the goings-on of the natural world, where processes can be even more bizarre. The inspiration for her latest work was an image of a dead ant that had succumbed to a fungal parasite, ophiocordyceps unilateralis s.l., which she came across in a scientific journal.

'It was quite grotesque and shocking,' she explains. The dead ant had a stem sticking out of its skull. The fungus infects the ant, scrambles its brain and sends it packing down to the forest floor, where the parasite has a chance to take root and grow. The possessed ant sleepwalks to a leaf, bites one of the veins and dies. A stem grows; a sack emerges; a new set of parasitical spores explode into the air, floating towards their next victim.

Sounds flowed from images. Form flowed from research on the exact spread of the infection. 'I discovered the death bite of an ant tends to happen around noon during the day, when the sun is at its strongest. So this became my central section.'

As the infection takes hold, timbral differences reveal themselves. Gestures start to break up the piece. The infection spreads, instrument by instrument. Noon strikes and the death bite hits. The music collapses.

BERTRAM WEE

(BORN 1992)

Dithyrambs (2015)
world premiere

PCM 4 • 10 AUGUST

A new work by a new composer confronting a new instrument. Bertram Wee's *Dithyrambs* offers an entry into the unknown. An unknown world that, nonetheless, comes highly recommended. Wee won a British Composer Award last year for *Sonicalia*, a duet for tenor trombone and tuba – imagine a Mike Leigh domestic drama for a pair of elephants and you'll get a good impression of it. The strange, the new, the demanding: Wee laps it all up.

He came across the Aluphone (a new type of vibraphone) on television as part of Dame Evelyn Glennie's performance at the London 2012 Olympics Opening Ceremony. Glennie later met Wee at the Royal College of Music, where he is a student, and commissioned him to write two works, one of which is *Dithyrambs*.

Although born in Singapore, and acknowledging similarities between the Aluphone and the Javanese gamelan instrument, the bonang barung, Wee wants to avoid any South-East Asian sounds. There's enough to explore in the instrument itself. 'It is a challenge to write for,' he admits. 'Certain things about the instrument are very clumsy. My main worry is that the sound can get too cloying and overstays its welcome.'

There are no dampers, so it rings and rings. 'It's very rich, very resonant.' It produces a bell-like tone that he's never heard before. 'It's like a cross between a vibraphone and a steel drum – it's quite crazy.'

ERIC WHITACRE
(BORN 1970)

Deep Field (2015)
BBC co-commission with the Minnesota Orchestra: European premiere

PROM 32 • 9 AUGUST

Eric Whitacre, the popular American choral specialist and YouTube sensation, has never shied away from technological innovation. For his latest work, *Deep Field*, his inspiration is the Hubble Telescope Deep Field Image.

'In 1990, NASA launched the Hubble Telescope into space. For its first exposure, the telescope was aimed towards one tiny area of the sky – just one 28 millionth of the total area. The exposure lasted 11 days and the results were breathtaking. There were over 3,000 galaxies, 12 to 13 light years away. Not only breathtakingly beautiful but it showed the incomprehensible magnitude of the universe. I wanted to write a piece that captured the wonder and awe I felt when looking at the image for the first time.

'The piece, for chorus and orchestra, moves from chords that are out of focus, musically, and then come into focus, very slowly in a grand majestic way. As it nears the end, there's a big climax where the work comes into focus, at which point I'll turn to the audience, give a downbeat and invite them to participate using their mobile phones, recreating the spectra of the Deep Field image. I hope that the audience will feel a similar sense of wonder and awe.'

HUGH WOOD
(BORN 1932)

Epithalamium (2014–15)
BBC commission: world premiere

PROM 7 • 22 JULY

A tongue-twister greets us. A tongue-twister that, should you try to unravel it, conceals something ancient and lovely: a wedding song.

Epithalamiums can be poetic and personal, like Spenser's ode to his bride, or musical and theatrical, like Wagner's 'Bridal March'. For Wood, one of the finest, and most direct and sensuous, is John Donne's *An Epithalamion, or Marriage Song on the Lady Elizabeth and Count Palatine being married on St Valentine's Day*.

'Donne's poem, addressed to "Bishop Valentine, whose day this is", is rich in high spirits and poetic fantasy, and is sensuously sexy and jubilant throughout,' explains Wood. 'I have known and loved it for many years, and have at last managed to set it for large and smaller chorus and full symphony orchestra.'

Wood's music often twists and turns with a kind of restlessness the Second Viennese School would have appreciated. The turmoil is usually calmed. But how, one wonders, will this dramatic language adapt to Donne's continuous stream of steamy loveliness. 'I've made some judicious cuts – where he gets too philosophical,' Wood admits. 'It's a jolly good work, though.'

Beyond that, he's keeping his cards close to his chest.

JOHN WOOLRICH
(BORN 1954)

Falling Down (2009)
London premiere

PROM 4 • 19 JULY

If some composers paint, and others draw, John Woolrich could be thought to sculpt his soundscapes. In his music, ideas lap against our eardrums. Shapes emerge, recede, conjoin. A steep slope headed for darkness opens his contra-bassoon concerto, *Falling Down*.

'The title explains itself: the piece begins and ends with music that tumbles from the top of the orchestra down to the depths, where the contra lives,' Woolrich writes. In these depths, light is scarce.

'The dark colours of the contra spread into the orchestra,' he writes. 'The cor anglais (sometimes doubling the contra-bassoon), the tuba, the bass drum and lion's roar are to the fore.'

Inspired by Goya's experimental print series *Los Caprichos*, Woolrich wrote a lyrical section for the shadowy middle. 'I'm haunted by Goya's *Caprichos*,' he writes. 'Like them, my piece combines the comic, the dark, the menacing and the grotesque.'

The perverse too. It's not every day the contra-bassoon gets a concerto written for it. 'It's easier if the solo instrument is high (like a violin) because the ear tends to be drawn upwards,' Woolrich admits. To stop the soloist being 'blotted out by the orchestra' he's asked for amplification. 'But otherwise the balance problems are solved by alternating lightly accompanied solos and big orchestral *tuttis*.'

RAYMOND YIU
(BORN 1973)

Symphony (2015)
BBC commission: world premiere

PROM 54 • 25 AUGUST

'When I first came to London in 1992, Aids was a big thing. You went out on the scene, you'd see someone for a while and they'd disappear. Years later you'd discover that they were dead. It was horrible. And the younger generation don't have any memory of this,' explains Raymond Yiu. 'For me it's still very vivid.'

The central pillar of Yiu's Symphony – a five-movement meditation on memory for orchestra and counter-tenor – is the fourth movement, which sets Thom Gunn's club scene poem to the lush orchestral sounds of 1970s disco. Around it four other movements grapple – through music and text – with the way our brains try to recover and hold on to the past.

The influences are wide-ranging: Scarlatti, Berio, the Bee Gees, Basil Bunting, Nielsen and Mahler.

We begin with an ear-opener from Walt Whitman, the musical fragments building and building till they break free of text. 'Now I will do nothing but listen,' proclaims Walt. We enter the second movement: 'a deconstruction of a Scarlatti sonata', twisted into a tone-row. Sonata form for Yiu is itself 'a way of trying to organise memories'.

It's the first of two dance movements. The second is the disco scene. In between these lies a lyrical, slow setting of *Come Back* by C. P. Cavafy, whose memories turn tactile. And we end with John Donne's *The Anniversarie* delivered as a hymn.

ALL AROUND THE PROMS

With lively pre-Prom introductions and a wealth of opportunities for your own music-making, **HANNAH NEPIL** steers a path through the myriad free events for all the family that complement the Proms concerts

When, in 1895, Henry Wood co-founded the annual Promenade Concerts, the aim was to 'train the public in easy stages'. Little could he have known how that mission would evolve. Now, 120 years on, the Proms is as much about learning and new experiences, as about showcasing leading international performers. Were you to take full advantage of the talks, late-night events and practical music-making sessions at this year's festival, you would have more than enough to fill your diary, and that's before you begin to factor in the concerts.

Whether you're a classical music novice or a loyal devotee, you're bound to find something to pique your interest. It may be the series of pre-concert talks and events taking place opposite the Royal Albert Hall at the Royal College of Music. Or it may be the chance to sit alongside professional musicians and have a go at playing yourself – perhaps even as part of a Prom, if you dare. All events are free and linked to the forthcoming Prom that evening, or to themes running throughout the season.

The Proms 'in the Round'

Among the most enjoyable aspects of the Proms are the pre-concert events. These include a series of introductions in which you can hear conductors, performers, composers and other experts discuss the music in the forthcoming Prom that evening. This year's topics are as wide-ranging as ever: the season launches with a lecture on music and the brain by the neuroscientist and musician Daniel Levitin (18 July), but later events include the story of swing, outlined by BBC Radio 3 *Jazz Record Requests* presenter Alyn Shipton (11 August), a focus on Leonard Bernstein (5 September) ahead of the Prom featuring his music for stage and screen, and *Gravity* soundtrack composer Steven Price's take on how Gustav Holst captured the sounds of the solar system so vividly in *The Planets*. Those who like to immerse themselves in the work of a particular composer will enjoy events across the summer linked to Sibelius, Nielsen and Beethoven. Meanwhile, a series of portraits profile contemporary composers, who discuss their new works to be premiered that evening

A young audience member at last year's CBeebies Prom

with BBC Radio 3 presenter Andrew McGregor and introduce live performances of their chamber works. This year's participants are Hugh Wood, Michael Finnissy, Alissa Firsova and B Tommy Andersson.

FREE PROMS EXTRA EVENTS FOR ALL THE FAMILY

Royal College of Music (*see page 168*)

PROMS EXTRA FAMILY

Family-friendly introductions to the music of the evening's Prom. Bring an instrument or just sit back and take it all in.

Suitable for ages 7-plus

Saturday 18 July • 4.30pm–5.30pm*
Tuesday 21 July • 5.00pm–6.00pm*
Monday 10 August • 5.30pm–6.30pm*
Tuesday 18 August • 5.30pm–6.30pm*
Friday 21 August • 5.00pm–6.00pm*
Sunday 23 August • 1.00pm–2.00pm*

PROMS EXTRA FAMILY ORCHESTRA AND CHORUS[†]

Play or sing alongside professional musicians, whatever your age or ability.

Suitable for ages 7-plus

Saturday 25 July • 10.30am–12.30pm
Saturday 15 August • 1.30pm–3.30pm
Monday 31 August • 2.00pm–4.30pm

PROMS EXTRA SING[†]

Explore the season's choral works by having a go yourself.

Suitable for ages 16-plus, except 25 July and 5 September, suitable for ages 7-plus

Sunday 19 July • 1.00pm–4.00pm
Saturday 25 July • 2.00pm–4.00pm
Sunday 2 August • 3.30pm–6.30pm
Saturday 5 September • 11.00am–1.00pm
Sunday 6 September • 2.30pm–5.30pm
Saturday 12 September • 5.00pm–5.45pm

PROMS SESSIONS

Proms sessions give access to many of the leading international artists and composers featuring at the Proms and are designed for young people interested in performing and making their own music.

Suitable for ages 12-plus

Proms Sessions with featured artists

Naughty Boy • Monday 20 July
Colin Currie • Wednesday 22 July
Alina Ibragimova • Sunday 26 July
Clare Teal • Saturday 1 August

Proms Sessions for young composers

Eric Whitacre/BBC Singers • Saturday 8 August
Michael Price • Sunday 16 August
Peter Wiegold and friends • Friday 21 August
Composers Q&A • Friday 28 August

For details of how to sign up, visit the BBC Proms website

*No ticket required; entry is on a first-come first-served basis (doors open 30 minutes before the event begins; capacity is limited)

[†]Places must be booked in advance; sign up at bbc.co.uk/proms; call 020 7765 0557 or email getinvolved@bbc.co.uk

Actor Henry Goodman talks about the role of Tevye ahead of the Proms performance of *Fiddler on the Roof* (25 July)

Other talks zoom in on 1895, the year the Proms began, drawing on significant events relating to Oscar Wilde, the National Trust and the pioneering cinematograph inventors, the Lumière brothers. There's also a focus on Hans Christian Andersen, to complement the performance of the Danish National Symphony Orchestra (20 August). And, if you're keen to scribble some lines of your own, then why not take part in the Proms Poetry Competition (*see page 103*)? Entrants write a poem inspired by the music of the 2015 Proms, and the winning poems are performed onstage by an actor at a special event at the Royal College of Music (8 September).

If what you crave is a chance to exercise your lungs, while getting to know the nuts and bolts of a work, then the Proms Extra Sing workshops provide just that. Choral leaders guide you through highlights of the season's choral works, which this year include Beethoven's Symphony No. 9, Bruckner's Mass in F minor and Verdi's *Requiem* (*see panel, left*). In the penultimate event of the series (6 September) you can sing sections of Carl Orff's *Carmina burana* before giving a scratch performance with the BBC Concert Orchestra.

Sven Arnstein

There are also post-concert events, for those loath to leave the Royal Albert Hall after the main-evening concert is over: a series of relaxed, intimate gatherings where you can enjoy jazz and poetry and the benefits of a late-night bar. All lates take place in the Royal Albert Hall's Elgar Room.

Nurturing Talent

As always, nurturing young talent is a key theme of the season. It comes to the fore over the opening weekend, when young performers from across the UK take part in two Ten Pieces Proms (18 and 19 July). In the culmination of a year-long project for primary-school pupils, there are live performances of the 10 chosen works of music (*see pages 74–75*) and a range of children's creative responses to them, from music to dance and digital art to animation. A couple of weeks later, the spotlight falls on young instrumentalists, who will perform, from memory, *Smatter Hauler* – a brand-new piece by Anna Meredith, side by side with the Aurora Orchestra (2 August).

Also on offer, in partnership with the Royal Albert Hall's education and outreach programme, are two series of Proms Sessions for young people (*see panel opposite*): the first

Ready to make some noise: anyone can have a bash in the Proms Extra Family events

Daniel Levitin gives the Proms Lecture on 'Unlocking the Mysteries of Music in Your Brain' (18 July)

led by Proms 2015 artists Alina Ibragimova, Colin Currie, Naughty Boy and Clare Teal; the other – as part of the BBC Proms Inspire scheme for young composers – focusing on choral music, writing for film and TV, improvisation and picking the brains of professional composers involved in the Inspire scheme. Inspire Lab composition workshops have also been running around the country since January in the lead-up to the BBC Proms Inspire Young Composers' Competition, open for entries until 21 May 2015. The winners will have their music performed in a special Proms Extra event on 28 August. They'll also receive a BBC commission and mentoring from a professional composer. You can hear the 2014 winners' commissions at the Royal College of Music on 8 August. All participants will be invited to attend this year's series of Proms Sessions for young composers.

Families

Decibel levels look set to soar this August bank holiday Monday (31 August), when the biggest Proms Family Orchestra and Chorus to date takes over the Royal Albert Hall for the afternoon. In a celebration of some of the American anniversaries of this year's Proms, you can help create a giant musical soup made up of the defining ingredients of 20th-century American music, from Copland to Dylan and from Bernstein to Cage. Other Family Orchestra sessions will draw on Proms repertoire ranging from *Fiddler on the Roof* to Sibelius (*see panel opposite*). The notes are learnt by ear, so there's no need to read music, and any instrument is welcome, as long as it is portable and acoustic. Professional musicians are strategically dotted around to keep participants on track.

Families can also take part in one of the interactive Proms Extra Family workshops

Owen Egan/McGill University (Levitin); Chris Christodoulou/BBC

Author Dame Hermione Lee discusses poetry
by American writer Willa Cather ahead of the
San Francisco Symphony's second Prom (31 August)

(*see panel, page 100*), where presenters guide
you through the music of the forthcoming
Prom. Professional musicians are on hand
to help, and the aim is to have as much fun
as possible. In a similar vein, RCM Sparks is
delivering workshops for children, young
people and families inspired by some of the
music featured this season – all held at the
Royal College of Music. Among the highlights
are two one-day workshops, linked to the
Ten Pieces Prom (18/19 July) and Stravinsky's
The Firebird (12 August).

This year, a series of Sunday Matinee
Proms offer programmes designed to fire up the
imagination. Among them is a Prom exploring
the musical mind of Sherlock Holmes (16
August). There's also the Life Story Prom,
featuring Sir David Attenborough (30 August).
But all Proms welcome children aged over 5,
with half-price tickets for under-18s. Not that
over-18s will need to break the bank: Arena and
Gallery tickets are still available to Prommers
for £5.00. For an evening's worth of music, plus
a workshop, pre-concert talk, or a singathon,
you'd be hard-pressed to find a better deal. ●

Journalist and music critic Hannah Nepil writes for the
*Financial Times, The Times, Gramophone, Time Out,
BBC Music Magazine, Classical Music* and *Opera*.

PROMS POETRY COMPETITION

The annual Proms Poetry Competition is chaired by the poet and presenter of BBC Radio 3's *The Verb*, Ian McMillan. The winners and runners-up in each of two categories – ages 12 to 18 and over-19 – are invited to the Proms Extra event at the Royal College of Music (8 September), where the winners talk about their poems, which are performed onstage. This year's competition will be launched in early June. Visit *The Verb* page on the Radio 3 website for more details.

Last year's winners were Sue Leigh, who teaches creative writing in Oxfordshire, and student Jade Cuttle. To launch this year's Proms Poetry Competition, we asked them to write a poem inspired by the Proms. Jade Cuttle's poem is inspired by Beethoven's setting of Schiller's 'Ode to Joy' in his Ninth Symphony (the 'Choral'). Sue Leigh's poem, 'Find', was inspired by the excavation of a fragment of the earliest stringed instrument in Western Europe.

Ode to Joy
The Ninth Symphony, Beethoven
by Jade Cuttle (ages 12 to 18 category winner)

The heart is a silent seed
that stays beneath the soil.
O Freunde, nicht diese Töne!

Flowers edge in on tiptoe
through cracks in the chest,
seeds scattered in staccato …
the hum of a heartbeat shivers
down the spine of a violin's bow.

*Freude, schöner Götterfunken,
Tochter aus Elysium,
Wir betreten feuertrunken,
Himmlische, dein Heiligtum.*

These bone-branches will not break;
punching palm and fist through flesh
to bruise a sky beyond their grasp,
the heart escapes its cage of a chest.

*Deine Zauber binden wieder,
Was die Mode streng geteilt;
Alle Menschen werden Brüder,
Wo dein sanfter Flügel weilt.*

A flock of hearts takes flight.
Freude! Freude! Freude!

Find
(c300BC)
by Sue Leigh (over-19 category winner)

Near the mouth
of High Pasture Cave
on Skye

among hearth leavings
antler, bone
they unearthed

a string-bearer
the broken bridge
of a lyre

imagine –
winter dark, wolf howl
the spit of the fire

then that sound strumming
the valley, running clear
as an underground stream –

how old this need
to make from our lives
a sounding, a song

A·L AROUND THE PROMS

Greg Solomonski/Photovile

UNIVERSITY OF
WEST LONDON
London College of **Music**

London College of Music is an internationally recognised music institution with a long tradition of providing innovative and creative courses. Many courses are specifically designed to fit around personal and professional commitments and are offered on a full or part time basis.

Our well established industry links and professional partnerships in London, the UK and abroad ensure that your studies are real and relevant to your musical interests.

UNDERGRADUATE PORTFOLIO:

- Composition
- Music Management
- Music Technology
- Musical Theatre
- Performance

POSTGRADUATE PORTFOLIO:

- Composition
- Music Management
- Music Technology
- Musical Theatre
- Performance

  London College of Music Examinations offer a wide range of external graded exams and diplomas.
uwl.ac.uk/lcmexams

 ENGLISH CHAMBER ORCHESTRA

uwl.ac.uk/ lcm

THE PROMS
WHERE YOU ARE

ANNA PICARD unravels the myriad ways in which you can experience the Proms, whether you're at home or on the move, and key BBC Radio personalities introduce the ever-growing series of Proms devised in collaboration with a range of BBC network radio stations

In August 2013, the actor Kevin Spacey delivered the MacTaggart Lecture at the Edinburgh International Television Festival. The watercooler moment, he said – where people gather to discuss the heart-stopping twists of last night's television – is dead. In an age of digital broadcasting, audiences are no longer experiencing drama in the same way and at the same time. The appetite, engagement and intense conversations continue, but now as much in the arena of social media. And so it is with the Proms, whether the moment that gets everyone talking is a subtle shift of dynamic in a Bach partita or the emotional climax of an opera. Audiences have evolved and the conversations continue, whether we are listening over the airwaves or online, watching television, using the BBC iPlayer, cheering or booing opinions on BBC Two's weekly *Proms Extra* show or exploring Radio 3's online archive of programmes and performances. As Director of the BBC Proms Edward Blakeman is keen to point out, 'It's a range of experiences that only the BBC can offer.'

From something originally reserved for those present at the performances, the Proms is now also open to anyone with access to a mobile phone, a tablet or a computer. For Andrew Downs, who, as Multiplatform Editorial Lead, develops the online content, 'there are many ways to think about what "digital" means and how it supports founder-conductor Henry Wood's vision. For me the key thing is access. Interpret "access" any way you like and I reckon I can point to something we do that reflects that.'

Downs sees part of his job as directing people to concerts, talks, reviews and the vast resources of the Radio 3 website. 'But beyond the riches of this related content,' he says, 'there's an awful lot of material and variety

From the Hall to your screen: BBC cameras will be at a range of Proms this season, and every one is live on BBC Radio 3

within the concerts themselves, so we have a particular challenge to help people navigate that, to create selections and make things meaningful in context.' Now, you may be reading this Proms Guide in printed form or as an app, complete with a search function for events. If you are planning your summer listening, there is also a brand-new Proms website to explore and an archive of over 2,000 programmes on the Radio 3 website. Do you want to learn more before, say, Sir John Eliot Gardiner's performance of Beethoven's Fifth and Berlioz's *Symphonie fantastique* in Prom 33? From *Discovering Music*'s analyses of those works to *CD Review*'s deliberations on the best available recordings to Donald Macleod's *Composer of the Week* podcasts (two on Berlioz, four on Beethoven), the website is the place to start. Then there is BBC Playlister, with expert recommendations on further listening. And then there is television.

Francesca Kemp, Executive Producer, BBC Music Television, has one of the most

challenging jobs in the festival, filming concerts for later transmission, overseeing the weekly magazine programme *Proms Extra* and managing live broadcasts. 'Serious television broadcasting of the Proms began in 1964,' she explains, 'with 10 concerts shown across the season. This century, with the launch of BBC Four, BBC Online and BBC iPlayer, there are more new ways of taking the Proms to our audiences.' Kemp is particularly keen to find ways to address viewers who may be curious about the Proms but nervous of unfamiliar music – an audience that Downs describes as 'dippers' rather than 'divers'. Launched in 2013, *Proms Extra* has been a great success, not least in terms of stimulating debate and a sense of connection with the performers, while the popularity of the Proms performances made available on YouTube last year suggests there is also a real appetite for sampling single works.

Kemp's plan for this summer is to create three distinctive strands of Proms broadcasts: 'Every Sunday night Sir Mark Elder will guide

Milos Photography/Corbis (page 106); Chris Christodoulou/BBC

BOBBY FRICTION ON LATE NIGHT WITH ... BBC ASIAN NETWORK

Prom 8 • 22 July

For me it's an immense pleasure to host this Late Night Prom with the new wave of Bollywood singers, Benny Dayal and Palak Muchhal, as well as Brit-Asian producer extraordinaire Naughty Boy in a unique musical clash of ideas, and all with a full-sized orchestra! This Prom is a radical coming-together of these massive forces destined to write a new musical language. Naughty Boy, an album artist in his own right, has been a regular at the top end of the UK Charts over the past couple of years, with collaborations and song-writing for artists including Emeli Sandé, JLS and Ed Sheeran.

PETE TONG ON LATE NIGHT WITH ... BBC RADIO 1

Prom 16 • 29 July

I've always been proud to be at the heart of dance music as it has continued to innovate and experiment, and this is exactly what we'll be doing in this Late Night Prom celebrating 20 years of programmes and live events from Europe's dance music capital, Ibiza. In this Prom we are reimagining some of the most enduring dance music tracks in the history of dance music and I'm very excited to help curate and guide that – as well as presenting. During the night we'll be re-working classics including Rhythm is Rhythm's 'Strings of Life' and Stardust's 'Music Sounds Better With You'.

MARY ANNE HOBBS ON LATE NIGHT WITH ... BBC RADIO 6 MUSIC

Prom 27 • 5 August

Nils Frahm and A Winged Victory for the Sullen are the shooting stars of a new generation of artists reimagining classical music. In this Prom they play individual sets as well as a specially composed collaboration. Nils Frahm is a Berlin-based, classically trained keyboard virtuoso and composer. A Winged Victory for the Sullen are two kindred American spirits, musicians and composers Adam Wiltzie and Dustin O'Halloran. These artists are rooted in classical music but also draw on contemporary electronic music, techno and drone, crossing every traditional boundary.

CLARE TEAL ON STORY OF SWING (WITH BBC RADIO 2)

Prom 35 • 11 August

This year marks the 80th anniversary of Benny Goodman's famed appearance at the Palomar Ballroom in Los Angeles when, seemingly overnight, swing became the pop music of America. 'Story of Swing' explores the roots of swing and revels in its many forms, from early pioneers Fletcher Henderson and Paul Whiteman to the great leaders Tommy Dorsey, Count Basie, Duke Ellington and, of course, the 'King of Swing' himself, Benny Goodman. Our two big bands comprise the cream of the British jazz and big-band scene and will battle against each other in high-octane duels.

MISTAJAM ON LATE NIGHT WITH ... BBC RADIO 1XTRA

Prom 37 • 12 August

BBC Radio 1Xtra is joining forces with one of Britain's finest lyrical rappers, Wretch 32, to present an evening of grime and hip hop in a style never heard before. Wretch will be joined by an all-star cast of the hottest prospects from the hip hop and grime world, performing their tracks with the Metropole Orkest. Grime and British hip hop are responsible for some of the most progressive sounds in UK music and have become a dominant force in UK youth music culture. It's going to be a night of musical alchemy, which we hope will show the true musicality of hip hop and grime to a classical audience.

JARVIS COCKER ON WIRELESS NIGHTS (WITH BBC RADIO 4)

Prom 74
10 September

Wireless Nights is my chance to see what people get up to at night without getting arrested. We call it 'a nocturnal investigation of the human condition' but, during its three-year run on Radio 4, it has also featured badgers, foxes, elves and the constellation known as Orion. We're hoping to bring some of the aforementioned to the Proms, based around pieces of music with a particular connection to the hours after sunset. I'm delighted that we now have the chance to further develop that collaboration in this Late Night Prom. What can you expect? Night terrors or visions of bliss? Both, probably …

Jay Brooks/BBC (Friction); Mark Elibeck/BBC (Tong), Laura Lewis/BBC (Hobbs), Ray Burmiston/BBC (MistaJam); Emma Russell/BBC (Cocker)

us through a symphony, starting with Beethoven's Ninth and ending with a new work by Scottish composer James MacMillan. On Thursdays we'll be focusing on soloists in both concerto and solo repertoire, from Nicola Benedetti to Yo-Yo Ma, while on Friday nights we'll be offering a hot ticket to the absolute highlight Proms of the season – from Daniel Barenboim and Bernard Haitink to swing and John Wilson.

For the vast majority of the audience, radio remains the leading Proms platform, though what we mean by 'radio' is changing. Every Proms concert is broadcast live on BBC Radio 3 and in HD Sound online – and an increasing number of listeners now listen online, while cooking, eating or sitting in the garden. For Radio 3's producers and engineers, it's the most exciting period of the year. Emma Bloxham, Radio 3's Editor, Live Music, says, 'We're fantastically lucky to have a dedicated team of expert sound-balancers, every one of whom relishes the challenge of bringing our listeners the very best seat in the house, night after night. In the space of a single day the team could be called upon to capture anything from the rich tapestry of a huge choral work to the intimacy of a string quartet.' Questions around which microphones to use, how many of them and where to place them, are debated endlessly: 'It's painstaking work, something we take incredibly seriously and are very proud of.' Aside from the concerts, many of the station's flagship shows gather behind the Proms. *Essential Classics*, *Composer of the Week* and *CD Review* survey the work of Proms composers and artists across the festival, while the drivetime show *In Tune* carries interviews with established and emerging performers.

The online resources of archived performances and programmes have immense educational value for all age-groups. And whether 'bespoke functionality' and 'connectivity' are music to your ears or anathema, the heartbeat of the Proms remains the relationship between the musicians and their audience, that mysterious energy created in a great performance from gut, wood, metal, the human voice and the human mind. As ever, the moments that get everyone talking this year will outlast the festival itself, with every performance available for 30 days via the Proms website: as Edward Blakeman points out, 'Your Proms are wherever and whenever you want them.' Andrew Downs agrees: 'I remember reading a tweet,' he says, 'during the Last Night a few years ago, from someone listening to the Proms in Sydney while watching the sunrise over the harbour bridge.' The Proms reach is truly global. •

Classical music critic of the *The Independent on Sunday* from 2000 to 2013, Anna Picard now writes for *The Times*, *The Spectator* and *Opera*, and contributes to BBC Radio 3's *CD Review*.

THE PROMS ON THE BBC

Every Prom broadcast live on **BBC Radio 3**
All broadcasts available on-demand for
30 days via the **BBC Proms** website

Many Proms broadcast across **BBC One**,
BBC Two and **BBC Four**

Selected Proms on **BBC Radio 1**, **1Xtra**,
2, 4, 6 Music and **BBC Asian Network**

The **BBC Proms Guide app**: search concerts,
organise your viewing and listening, plus all
the editorial content of the Proms Guide

Find details of all Proms performances
since 1895 on the **BBC Proms website**

Proms-related programmes on
BBC Radio 3 and **BBC Two**

Explore Proms-related archive programmes
and expert recommendations via the
BBC Proms website

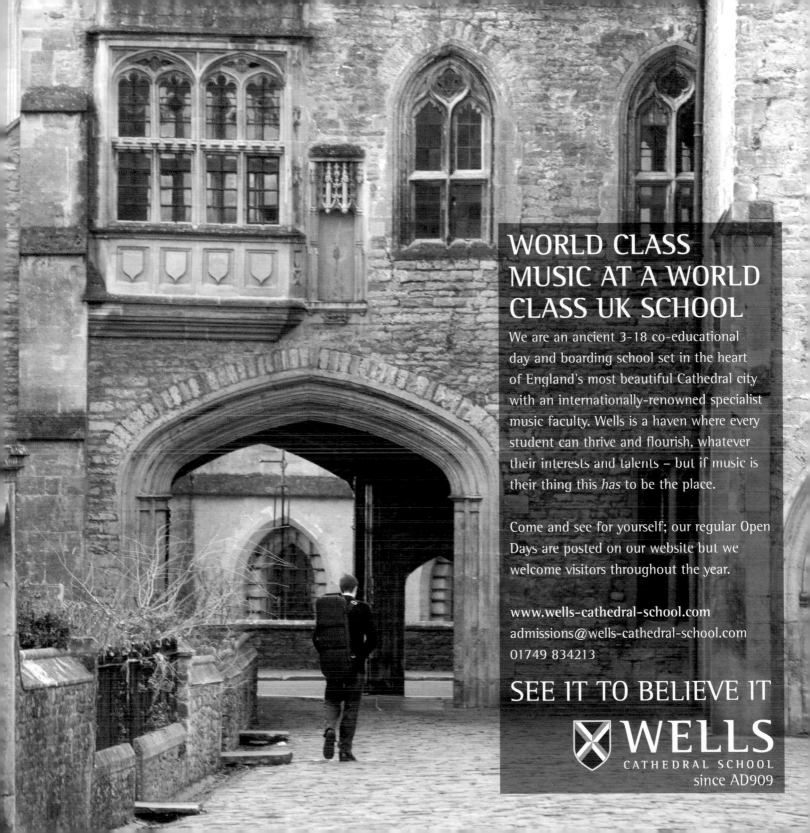

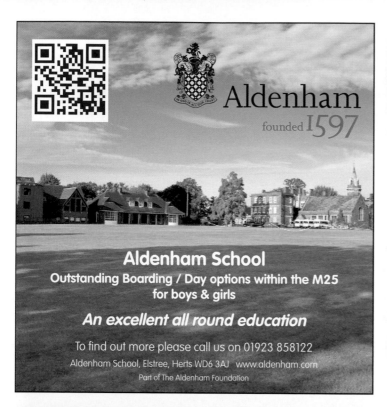

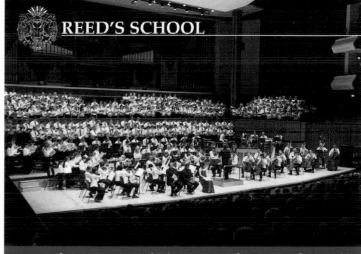

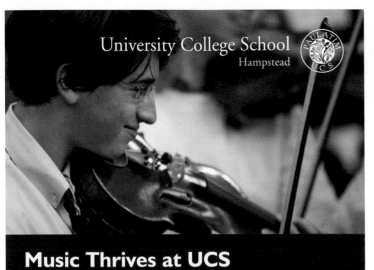

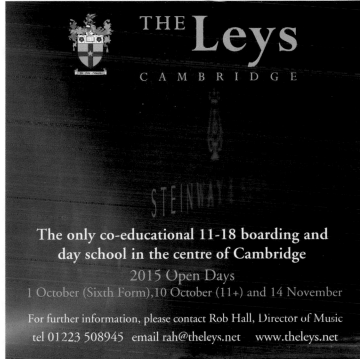

PIERINO

37 Thurloe Place, London SW7 2HP

Tel:0207 581 3770

Monday to Saturday
12 noon - 11.30pm

Sunday
12 noon - 11pm

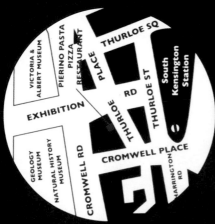

Prompt service guarenteed for you to be in time for the performance

We are within walking distance of the Royal Albert Hall, near South Kensington tube station.

You are welcome before and after the performance.

39 YEARS

EXPERIENCE OF SERVING GENUINE ITALAN FOOD AND FOR HOME-MADE PASTA AND THE BEST PIZZA IN LONDON

CONCERT LISTINGS

PROMS CONCERTS

Full details of all the 2015 BBC Proms concerts are in
this section *(pages 119–157)*

PROMS EXTRA

Look out, too, for the complementary series of free Proms
Extra events: find out more about the music through lively
introductions, or join in with workshops for all the family
(see also pages 98–103)

BOOKING

General booking opens at 9.00am on Saturday 16 May

Plan your Proms concert-going before tickets go on sale,
by using the Proms Planner at bbc.co.uk/proms from 2.00pm
on Thursday 23 April until midnight on Friday 15 May

For full booking and access information, see pages 159–169

ONLINE **bbc.co.uk/proms**
TELEPHONE **0845 401 5040†**

PRICE CODES A ▸ H

Each concert at the Royal Albert Hall falls
into one of eight price bands, colour-coded
for ease of reference. For a full list of prices
and booking fees, see page 162.

Please note: *concert start-times vary across the season – check before you book*
†see page 161 for call-cost information

FRIDAY 17 JULY

PROM 1
7.30pm–c9.55pm • Royal Albert Hall

PRICE BAND **B** *Seats £9.50 to £46 (plus booking fee*)*
WEEKEND PROMMING PASS *see page 164*

Nielsen Maskarade – overture	5'
Gary Carpenter Dadaville *BBC commission: world premiere*	c6'
Mozart Piano Concerto No. 20 in D minor, K466	31'

INTERVAL

Sibelius Belshazzar's Feast – suite	14'
Walton Belshazzar's Feast	34'

Lars Vogt *piano*
Christopher Maltman *bass-baritone*

BBC Singers
BBC National Chorus of Wales
BBC Symphony Chorus
BBC Symphony Orchestra
Sakari Oramo *conductor*

Two Nordic anniversaries launch this year's BBC Proms: Denmark's Carl Nielsen and Finland's Jean Sibelius both celebrate their 150th-birthday years. Two exotic musical retellings of the story of the Babylonian king Belshazzar include the first of this summer's feast of choral works. Celebrated German pianist Lars Vogt is soloist in the first of six late great Mozart piano concertos, and British composer Gary Carpenter spearheads the 32 premieres this season – a musical taste of things to come. *See 'A Force of Nature', pages 18–23; 'Nielsen and the Idea of Danishness', pages 26–31; 'With One Voice', pages 44–47; 'New Music', pages 88–95.*

RADIO *Live on BBC Radio 3*
TV *Broadcast on BBC Two this evening*
ONLINE *Listen, watch and catch up at bbc.co.uk/proms*

PROMS EXTRA
4.30pm–6.30pm • Royal College of Music A live Proms edition of BBC Radio 3's *In Tune*, presented by Sean Rafferty and Suzy Klein – with interviews and live performances from artists appearing this season. *Tickets available from BBC Studio Audiences, bbc.co.uk/tickets. Broadcast live on BBC Radio 3*

SPOTLIGHT ON...
Sakari Oramo • Prom 1

It was at the First Night of the Proms in 2013 that Sakari Oramo made his debut as Chief Conductor of the BBC Symphony Orchestra. So this year's opening Prom should bring back warm memories. That first appearance included Vaughan Williams's *A Sea Symphony*; two years later another British masterpiece is the focus of the second half – *Belshazzar's Feast* by Walton. 'It's such a rousing piece and surely suitable for this occasion,' says Oramo. 'It'll be important to create the utmost clarity as it's so fast and exciting.'

It was only natural, says Oramo, to mark the 150th anniversaries of Nielsen and Sibelius on the First Night. By happy coincidence Sibelius also wrote music inspired by *Belshazzar's Feast*, although Oramo points out that the pieces 'are diametrically opposed. Nothing, bar the name, tells us they are about the same material. Of course, Walton offers a narrative, whereas Sibelius was just adding incidental colour to a stage version of the Bible story.'

In the first half of the Prom, soloist Lars Vogt joins Oramo and the BBC Symphony Orchestra for Mozart's Piano Concerto No. 20 in D minor – one of only two of the composer's 27 piano concertos to be written in a minor key. 'I find the way Mozart uses the key of D minor really mystical,' says Oramo. 'There is tragedy but also a smile behind the tears.'

SATURDAY 18 JULY

PROM 2
6.30pm–c8.30pm • Royal Albert Hall

PRICE BAND **H** *Seats £6/£12 (plus booking fee*)*

TEN PIECES PROM

Programme to include excerpts from:

John Adams Short Ride in a Fast Machine

Beethoven Symphony No. 5 in C minor – first movement

Britten 'Storm' Interlude (from *Peter Grimes*)

Grieg In the Hall of the Mountain King (from *Peer Gynt*)

Handel Zadok the Priest

Holst Mars (from *The Planets*)

Anna Meredith Connect It
BBC commission: London premiere

Mozart Horn Concerto No. 4 – third movement

Mussorgsky A Night on the Bare Mountain

Stravinsky The Firebird (Suite 1910) – Finale

Barney Harwood
Dick and Dom
Tim Thorpe *horn*

Ten Pieces Children's Choir
BBC National Orchestra of Wales
Thomas Søndergård *conductor*

There will be one interval

For concert description, see Prom 3

PROMS EXTRA
2.30pm–3.45pm • Royal College of Music • Proms Lecture 'Unlocking the Mysteries of Music in Your Brain': Neuroscientist and author Daniel Levitin explores the fascinating relationship between music and the mind. *Edited version broadcast on BBC Radio 3 after tonight's Prom*

4.30pm–5.30pm • Royal College of Music Join professional musicians for a family-friendly introduction to tonight's Prom. Bring your instrument and join in! *See pages 98–103 for details*

CONCERT LISTINGS

120

BOOK ONLINE AT BBC.CO.UK/PROMS • BY TELEPHONE 0845 401 5040† • IN PERSON AT THE ROYAL ALBERT HALL • BOOKING OPENS 9.00AM ON 16 MAY

SUNDAY 19 JULY

PROM 3
11.00am–c1.00pm • Royal Albert Hall

PRICE BAND H *Seats £6/£12 (plus booking fee*)*

BARNEY HARWOOD

TEN PIECES PROM

For programme and artist details, see Prom 2

Since the Ten Pieces film launched last October, children in schools across the UK have been working on their own creative responses to music by Beethoven, Britten, Mozart, Mussorgsky and others, with the help of BBC ensembles. Some of the results now come to the Royal Albert Hall, where they will be performed alongside extracts from the Ten Pieces that inspired them. These two Proms are a musical celebration showcasing digital art, dance and new composition, bringing the first year of the BBC's Ten Pieces project to a triumphant close. Barney Harwood and Dick and Dom join in the fun. See 'Ten Pieces', pages 74–75.

Signed performance (Prom 3): see page 169 for details.

RADIO *Prom 2 Live on BBC Radio 3; Prom 3 recorded for future broadcast on BBC Radio 2*
TV *Ten Pieces Prom recorded for future broadcast on CBBC*
ONLINE *Listen, watch and catch up at bbc.co.uk/proms*

SUNDAY 19 JULY

PROM 4
7.30pm–c9.40pm • Royal Albert Hall

PRICE BAND B *Seats £9.50 to £46 (plus booking fee*)*
WEEKEND PROMMING PASS *see page 164*

Beethoven The Creatures of
Prometheus – overture   5'

John Woolrich Falling Down   15'
London premiere

INTERVAL

Beethoven
Symphony No. 9 in D minor, 'Choral'   68'

Margaret Cookhorn *contra-bassoon*
Lucy Crowe *soprano*
Gerhild Romberger *mezzo-soprano*
Dmitry Popov *tenor*
Kostas Smoriginas *bass-baritone*

CBSO Chorus
City of Birmingham Symphony Orchestra
Andris Nelsons *conductor*

Beethoven's 'Choral' Symphony is a celebration of human endeavour, as is his ballet score *The Creatures of Prometheus*. Latvian Andris Nelsons is reunited with the CBSO, having ended his Music Directorship on a high in June. (He returns in Proms 49 and 51 with the Boston Symphony Orchestra). John Woolrich's dark, sardonic contra-bassoon concerto was written for the CBSO's own contra-bassoonist Margaret Cookhorn. See 'With One Voice', pages 44–47; 'New Music', pages 88–95.

RADIO *Live on BBC Radio 3*
TV *Beethoven's Symphony No. 9 broadcast on BBC Four this evening*
ONLINE *Complete Prom available to listen, watch and catch up at bbc.co.uk/proms*

PROMS EXTRA
1.00pm–4.00pm • **Royal College of Music** Join Mary King and members of the BBC Singers to sing excerpts from Beethoven's Symphony No. 9. Experience in sight-reading or a knowledge of the piece is an advantage but not essential. *See pages 98–103 for details*

5.45pm–6.30pm • **Royal College of Music** Sir Nicholas Kenyon, Managing Director of the Barbican and former Director of the Proms, discusses the history of the festival. *Edited version broadcast on BBC Radio 3 during tonight's interval*

SPOTLIGHT ON...
Lucy Crowe • Prom 4

The last time Lucy Crowe performed Beethoven at the Proms – the *Missa solemnis* under Sir John Eliot Gardiner last year – she gave birth four days later. 'There's nothing more exciting than singing in a packed Royal Albert Hall and, clearly, hearing the work made my son want to enter the world!'

This year she's performing in another great Beethoven work, the Ninth Symphony. 'What I love about Beethoven's writing is that he pushes you to your limits,' she explains. 'In the Ninth he writes such demanding music for every instrument and every voice. He composed it towards the end of his life and it's almost as if he's saying, "I'm near to the end, I'm going to write something that's going to challenge everybody".'

The soprano part is no exception, says Crowe: 'the moment I most look forward to is the very end when I have to float a top B. It's really quite demanding but because of that it's massively exciting, and very rewarding if you nail it.'

One of the main challenges of performing such a well-known work is making it seem fresh, as Crowe is well aware. 'Everybody knows this piece, it's like an international anthem. But you've got to try and come to it with a fresh pair of eyes and ears. You've got to look at the music and perform it as if people haven't heard it before.'

MONDAY 20 JULY

PROMS CHAMBER MUSIC I
1.00pm–c2.00pm • Cadogan Hall

Seats £10/£12 (plus booking fee*)

THE CARDINALL'S MUSICK

Tallis

Videte miraculum	*9'*
O Lord, give thy Holy Spirit	*3'*
Hear the voice and prayer	*3'*
Why fum'th in fight?	*4'*
Suscipe quaeso	*9'*
O nata lux de lumine	*2'*
O sacrum convivium	*4'*
O salutaris hostia	*3'*

Cheryl Frances-Hoad

Homage to Tallis   *c7'*
world premiere

Tallis Spem in alium   *10'*

The Cardinall's Musick
Andrew Carwood *director*

There will be no interval

The Cardinall's Musick returns to the BBC Proms with director Andrew Carwood to launch a major new project: the Tallis Edition, aiming to throw new light on the music of this most lyrical of English polyphonists. As well as a selection of the composer's liturgical music, the concert includes his extraordinary 40-part motet *Spem in alium*, in addition to the world premiere of a new tribute to Tallis by British composer Cheryl Frances-Hoad. *See 'With One Voice', pages 44–47; 'New Music', pages 88–95.*

RADIO *Live on BBC Radio 3*
ONLINE *Listen and catch up at bbc.co.uk/proms*

MONDAY 20 JULY

PROM 5
7.30pm–c9.40pm • Royal Albert Hall

PRICE BAND Ⓐ *Seats £7.50 to £38 (plus booking fee*)*

Haydn Symphony No. 85 in B flat major, 'La reine'   *23'*

INTERVAL

HK Gruber into the open …   *c25'*
world premiere

Stravinsky Petrushka (1911 version)   *35'*

Colin Currie *percussion*

BBC Philharmonic
John Storgårds *conductor*

Petrushka, with its bustling Shrovetide fair and colourful carnival characters, launches a week dominated by the music of Stravinsky. All three of the composer's great scores for Diaghilev's Ballets Russes are performed this season – bright, folkloric textures gradually giving way to new musical brutality. Haydn's 'Paris' Symphony set the City of Light talking over a century earlier. The second movement of 'La reine' (The Queen) shares Stravinsky's sophisticated approach to folk music, while Viennese maverick HK Gruber's *into the open …* echoes the ballet's vivid scoring with instruments from Thailand, Africa and South America. Former BBC Young Musician of the Year Colin Currie joins the BBC Philharmonic under its Principal Guest Conductor John Storgårds. *See 'New Music', pages 88–95.*

RADIO *Live on BBC Radio 3*
TV *HK Gruber and Stravinsky recorded for broadcast on BBC Four on 6 August*
ONLINE *Complete Prom available to listen, watch and catch up at bbc.co.uk/proms*

PROMS EXTRA
5.45pm–6.30pm • Royal College of Music HK Gruber discusses the world premiere of his percussion concerto *into the open …*
Edited version broadcast on BBC Radio 3 during tonight's interval

TUESDAY 21 JULY

PROM 6
7.00pm–c9.15pm • Royal Albert Hall

PRICE BAND Ⓐ *Seats £7.50 to £38 (plus booking fee*)*

THOMAS SØNDERGÅRD

Poulenc Organ Concerto   *23'*

Stravinsky Symphony of Psalms   *21'*

INTERVAL

Haydn Te Deum in C major, Hob. XXIIIc:2   *10'*

Mozart Symphony No. 41 in C major, K551 'Jupiter'   *36'*

James O'Donnell *organ*

BBC National Chorus of Wales
BBC National Orchestra of Wales
Thomas Søndergård *conductor*

The Royal Albert Hall's great organ is showcased in a series of Proms this year, starting with Poulenc's Baroque-inspired Organ Concerto – all Gothic flourishes and grand gestures. Also gazing back to the Baroque, Stravinsky's *Symphony of Psalms* is a devout musical gesture, reimagining religious rituals on a symphonic scale. The second half pairs two Classical masterpieces: Haydn's cheery *Te Deum* and Mozart's enduringly popular 'Jupiter' Symphony. *See 'With One Voice', pages 44–47.*

RADIO *Live on BBC Radio 3*
TV *Stravinsky and Mozart recorded for broadcast on BBC Four on 26 July*
ONLINE *Complete Prom available to listen, watch and catch up at bbc.co.uk/proms*

PROMS EXTRA
5.00pm–6.00pm • Royal College of Music Join professional musicians for a family-friendly introduction to tonight's Prom. Bring your instrument and join in! *See pages 98–103 for details*

Dmitri Gulg.hin (The Cardinall's Musick); Andy Buchanan (Søndergård)

WEDNESDAY 22 JULY

PROM 7
7.00pm–c9.05pm • Royal Albert Hall

PRICE BAND **A** *Seats £7.50 to £38 (plus booking fee*)*

SIR ANDREW DAVIS

Delius In a Summer Garden   15'

Nielsen Clarinet Concerto   24'

INTERVAL

Hugh Wood Epithalamium   c25'
BBC commission: world premiere

Ravel Daphnis and Chloe – Suite No. 2   16'

Mark Simpson *clarinet*

BBC Symphony Chorus
BBC Symphony Orchestra
Sir Andrew Davis *conductor*

Afternoon heat breeds musical languor in a Prom that drifts from Delius's summer garden to the classical landscapes of Ravel's lovers Daphnis and Chloe. Former BBC Radio 3 New Generation Artist Mark Simpson is the soloist in anniversary composer Nielsen's intimate, playful Clarinet Concerto. Hugh Wood's *Epithalamium* is a new cantata that delights in John Donne's sensuous and jubilant verse. See 'Nielsen and the Idea of Danishness', pages 26–31; 'With One Voice', pages 44–47; 'New Music', pages 88–95.

RADIO *Live on BBC Radio 3*
TV *Nielsen and Hugh Wood recorded for broadcast on BBC Four on 30 July*
ONLINE *Complete Prom available to listen, watch and catch up at bbc.co.uk/proms*

PROMS EXTRA
5.15pm–6.00pm • Royal College of Music Hugh Wood, in conversation with Andrew McGregor, discusses the world premiere of *Epithalamium* and introduces performances of his chamber works.
Edited version broadcast on BBC Radio 3 after tonight's first Prom

---

SPOTLIGHT ON…
Mark Simpson • Prom 7

When Mark Simpson steps out on stage to play Nielsen's Clarinet Concerto this summer, it'll be the first time he's played it in public since 2006 – when it won him the title of BBC Young Musician of the Year. 'It's both exciting and daunting,' says Simpson. 'The piece itself is a mammoth undertaking. Also, performing it at the Proms for the first time is going to be pretty crazy.' Nielsen wrote his 1928 concerto for the Danish virtuoso Aage Oxenvad, with his character in mind. 'Oxenvad was quite frenetic and wild, so this piece is explosive,' says Simpson. 'As a performer you've got to be completely in control but also completely able to lose control. When I played it the first time, I just wanted to get the notes right and get to the end. It's a tumultuous journey but the ending is beautiful, quiet and serene.'

Since that award-winning performance, Simpson has been busy carving out a career as both a clarinettist and a composer. He's just about to finish his stint as a BBC Radio 3 New Generation Artist and next season sees the start of a four-year residency as Composer-in-Association with the BBC Philharmonic. 'I'm a composer, listener and performer,' he explains. 'I love this combination. Nielsen was a violinist himself and I suppose this concerto makes sense to me because it's performers' music. It feels comfortable.'

WEDNESDAY 22 JULY

PROM 8
10.15pm–c11.30pm • Royal Albert Hall

PRICE BAND **E** *Seats £7.50 to £24 (plus booking fee*)*

BOBBY FRICTION

LATE NIGHT WITH … BBC ASIAN NETWORK

Benny Dayal *vocalist*
Palak Muchhal *vocalist*
Naughty Boy *live producer*

Bobby Friction *presenter*
BBC Philharmonic
Richard Davis *conductor*

There will be no interval

Indian singers Benny Dayal and Palak Muchhal, together with British Asian DJ, songwriter and producer Naughty Boy, headline a Prom in association with BBC Asian Network and as part of the 50th anniversary this year of Asian Programmes on the BBC. The event launches a new series of Proms curated in collaboration with six BBC national radio stations – including 6 Music, Radio 1 and Radio 2 – and BBC Music. Bobby Friction presents the very best of South Asian music, from Bollywood to contemporary sounds. See 'The Proms Where You Are', pages 106–109.

RADIO *Live on BBC Radio 3 and BBC Asian Network*
ONLINE *Listen and catch up at bbc.co.uk/proms*

THURSDAY 23 JULY

PROM 9
7.30pm–c9.45pm • Royal Albert Hall

PRICE BAND C *Seats £14 to £57 (plus booking fee*)*

LEIF OVE ANDSNES

Beethoven
Piano Concerto No. 1 in C major   33'

Stravinsky
Apollon musagète (1947 version)   30'

INTERVAL

Beethoven
Piano Concerto No. 4 in G major   33'

Mahler Chamber Orchestra
Leif Ove Andsnes *piano/director*

Norwegian pianist Leif Ove Andsnes embarks
on his Proms cycle of Beethoven piano concertos
(see also Proms 10 & 12), directing the dynamic
Mahler Chamber Orchestra. Each concert features
a work by Stravinsky (in this case the composer's
classically inspired ballet *Apollon musagète* ('Apollo,
Leader of the Muses') – music, the impresario
Diaghilev claimed, 'not of this world, but of
somewhere above'. See *'Back to Beethoven'*,
pages 38–41.

RADIO *Live on BBC Radio 3*
ONLINE *Listen and catch up at bbc.co.uk/proms*

PROMS EXTRA
5.45pm–6.30pm • Royal College of Music Explore the
myths around Beethoven's life and music with guests
including Misha Donat.
Edited version broadcast on BBC Radio 3 during tonight's interval

c10.00pm–c11.00pm • Elgar Room, Royal Albert Hall
Informal late-night music and poetry, featuring young talent.
For details see bbc.co.uk/proms

FRIDAY 24 JULY

PROM 10
7.30pm–c9.35pm • Royal Albert Hall

PRICE BAND C *Seats £14 to £57 (plus booking fee*)*
WEEKEND PROMMING PASS *see page 164*

Stravinsky Concerto in E flat major,
'Dumbarton Oaks'   16'

Beethoven
Piano Concerto No. 3 in C minor   36'

INTERVAL

Schoenberg Friede auf Erden*   10'

Beethoven Fantasia in C minor for piano,
chorus and orchestra, 'Choral Fantasy'   20'

BBC Singers

Mahler Chamber Orchestra
Leif Ove Andsnes *piano/director*
*David Hill *conductor*

In his Third Piano Concerto Beethoven opened
up a new dramatic and physical scope, pushing the
instrument to new expressive lengths. The same
maverick energy pulses through the 'Choral Fantasy',
anticipating the Ninth Symphony in its unexpected
resort to words in its finale. In Schoenberg's
tour de force *Friede auf Erden* ('Peace on Earth')
the composer takes tonality to its limits. Stravinsky's
'Dumbarton Oaks' Concerto is a delightful
neo-Classical romp, an elegant homage to the
18th century. See *'Back to Beethoven'*, *pages 38–41.*

RADIO *Live on BBC Radio 3*
TV *Broadcast on BBC Four this evening*
ONLINE *Listen, watch and catch up at bbc.co.uk/proms*

PROMS EXTRA
5.45pm–6.30pm • Royal College of Music German culture
expert Karen Leeder on the great German Romantic poetry
that inspired Beethoven throughout his life, from Schiller's
Ode to Joy to Goethe's *Egmont* and Treitschke's *Fidelio*.
Edited version broadcast on BBC Radio 3 during tonight's interval

SATURDAY 25 JULY

PROMS SATURDAY MATINEE 1
3.00pm–c4.30pm • Cadogan Hall

Seats £10/£12 (plus booking fee*)

Pierre Boulez, arr. Schöllhorn
Notations 2, 12 & 10; La treizième   4'
UK premiere

Shiori Usui
Ophiocordyceps unilateralis s.l.   c7'
BBC commission: world premiere

Betsy Jolas Wanderlied   12'
UK premiere

Joanna Lee Hammer of Solitude   c7'
BBC commission: world premiere

Pierre Boulez Dérive 2   45'

Ulrich Heinen *cello*
Hilary Summers *contralto*

**Birmingham Contemporary
Music Group**
Franck Ollu *conductor*

There will be no interval

French conductor Franck Ollu makes his Proms
debut, directing the Birmingham Contemporary
Music Group in the first of two concerts celebrating
composer Pierre Boulez's 90th-birthday year.
Boulez's own *Notations* – written while he was
still a student – sits alongside his *Dérive 2*, both
works embedded in the 'family tree' of a composer
whose works interconnect in ever-evolving ways.
The concert also features *Wanderlied* for cello
and ensemble by Boulez's French-American
contemporary Betsy Jolas, as well as music by two
young composers new to the Proms: Shiori Usui
and Joanna Lee. See *'Beautiful Logic'*, *pages 50–53*;
'New Music', *pages 88–95.*

RADIO *Live on BBC Radio 3*
ONLINE *Listen and catch up at bbc.co.uk/proms*

Özgür Albayrak

SATURDAY 25 JULY

PROM 11
7.00pm–c10.10pm • Royal Albert Hall

PRICE BAND **D** *Seats £18 to £68 (plus booking fee*)*
WEEKEND PROMMING PASS *see page 164*

Bock Fiddler on the Roof   165'
(semi-staged)

Cast to include:

Bryn Terfel *Tevye*

Grange Park Opera
BBC Concert Orchestra
David Charles Abell *conductor*

There will be one interval

Fiddler on the Roof brims with numbers such as 'If I were a rich man', 'Sunrise, sunset' and 'Miracle of Miracles'. Hampshire's Grange Park Opera makes its Proms debut with a semi-staged performance of its new production starring Bryn Terfel as Tevye, the village milkman in pre-Revolutionary Russia trying, in vain, to bring up his five daughters within the time-honoured traditions of his Jewish forebears. See 'Miracle of Miracles', pages 62–67.

RADIO *Live on BBC Radio 3*
ONLINE *Listen and catch up at bbc.co.uk/proms*

PROMS EXTRA
10.30am–12.30pm • Royal College of Music
Join professional musicians and create your own music inspired by this evening's Prom. Suitable for all the family (ages 7-plus). *See pages 98–103 for details*

2.00pm–4.00pm • Royal College of Music Join Mary King and members of the BBC Singers to sing excerpts from *Fiddler on the Roof*. Suitable for all abilities. *See pages 98–103 for details*

5.15pm–6.00pm • Royal College of Music Award-winning actor Henry Goodman, who played the role of Tevye in a recent revival of *Fiddler on the Roof*, discusses the appeal of the hit 1964 musical.
Edited version broadcast on BBC Radio 3 during tonight's interval

SPOTLIGHT ON...

David Charles Abell • Prom 11

Fiddler on the Roof is a musical close to David Charles Abell's heart. 'I played the Fiddler in a production at high school. Prior to that I'd played the viola in the school orchestra, so I had to learn the violin,' he recalls. 'Playing in tune was a bit of a challenge, as was playing on the roof. But I fell in love with this show.'

This summer Abell will be conducting the ever-popular 1964 musical in a production at Grange Park Opera before bringing it to the Proms. Bass-baritone Bryn Terfel stars as Tevye. 'It's a perfect role for him,' says Abell. 'I'm doing *Sweeney Todd* with him at English National Opera in the spring, so he'll go from being scary to being lovable!'

Abell and his husband, pianist Seann Alderking, have spent months restoring the score by the original orchestrator Don Walker and incorporating some changes made for a 2004 Broadway revival. 'Two of the particular sounds for this show are the mandolin and the accordion,' says Abell. 'They were played in klezmer music, which very much influenced our orchestration, so we're thrilled to be including them.'

Does Abell have a favourite moment? 'The song "Do you love me?",' he says. 'I met Sheldon Harnick, one of the creators, last year. He and his wife are in their early nineties and the cutest couple you'll ever encounter. I could understand how he could write that song.'

SUNDAY 26 JULY

PROM 12
7.30pm–c9.35pm • Royal Albert Hall

PRICE BAND **C** *Seats £14 to £57 (plus booking fee*)*
WEEKEND PROMMING PASS *see page 164*

LEIF OVE ANDSNES

Stravinsky Octet   16'

Beethoven
Piano Concerto No. 2 in B flat major   29'

INTERVAL

Beethoven Piano Concerto No. 5
in E flat major, 'Emperor'   38'

Mahler Chamber Orchestra
Leif Ove Andsnes *piano/director*

Leif Ove Andsnes and the Mahler Chamber Orchestra complete their cycle of Beethoven Piano Concertos with Nos. 2 and 5 – the composer's first and final experiments in the genre. In No. 2 a spacious and lovely central Adagio is framed with Mozartean grace in the outer movements, while the Fifth is the composer's last word on the subject – a musical emancipation of the soloist that anticipates the Romantic concertos of Beethoven's successors. Looking to the musical past for inspiration once again, Stravinsky's Octet pastiches the forms and textures of the 18th century, colouring them with a mood and mischief all his own. See 'Back to Beethoven', pages 38–41.

RADIO *Live on BBC Radio 3*
ONLINE *Listen and catch up at bbc.co.uk/proms*

PROMS EXTRA
5.45pm–6.30pm • Royal College of Music Pianist Leif Ove Andsnes looks back over his four-year project with the Mahler Chamber Orchestra and discusses Beethoven's piano concertos.
Edited version broadcast on BBC Radio 3 during tonight's interval

MONDAY 27 JULY

PROMS CHAMBER MUSIC 2
1.00pm–c2.00pm • Cadogan Hall

Seats £10/£12 (plus booking fee*)

ROYAL NORTHERN SINFONIA WINDS

Nielsen Wind Quintet   26'

Mozart Quintet in E flat major
for piano and winds, K452   24'

Christian Blackshaw piano
Royal Northern Sinfonia Winds

There will be no interval

After many years away from the limelight, pianist Christian Blackshaw has recently returned with a series of recordings that have established him at the top of his profession. This lunchtime he is joined by the Royal Northern Sinfonia Winds for Mozart's Quintet for piano and winds, paired with anniversary composer Nielsen's Wind Quintet. Mozart's Quintet is a charming affair, described by the 28-year-old composer as 'the best thing I have written in my life so far', while Nielsen's – which was influenced by Mozart's – is a showcase for the different tones of the five wind instruments, a distinctive blend of contemporary and neo-Classical gestures. See 'Nielsen and the Idea of Danishness', pages 26–31.

RADIO *Live on BBC Radio 3*
ONLINE *Listen and catch up at bbc.co.uk/proms*

MONDAY 27 JULY

PROM 13
7.30pm–c9.50pm • Royal Albert Hall

PRICE BAND (A) *Seats £7.50 to £38 (plus booking fee*)*

SUSANNA MÄLKKI

Pierre Boulez Notations 1–4 & 7   17'

Luca Francesconi
Duende – The Dark Notes   26'
BBC co-commission: UK premiere

INTERVAL

Holst The Planets   51'

Leila Josefowicz violin

Elysian Singers (women's voices)
BBC Symphony Orchestra
Susanna Mälkki conductor

Once an irascible *enfant terrible*, Pierre Boulez was born 90 years ago. The Proms celebrations continue with one of his earliest works. Originally a series of 12 brilliant miniatures for piano, *Notations* is gradually being expanded by the composer into an orchestral cycle. Holst's *The Planets* brings musical imagery of a different kind. Violinist Leila Josefowicz makes a welcome return to the Proms, with a new concerto composed specially for her by one of Italy's greatest living composers. See 'Beautiful Logic', pages 50–53; 'New Music', pages 88–95.

RADIO *Live on BBC Radio 3*
TV *Pierre Boulez and Holst recorded for broadcast on BBC Four on 31 July*
ONLINE *Complete Prom available to listen, watch and catch up at bbc.co.uk/proms*

PROMS EXTRA
5.45pm–6.30pm • Royal College of Music Composer Steven Price, who won an Oscar for his soundtrack to *Gravity*, discusses the ways in which Holst's *The Planets* is still inspiring film composers almost 100 years after its premiere. *Edited version broadcast on BBC Radio 3 during tonight's interval*

SPOTLIGHT ON...

Leila Josefowicz • Prom 13

'*Duende* is an inner fire, the unleashing of an almost diabolical energy,' says violinist Leila Josefowicz. 'It has a lot to do with the flamenco spirit and an intense, visceral, dark energy. It's not something that can be learnt. You either have it or you don't.' It's also the title of a concerto written last year for Josefowicz by Italian composer Luca Francesconi. 'We first met in Milan with a mutual friend, the conductor Susanna Mälkki,' she says. 'We were talking about *duende* and he said, "You have it" – and was inspired to write a piece for me that unleashes this energy.'

Josefowicz and Mälkki give the first UK performance of *Duende – The Dark Notes* this year at the Proms; they premiered it last year in Stockholm. 'The piece is bursting with colour, rhythm and atmosphere,' says Josefowicz – 'from the very first note you're grabbed by the sense of suspense and the colours bouncing around. At first the orchestras we've played this with are always sort of shocked and then there's this glee as they really let loose.'

It's that shock of the new that Josefowicz loves as a performer, preferring it to playing more traditional concert-hall fare: 'It's an utterly different universe and one that I'm sort of addicted to more than ever before. I want to play things that are unexpected and improvisatory. Music is about exploration.'

TUESDAY 28 JULY

PROM 14
7.00pm–c10.20pm • Royal Albert Hall

PRICE BAND B Seats £9.50 to £46 (plus booking fee*)

Prokofiev

Piano Concerto No. 1 in D flat major*   16'

Piano Concerto No. 2 in G minor†   37'

INTERVAL

Piano Concerto No. 3 in C major*   29'

INTERVAL

Piano Concerto No. 4 in B flat major‡   22'

Piano Concerto No. 5 in G major†   24'

*Daniil Trifonov piano
†Sergei Babayan piano
‡Alexei Volodin piano

London Symphony Orchestra
Valery Gergiev conductor

All five Prokofiev piano concertos in one concert – it's a feat conductor Valery Gergiev achieved in 2012 at the Mariinsky and now brings to the Proms, along with three of his original pianists. It's a rare opportunity to hear three international soloists back-to-back, to compare styles and approaches, as well as to explore the composer's later, lesser-known concertos with their newly expressive tenderness. Daniil Trifonov, the prodigious young winner of the Tchaikovsky and Chopin competitions, shares the bill with his teacher Sergei Babayan, while Alexei Volodin tackles the rarely heard Fourth, commissioned, like Ravel's Piano Concerto for the Left Hand (Prom 36), by the one-armed pianist Paul Wittgenstein. See 'Playing Prokofiev', pages 56–59.

RADIO Live on BBC Radio 3
ONLINE Listen and catch up at bbc.co.uk/proms

PROMS EXTRA
5.15pm–6.00pm • Royal College of Music Delve into the life of Prokofiev and his five piano concertos with guests including David Nice.
Edited version broadcast on BBC Radio 3 during tonight's first interval

---

WEDNESDAY 29 JULY

PROM 15
6.30pm–c9.00pm • Royal Albert Hall

PRICE BAND A Seats £7.50 to £38 (plus booking fee*)

Prokofiev

Symphony No. 1 in D major, 'Classical'   15'

Qigang Chen Iris dévoilée   40'
London premiere

INTERVAL

Rachmaninov

Symphony No. 2 in E minor   59'

Meng Meng soprano
Anu Komsi soprano
Piia Komsi soprano
Jia Li pipa
Jing Chang zheng
Nan Wang erhu

BBC National Orchestra of Wales
Xian Zhang conductor

Following last night's Prokofiev piano concerto cycle, tonight's Prom opens with the Russian's bright and joyous 'Classical' Symphony, which surprised critics of the young firebrand composer with its formal elegance. It's paired with Rachmaninov's Second Symphony – beloved for its intimate, lyrical slow movement. Rachmaninov might be the original composer of the 'big tune', but it's an instinct China's Qigang Chen – a pupil of Messiaen – shares. East and West come together for his evocative *Iris dévoilée*, pairing traditional Chinese instruments with Western harmonies. See 'New Music', pages 88–95.

RADIO Live on BBC Radio 3
ONLINE Listen and catch up at bbc.co.uk/proms

PROMS EXTRA
4.45pm–5.30pm • Royal College of Music In 1915 Ezra Pound published *Cathay*, a collection of poems translated from classical Chinese. Poets Jo Shapcott and Sean O'Brien discuss these poems, once hailed as being of 'a supreme beauty'.
Edited version broadcast on BBC Radio 3 during tonight's interval

---

WEDNESDAY 29 JULY

PROM 16
10.15pm–c11.30pm • Royal Albert Hall

PRICE BAND F Seats £10 to £30 (plus booking fee*)

PETE TONG

LATE NIGHT WITH … BBC RADIO 1

Pete Tong presenter

Heritage Orchestra
Jules Buckley conductor

There will be no interval

Radio 1's first ever Prom is less concert and more dance-party – a musical homage to Ibiza and its infectious, energetic brand of club music. 2015 marks the 20th anniversary of Radio 1 in Ibiza and this will be a celebration to remember. Veteran British DJ Pete Tong presents a line-up of live artists, who perform with Jules Buckley and his Heritage Orchestra. See 'The Proms Where You Are', pages 106–109.

RADIO Live on BBC Radio 3 and BBC Radio 1
ONLINE Listen and catch up at bbc.co.uk/proms

---

*SEE PAGE 162 FOR BOOKING FEES • †SEE PAGE 161 FOR CALL-COST INFORMATION   UNDER-18s GO HALF-PRICE (SEE PAGE 163)

THURSDAY 30 JULY

PROM 17
7.30pm–c9.50pm • Royal Albert Hall

PRICE BAND **A** *Seats £7.50 to £38 (plus booking fee*)*

Debussy Prélude à l'après-midi
d'un faune   11'

Vaughan Williams Sancta civitas   35'

INTERVAL

Elgar Symphony No. 2 in E flat major 57'

Robin Tritschler *tenor*
Iain Paterson *baritone*

Hallé Youth Choir
Trinity Boys Choir
Hallé Choir
London Philharmonic Choir
Hallé
Sir Mark Elder *conductor*

Sir Mark Elder and the Hallé champion Vaughan
Williams's neglected oratorio *Sancta civitas* – an
ecstatic vision of post-apocalyptic salvation. It's a
piece made for the huge space of the Royal Albert
Hall, where its heavenly trumpets and choirs can
swell to full force. Described by Elgar's wife as 'vast
in design and supremely beautiful', his Second
Symphony took a while to win public affection, but
is now almost as cherished as Debussy's evocative
tone-poem depicting the lascivious thoughts of a
sleepy faun – a work the composer Pierre Boulez
has hailed as signalling the beginning of modern
music. See *'With One Voice'*, pages 44–47.

RADIO *Live on BBC Radio 3*
TV *Elgar recorded for broadcast on BBC Four on 2 August*
ONLINE *Complete Prom available to listen, watch
and catch up at bbc.co.uk/proms*

PROMS EXTRA
5.45pm–6.30pm • Royal College of Music 150 years after
its publication, writers Lynne Truss and Philip Ardagh discuss
Lewis Carroll's *Alice's Adventures in Wonderland* and its
enduring appeal to readers, writers and film-makers.
Edited version broadcast on BBC Radio 3 during tonight's interval

c10.15pm–c11.15pm • Elgar Room, Royal Albert Hall
Informal late-night music and poetry, featuring young talent.
For details see bbc.co.uk/proms

FRIDAY 31 JULY

PROM 18
7.00pm–c9.15pm • Royal Albert Hall

PRICE BAND **B** *Seats £9.50 to £46 (plus booking fee*)*
WEEKEND PROMMING PASS *see page 164*

KATIA AND MARIELLE LABÈQUE

Mozart Concerto for two pianos
in E flat major, K365   24'

INTERVAL

Shostakovich Symphony No. 7
in C major, 'Leningrad'   73'

Katia and Marielle Labèque *pianos*

BBC Symphony Orchestra
Semyon Bychkov *conductor*

Sisters Katia and Marielle Labèque perform
Mozart's Concerto for two pianos as a complement
to our focus on the composer's late piano
concertos. Written in the 1770s for Mozart and
his own sister 'Nannerl' to perform, it's a work that
delights in the interplay of dialogue, with a slow
movement that is a tender conversation between
friends. Intimacy gives way to epic gestures in
Shostakovich's sprawling 'Leningrad' Symphony
– one of the giants of the symphonic repertoire,
and a passionate musical testament to the 25 million
Soviet citizens killed in the Second World War.

RADIO *Live on BBC Radio 3*
ONLINE *Listen and catch up at bbc.co.uk/proms*

PROMS EXTRA
5.15pm–6.00pm • Royal College of Music Explore the
historical context of Shostakovich's 'Leningrad' Symphony
with Marina Frolova-Walker.
Edited version broadcast on BBC Radio 3 during tonight's interval

FRIDAY 31 JULY

PROM 19
10.15pm–c11.30pm • Royal Albert Hall

PRICE BAND **E** *Seats £7.50 to £24 (plus booking fee*)*
WEEKEND PROMMING PASS *see page 164*

ALINA IBRAGIMOVA

J. S. Bach

Sonata No. 1 in G minor for solo violin,
BWV 1001   17'

Partita No. 1 in B minor for solo violin,
BWV 1002   28'

Sonata No. 2 in A minor for solo violin,
BWV 1003   24'

Alina Ibragimova *violin*

There will be no interval

When you place a single, solo instrumentalist in
the Royal Albert Hall, a peculiar alchemy occurs.
Suddenly the huge space becomes charged with
a collective energy, a concentration that amplifies
the emotions and gestures of the music performed.
When that happens at a Late Night Prom, it's
particularly magical. Violinist Alina Ibragimova,
making the first of several appearances this season,
takes us back to what can seem like the purest
expression of music, performing Bach's complete
Sonatas and Partitas for solo violin, split across
two concerts (see also Prom 21). See *'Me, Myself
and Bach'*, pages 78–81.

RADIO *Live on BBC Radio 3*
TV *Recorded for broadcast on BBC Four on 20 August*
ONLINE *Listen, watch and catch up at bbc.co.uk/proms*

Umberto Nicoletti (Labèques); Eva Vermandel (Ibragimova)

SPOTLIGHT ON...

Alina Ibragimova • Prom 19

'I began to play Bach when I was at school and it was a struggle at first,' says Alina Ibragimova. 'It took a while to find what I wanted to do with the stylistic and expressive aspects. But I started to play Baroque violin and little by little I developed an approach that was close to me. I needed to live with the music for years and let it grow with me.'

Now, with an acclaimed solo Bach recording to her name, the Russian-born violinist will be playing Bach's six solo Sonatas and Partitas at the Proms during two late-night concerts. It's the first time this has been done at the Proms, and the first of this year's series of late-night solo Bach. 'It always feels great to play them close together,' says Ibragimova, 'In a way they are one big journey from the very first chord of the G minor Sonata, with the climax of the set being the Partita in D minor and its famous Chaconne, the first piece Bach wrote after his wife died. It's full of pain. But the C major Sonata that follows is full of acceptance. And after that the E major Partita is a party.'

But how well will these solo violin pieces come across in the vast space of the Royal Albert Hall?

'The intimacy of the works, wherever you play them, tends to bring people in,' she says. 'I think that will happen here as well.'

Chris Christofoulou/BBC (Ibragimova), Sussie Ahlburg (Mena), Eva Vermandel (Ibragimova)

SATURDAY 1 AUGUST

PROM 20

6.30pm–c9.00pm • Royal Albert Hall

PRICE BAND A Seats £7.50 to £38 (plus booking fee*)
WEEKEND PROMMING PASS see page 164

JUANJO MENA

Schubert
Symphony No. 4 in C minor, 'Tragic'   29'

Luke Bedford Instability   c25'
BBC commission: world premiere

INTERVAL

Bruckner Mass No. 3 in F minor   59'

Luba Orgonášová soprano
Jennifer Johnston mezzo-soprano
Robert Dean Smith tenor
Derek Welton bass-baritone

Orfeón Pamplonés
BBC Philharmonic
Juanjo Mena conductor

Although composed for the church, it is in the concert hall that the dramatic scale of Bruckner's mighty Mass in F minor comes into its own. A new commission from Luke Bedford puts the Royal Albert Hall's great organ in the spotlight, while opening the concert is Schubert's 'Tragic' Symphony – a work whose heart-on-sleeve emotions are those of a composer still in his teens. See 'With One Voice', pages 44–47; 'New Music', pages 88–95.

RADIO Live on BBC Radio 3
ONLINE Listen and catch up at bbc.co.uk/proms

PROMS EXTRA
4.45pm–5.30pm • Royal College of Music Erik Levi discusses the relationship between Bruckner's Mass in F minor and the Viennese tradition of sacred music.
Edited version broadcast on BBC Radio 3 during tonight's interval

SATURDAY 1 AUGUST

PROM 21

10.15pm–c11.30pm • Royal Albert Hall

PRICE BAND E Seats £7.50 to £24 (plus booking fee*)
WEEKEND PROMMING PASS see page 164

ALINA IBRAGIMOVA

J. S. Bach
Partita No. 2 in D minor for solo violin, BWV 1004   30'

Sonata No. 3 in C major for solo violin, BWV 1005   23'

Partita No. 3 in E major for solo violin, BWV 1006   19'

Alina Ibragimova violin

There will be no interval

Russian-born Alina Ibragimova gives the second of her two Late Night recitals of solo Bach. Her natural tendency towards a historically informed style of playing these works was formed while she was a teenager at the Yehudi Menuhin School. Her teachers at the time called for more vibrato, bigger gestures. 'I wanted something more direct,' she recalls. 'Less about me.' See 'Me, Myself and Bach', pages 78–81.

RADIO Live on BBC Radio 3
TV Recorded for broadcast on BBC Four on 27 August
ONLINE Listen, watch and catch up at bbc.co.uk/proms

SUNDAY 2 AUGUST

PROM 22
3.30pm–c5.45pm • Royal Albert Hall

PRICE BAND A Seats £7.50 to £38 (plus booking fee*)
WEEKEND PROMMING PASS see page 164

Brett Dean Pastoral Symphony   15'

Mozart Piano Concerto No. 26
in D major, K537 'Coronation'   32'

INTERVAL

Anna Meredith Smatter Hauler   c5'
BBC commission: world premiere

Beethoven Symphony No. 6
in F major, 'Pastoral'   40'

Francesco Piemontesi *piano*

Aurora Orchestra
Nicholas Collon *conductor*

The Aurora Orchestra staged a Proms first last year when it performed Mozart's Symphony No. 40 from memory. Now the dynamic young ensemble returns to continue this season's sequence of family-friendly matinees, giving Beethoven's 'Pastoral' Symphony the same direct, communicative treatment. It is paired with Australian composer Brett Dean's own homage to nature – a work, he explains, inspired by 'glorious birdsong, the threat that it faces, the loss, and the soulless noise that we're left with when they're all gone'. Former BBC Radio 3 New Generation Artist Francesco Piemontesi joins the orchestra for Mozart's late 'Coronation' Concerto, and the afternoon also features the premiere of a new commission from British composer Anna Meredith – also performed from memory. See 'Learning by Heart', pages 32–35; 'New Music', pages 88–95.

RADIO *Live on BBC Radio 3*
TV *Brett Dean and Beethoven recorded for broadcast on BBC Four on 9 August*
ONLINE *Complete Prom available to listen, watch and catch up at bbc.co.uk/proms*

PROMS EXTRA
1.45pm–2.30pm • Royal College of Music As Beethoven's 'Pastoral' Symphony is played from memory, actress Lisa Dwan, who has performed Samuel Beckett's monologues, and musician soprano Susan Bullock, discuss the role of memory in performance.
Edited version broadcast on BBC Radio 3 during this afternoon's interval

SPOTLIGHT ON...
Francesco Piemontesi • Prom 22

'I'm someone who loves to analyse a piece,' says Francesco Piemontesi. 'But with Mozart, once you've done that, there is still something you cannot explain.'

The Swiss pianist, who performs the 'Coronation' Piano Concerto at the Proms this year, has made a name for himself as an interpreter of Mozart. And this concerto is one of his favourites: 'There is a simplicity which composers seem to get in their last works. This concerto may be less elaborate than the middle-period concertos but under that smooth surface you find so many different aspects.'

Something else that's particular to this concerto is that large sections of the left-hand part are missing. So Piemontesi has written his own. 'I wasn't very happy with the part given in the existing edition – it's not completely what I would have expected. So I studied the way Mozart had written the left hand in other concertos and made my own version. It was a lot of work, but to be able to compose this was wonderful.'

The conductor is Nicholas Collon, one of Piemontesi's favourite musicians to work with, and also a great friend. 'There are some musicians whose breathing is exactly the same as yours,' says Piemontesi: 'you don't have to look for every upbeat, you're both receptive to the other person. We know we can trust each other.'

SUNDAY 2 AUGUST

PROM 23
8.00pm–c9.30pm • Royal Albert Hall

PRICE BAND B Seats £9.50 to £46 (plus booking fee*)
WEEKEND PROMMING PASS see page 164

KAREN CARGILL

Verdi Requiem   81'

Angela Meade *soprano*
Karen Cargill *mezzo-soprano*
Yosep Kang *tenor*
Raymond Aceto *bass*

**Concert Association of the Chorus
of the Deutsche Oper Berlin**
BBC Scottish Symphony Orchestra
Donald Runnicles *conductor*

There will be no interval

After a powerfully disquieting performance of Strauss's *Salome* last year, Donald Runnicles returns for the first of two appearances this summer, bringing the chorus of the Deutsche Oper Berlin and the BBC SSO together for Verdi's *Requiem* – a work conductor Hans von Bülow described as 'an opera in ecclesiastical garb', written for the concert hall but distilling all the drama and intensity of the stage. At its core is the extended *Dies irae* sequence – a Day of Judgement whose terrors are not easily forgotten. The international cast of soloists includes Scottish mezzo-soprano Karen Cargill. See 'With One Voice', pages 44–47.

RADIO *Live on BBC Radio 3*
ONLINE *Listen and catch up at bbc.co.uk/proms*

PROMS EXTRA
3.30pm–6.30pm • Royal College of Music Join Mary King and members of the BBC Singers to sing excerpts from Verdi's *Requiem*. Experience in sight-reading or a knowledge of the piece is an advantage but not essential. See pages 98–103 for details

Marco Borggreve (Piemontesi); K. K. Dundas (Cargill)

MONDAY 3 AUGUST

PROMS CHAMBER MUSIC 3
1.00pm–c2.00pm • Cadogan Hall

Seats £10/£12 (plus booking fee*)

APOLLON MUSAGÈTE QUARTET

Webern Langsamer Satz *12'*

Colin Matthews
String Quartet No. 5 *12'*
European premiere

Beethoven
String Quartet in D major, Op. 18 No. 3 *26'*

Apollon Musagète Quartet

There will be no interval

The Apollon Musagète Quartet — former BBC Radio 3 New Generation Artists and eloquent champions of contemporary music — makes its Proms debut, bringing the European premiere of the Fifth Quartet by one of Britain's leading living composers, Colin Matthews — a work commissioned for the 75th anniversary of the Tanglewood Festival. It is paired with Webern's youthful *Langsamer Satz*, an ecstatic piece that showcases the composer's formal skill within a lyrical idiom. Of Beethoven's six Op. 18 quartets, No. 3 is the lightest, and the hardest to pin down. The scherzo is fleeting, and even the framing movements have an unusual delicacy and wistfulness about them. See 'New Music', pages 88–95.

RADIO *Live on BBC Radio 3*
ONLINE *Listen and catch up at bbc.co.uk/proms*

MONDAY 3 AUGUST

PROM 24
7.30pm–c9.45pm • Royal Albert Hall

PRICE BAND **A** Seats £7.50 to £38 (plus booking fee*)

DONALD RUNNICLES

James MacMillan Symphony No. 4 *c25'*
BBC commission: world premiere

INTERVAL

Mahler
Symphony No. 5 in C sharp minor *72'*

BBC Scottish Symphony Orchestra
Donald Runnicles conductor

Mahler's mighty Symphony No. 5 is the climax of this second Prom from Donald Runnicles and the BBC Scottish Symphony Orchestra. The work's intense, contrasting moods — the bitter solemnity of the funeral march, the violence of the second movement and the tenderness of the famous Adagietto — make this one of the great orchestral showpieces. The evening opens with the world premiere of a dramatic new symphony from Scottish composer James MacMillan. See 'New Music', pages 88–95.

RADIO *Live on BBC Radio 3*
TV *James MacMillan recorded for broadcast on BBC Four on 6 September*
ONLINE *Complete Prom available to listen, watch and catch up at bbc.co.uk/proms*

PROMS EXTRA
5.45pm–6.30pm • Royal College of Music The year of the first Proms concerts, 1895, was a critical one for Oscar Wilde. His plays *The Importance of Being Earnest* and *An Ideal Husband* were first performed and he underwent three trials in the High Court. Philip Hoare, author of *Oscar Wilde's Last Stand*, explores this tumultuous year. *Edited version broadcast on BBC Radio 3 during tonight's interval*

TUESDAY 4 AUGUST

PROM 25
7.30pm–c10.00pm • Royal Albert Hall

PRICE BAND **C** Seats £14 to £57 (plus booking fee*)

Monteverdi Orfeo *107'*
(sung in Italian)

Cast to include (in alphabetical order):

Krystian Adam *tenor*
Francesca Aspromonte *soprano*
Francesca Boncompagni *soprano*
Gianluca Buratto *bass*
Mariana Flores *soprano*
Silvia Frigato *soprano*
Nicholas Mulroy *tenor*
David Shipley *bass*
Andrew Tortise *tenor*
Gareth Treseder *tenor*

Monteverdi Choir
English Baroque Soloists
Sir John Eliot Gardiner *conductor*

There will be one interval

Monteverdi's *Orfeo* is the first great opera — the moment when psychological truth and musical virtuosity came together to tell a story of love, loss and the power of art. Sir John Eliot Gardiner — making the first of two appearances this year, tonight with the English Baroque Soloists — transforms the Royal Albert Hall into the 17th-century Mantuan court of the Gonzagas with some of Monteverdi's loveliest melodies and most colourful instrumental writing, bringing the tale of Orpheus and his beloved Eurydice to fresh musical life. See 'A Grand Arrival', pages 84–85.

RADIO *Live on BBC Radio 3*
ONLINE *Listen and catch up at bbc.co.uk/proms*

PROMS EXTRA
5.45pm–6.30pm • Royal College of Music An introduction to Monteverdi's *Orfeo*, with guests including Sarah Lenton. *Edited version broadcast on BBC Radio 3 during tonight's interval*

Marco Borggreve (Apollon Musagète Quartet); Simon Pauly (Runnicles)

WEDNESDAY 5 AUGUST

PROM 26
6.30pm–c8.45pm • Royal Albert Hall

PRICE BAND Ⓐ *Seats £7.50 to £38 (plus booking fee*)*

CHLOË HANSLIP

Walton Spitfire Prelude and Fugue   8'

Vaughan Williams
Concerto accademico   17'

Grace Williams Fairest of Stars   15'

INTERVAL

Elgar Overture 'Froissart'   15'

Walton Symphony No. 2   30'

Chloë Hanslip *violin*
Ailish Tynan *soprano*

BBC National Orchestra of Wales
Tadaaki Otaka *conductor*

Elgar's *Froissart* overture throbs with national pride
and swagger, while Walton's Second Symphony
sustains an altogether darker, more contemplative
mood. Former BBC Young Musician Chloë Hanslip
is the soloist in Vaughan Williams's rarely heard
Concerto accademico – a work whose lyrical slow
movement and dancing finale are anything but
'academic'. The concert also features Welsh
composer Grace Williams's ecstatic, neo-Straussian
Fairest of Stars for soprano and orchestra, a musical
celebration of Milton's poetry.

RADIO *Live on BBC Radio 3*
ONLINE *Listen and catch up at bbc.co.uk/proms*

PROMS EXTRA
4.45pm–5.30pm • Royal College of Music J. P. E. Harper-
Scott introduces Walton's Symphony No. 2 in the context
of 20th-century British music.
Edited version broadcast on BBC Radio 3 during tonight's interval

WEDNESDAY 5 AUGUST

PROM 27
10.15pm–c11.30pm • Royal Albert Hall

PRICE BAND Ⓔ *Seats £7.50 to £24 (plus booking fee*)*

MARY ANNE HOBBS

LATE NIGHT WITH …
BBC RADIO 6 MUSIC

Mary Anne Hobbs *presenter*
Nils Frahm *piano/keyboards*
A Winged Victory for the Sullen

London Brass

There will be no interval

Mary Anne Hobbs of BBC Radio 6 Music presents
an evening exploring the borderlands of classical
music, with the pioneers of a new generation of
musicians who draw on contemporary electronic
influences. Piano and keyboard virtuoso Nils Frahm
makes his Proms debut, as does atmospheric duo
A Winged Victory for the Sullen, and together they
create an exclusive centrepiece collaboration.
See 'The Proms Where You Are', pages 106–109.

RADIO *Live on BBC Radio 3 and BBC Radio 6 Music*
ONLINE *Listen and catch up at bbc.co.uk/proms*

THURSDAY 6 AUGUST

PROM 28
7.30pm–c9.35pm • Royal Albert Hall

PRICE BAND Ⓐ *Seats £7.50 to £38 (plus booking fee*)*

OLIVER KNUSSEN

Dukas The Sorcerer's Apprentice   12'

Mark-Anthony Turnage
On Opened Ground   24'

INTERVAL

Gunther Schuller Seven Studies
on Themes of Paul Klee   22'

Scriabin The Poem of Ecstasy   22'

Lawrence Power *viola*

BBC Symphony Orchestra
Oliver Knussen *conductor*

Poetry, art and music itself inspire this programme.
Scriabin's *The Poem of Ecstasy* fuses poetry and
music in pursuit of sexual bliss and spiritual
transcendence. Turnage's *On Opened Ground* pays
tribute to the poet Seamus Heaney. Schuller's
Seven Studies explore Paul Klee's paintings in sound,
while Dukas transforms a ballad by Goethe into a
musical tale of magic and mischief.

RADIO *Live on BBC Radio 3*
ONLINE *Listen and catch up at bbc.co.uk/proms*

PROMS EXTRA
5.45pm–6.30pm • Royal College of Music Musicologist
Marina Frolova-Walker offers insights into Scriabin's
The Poem of Ecstasy and the world of the composer.
Edited version broadcast on BBC Radio 3 during tonight's interval

c9.45pm–c10.45pm • Elgar Room, Royal Albert Hall
Informal late-night music and poetry, featuring young talent.
For details see bbc.co.uk/proms

Benjamin Ealovega (Hanslip); Laura Lewis/BBC (Hobbs); Chris Christodoulou/BBC (Knussen)

SPOTLIGHT ON...
Lawrence Power • Prom 28

Lawrence Power has both performed and recorded *On Opened Ground*, Mark-Anthony Turnage's viola concerto, since giving its UK premiere in 2004. 'It's a wonderful piece,' he says. 'There are moments of raw, guttural screaming, but there's also touching intimacy. Actually, it's quite inherently English in its expression. It taps into the viola's character and history.' That heritage, Power explains, includes music by Walton, Vaughan Williams, York Bowen, Benjamin Dale and Cecil Forsyth. 'That's what makes Turnage such a great composer – he has incorporated them in his own way, and he's such a unique voice.'

'What I love here is the way the viola goes in and out of the texture,' says Power: 'there are moments where it's part of the orchestra and others where it's in dialogue. At the most intimate moments Turnage pares down the orchestration, sometimes to just two solo violins playing. He's a master of that.'

Turnage recently wrote Power a piece for viola and piano, *Powerplay*. 'He's such a joy to work with,' says Power. 'But in a way it's my job just to put across what he's written and not be involved in long dialogues with composers beforehand. Mark is quite refreshing in that he really trusts the performer to create nuances. Perhaps it ties in to his passion for jazz, that he trusts soloists to bring their own stamp to his music.'

FRIDAY 7 AUGUST

PROM 29
6.30pm–c8.50pm • Royal Albert Hall

PRICE BAND Ⓐ *Seats £7.50 to £38 (plus booking fee*)*
WEEKEND PROMMING PASS *see page 164*

Mozart
Idomeneo – ballet music   24'

Ravel
Piano Concerto in G major   23'

INTERVAL

Ravel, arr. C. Matthews
Miroirs – Oiseaux tristes   4'
BBC commission: world premiere

Messiaen, orch. C. Dingle
Un oiseau des arbres de Vie (Oiseau tui)   c4'
world premiere

Stravinsky Symphony in
Three Movements   22'

Ravel La valse   11'

Jean-Efflam Bavouzet *piano*

BBC Philharmonic
Nicholas Collon *conductor*

Mozart's *Idomeneo* owes its ballet sequence to the influence of French opera, and it launches a programme featuring two Frenchmen who idolised Mozart: Ravel and Messiaen. Ravel's Piano Concerto in G adds a jazzy colouring to its Classical influences, while *Oiseaux tristes* and *La valse* contrast the doleful calls of lost forest birds with a dark, swirling portrait of the disintegration of Vienna. The world premiere of a recently rediscovered work by Messiaen originally intended for the composer's *Éclairs sur l'au-delà* – brings more birdsong (that of the tui from New Zealand), while Stravinsky's urbane neo-Classical Symphony combines piquancy and elegance. See 'New Music', pages 88–95.

RADIO *Live on BBC Radio 3*
ONLINE *Listen and catch up at bbc.co.uk/proms*

PROMS EXTRA
4.45pm–5.30pm • **Royal College of Music** Join Christopher Dingle to explore the life and works of Olivier Messiaen, with a particular focus on the newly orchestrated *Un oiseau des arbres de Vie (Oiseau tui)*.
Edited version broadcast on BBC Radio 3 during tonight's interval

---

FRIDAY 7 AUGUST

PROM 30
10.15pm–c11.30pm • Royal Albert Hall

PRICE BAND Ⓕ *Seats £10 to £30 (plus booking fee*)*
WEEKEND PROMMING PASS *see page 164*

SETH MACFARLANE

LATE NIGHT SINATRA

Cast to include:

Seth MacFarlane *vocalist*

John Wilson Orchestra
John Wilson *conductor*

There will be no interval

'The Voice' … 'Ol' Blue Eyes' … 'The Sultan of Swoon': the mythology surrounding Frank Sinatra is overwhelming. A gifted entertainer, screen actor and ubiquitous personality, his real legacy as a pioneer of popular song can sometimes get lost in the clamour. This Late Night Prom celebrates the centenary of this musical legend in a concert that brings together some of the great voices of our own time, led by the multitalented Seth MacFarlane. Join John Wilson and his orchestra for an after-hours sequence of big tunes and even bigger performances. See 'Popular Idols', pages 66–67.

RADIO *Live on BBC Radio 3*
TV *Broadcast on BBC Four this evening*
ONLINE *Listen, watch and catch up at bbc.co.uk/proms*

Dmitry Sinkovsky • PSM 2

A virtuoso Baroque violinist who is equally skilled as a director and a counter-tenor? It seems Dmitry Sinkovsky is the nearest we'll get to a modern-day Orpheus. He will wear all his many hats with the innovative Ghent-based period ensemble B'Rock at Cadogan Hall.

Appropriately, it was an English counter-tenor who inspired him. 'I trained as a modern violinist; then, through Marie Leonhardt, I became fascinated by the Baroque violin, which became my instrument. In 2003 I had the fortune to tour the UK with an ensemble supporting Emma Kirkby and Michael Chance and I became very curious about singing.

'I naturally sang high, perhaps because of the violin's natural range. Michael was kind enough to give me lessons, but advised me to find a teacher. So, back in Russia, I studied vocal technique for seven years; I was smitten!'

Sinkovsky says that singing has transformed his approach to the violin. 'The two arts complement each other. Violin playing is more physical and technical, while singing is more naked, sincere, but a revelation in terms of phrasing, colour and timbre.' He also leads his own Russian ensemble, La Voce Strumentale, and works with many prominent groups: 'B'Rock is an exciting group with a strong identity, which is developing in a special way. I always enjoy the variety in the group's continuo playing; each player brings something to the conversation.'

SATURDAY 8 AUGUST

PROMS SATURDAY MATINEE 2
3.00pm–c4.30pm • Cadogan Hall

Seats £10/£12 (plus booking fee*)

MARY-ELLEN NESI

Vivaldi
Violin Concerto in C major,
RV 177 – Allegro ma poco; Largo   8'
Sinfonia al Santo Sepolcro, RV 169   4'

Caldara La morte d'Abel –
'Quel buon pastor son io'   10'

Geminiani Concerto grosso
in D minor, Op. 5 No. 12 'La folia'   12'

Vivaldi
Longe mala, umbrae, terrores, RV 629   15'
Violin Concerto in D major, RV 208
'Grosso Mogul'   13'
In furore iustissimae irae, RV 626   12'

Mary-Ellen Nesi mezzo-soprano

B'Rock – Baroque Orchestra Ghent
Dmitry Sinkovsky violin/counter-tenor/director

There will be no interval

In the first of a pair of Proms Saturday Matinees dedicated to early music, Belgian Baroque ensemble B'Rock makes its Proms debut with a programme of 18th-century Italian music. Orchestral pieces and solo motets by Vivaldi sit alongside music by Caldara – a famous castrato showpiece – and Geminiani, whose variations on the famous 'La folia' theme rival Scarlatti's, Lully's and Corelli's for rhythmic urgency and virtuosity.

RADIO Live on BBC Radio 3
ONLINE Listen and catch up at bbc.co.uk/proms

SATURDAY 8 AUGUST

PROM 31
7.30pm–c9.20pm • Royal Albert Hall

PRICE BAND Ⓐ Seats £7.50 to £38 (plus booking fee*)
WEEKEND PROMMING PASS see page 164

SIR MARK ELDER

Tansy Davies Re-greening   c7'
world premiere

Mahler Symphony No. 9   85'

**National Youth Orchestra
of Great Britain**
Sir Mark Elder conductor

There will be no interval

Mahler's bitterly beautiful Ninth Symphony is the focus for the National Youth Orchestra's annual visit to the Proms. Still unperformed at the time of the composer's death, the symphony was the last Mahler would complete – a requiem in all but name from a man who had already lost his daughter and knew his own death was imminent. The work's rich writing for brass and strings makes it one of the greats of the orchestral repertoire. The concert opens with the world premiere of Tansy Davies's Re-greening, a celebration of spring written specially as a complement to Mahler's Symphony No. 9. See 'New Music', pages 88–95.

RADIO Live on BBC Radio 3
TV Mahler recorded for broadcast on BBC Four on 16 August
ONLINE Complete Prom available to listen, watch and catch up at bbc.co.uk/proms

---

PROMS EXTRA
5.30pm–6.30pm • Royal College of Music World-premiere performances of commissions from the 2014 BBC Proms Inspire Young Composers' Competition winners.

SPOTLIGHT ON...

Martin James Bartlett • Prom 32

Since winning BBC Young Musician last year, life has been 'amazing', says Martin James Bartlett. Among the highlights has been a performance of Gershwin's *Rhapsody in Blue* at Proms in the Park in Belfast – 'although it was freezing, so I'm looking forward to playing it in the warmth of the Royal Albert Hall this year.'

'*Rhapsody in Blue* is hard to perform because it's so jazzy,' says Bartlett. 'You can practise for hours and hours but you have to feel it on the spot and have a spark.' And, while the collaboration between piano and orchestra is one of the piece's most exciting aspects for the pianist (who turns 19 just before his Prom), what he really hopes to do is make Gershwin's ever-popular work sound fresh: 'I want to give a new and spontaneous performance.'

Bartlett counts jazz among his inspirations, along with 'so many things! Mozart, Tchaikovsky symphonies, Mahler, avant-garde composers.' When it comes to pianists, his heroes fall into two camps: 'I love Martha Argerich because you never know what she's going to do on stage. Vladimir Horowitz too. But I also love pianists like Alfred Brendel, Murray Perahia and Stephen Hough who have such a huge intellectual knowledge.' And, when it comes to *Rhapsody in Blue*, whose performance does he like? 'Leonard Bernstein with the Columbia Symphony Orchestra' is the instant answer. 'He was such a genius with the different colours and whole atmosphere.'

SUNDAY 9 AUGUST

PROM 32
3.30pm–c.5.35pm • Royal Albert Hall

PRICE BAND **A** *Seats £7.50 to £38 (plus booking fee*)*
WEEKEND PROMMING PASS *see page 164*

ERIC WHITACRE

Jonathan Newman
Blow It Up, Start Again   4'
European premiere

Eric Whitacre
The River Cam   12'

Cloudburst   9'

Gershwin, orch. Grofé
Rhapsody in Blue   16'

INTERVAL

Copland Quiet City   9'

Eric Whitacre
Equus   9'

Deep Field   20'
BBC co-commission: European premiere

Martin James Bartlett *piano*
Leonard Elschenbroich *cello*

BBC Singers
BBC Symphony Chorus
Royal Philharmonic Orchestra
Eric Whitacre *conductor*

Eric Whitacre's new work *Deep Field* is inspired by images taken from the Hubble Space Telescope – and offers the audience a chance to participate in a novel way. In his popular *Cloudburst*, too, you can help create the sound of rain falling. Plus, American classics by Copland and Gershwin. See 'With One Voice', pages 44–47; 'New Music', pages 88–95.

RADIO *Live on BBC Radio 3*
TV *Recorded for broadcast on BBC Four on 14 August*
ONLINE *Listen, watch and catch up at bbc.co.uk/proms*

SUNDAY 9 AUGUST

PROM 33
8.00pm–c.10.00pm • Royal Albert Hall

PRICE BAND **C** *Seats £14 to £57 (plus booking fee*)*
WEEKEND PROMMING PASS *see page 164*

SIR JOHN ELIOT GARDINER

Beethoven
Symphony No. 5 in C minor   33'

INTERVAL

Berlioz Symphonie fantastique   54'

**Orchestre Révolutionnaire
et Romantique**
Sir John Eliot Gardiner *conductor*

Sir John Eliot Gardiner's second appearance of the season showcases the work of the conductor's other period-instrument ensemble – the Orchestre Révolutionnaire et Romantique, specialists in 19th- and 20th-century repertoire. Gardiner's brisk and brilliant take on Beethoven's Fifth Symphony promises to find fresh energy within a familiar work – a Classical curtain-raiser to Berlioz's extravagant *Symphonie fantastique*, the height of Romantic excess, with its quasi-cinematic storytelling and vivid, ghoulish soundscapes.

RADIO *Live on BBC Radio 3*
ONLINE *Listen and catch up at bbc.co.uk/proms*

PROMS EXTRA
6.15pm–7.00pm • Royal College of Music Novelists Amit Chaudhuri and Louise Welsh discuss D. H. Lawrence's *The Rainbow*, first published 100 years ago. The novel, which was banned on publication, tells the story of the Brangwen family as they face the decline of their pastoral life in the face of industrialisation.
Edited version broadcast on BBC Radio 3 during tonight's interval

Marc Royce (Whitacre); Sim Canetty-Clarke (Gardiner)

8–9 AUGUST

135

MONDAY 10 AUGUST

PROMS CHAMBER MUSIC 4
1.00pm–c2.00pm • Cadogan Hall

Seats £10/£12 (plus booking fee*)

Keiko Abe Prism Rhapsody   *15'*

Evelyn Glennie & Philip Sheppard
Orologeria aureola   *5'*

Bertram Wee Dithyrambs   *c7'*
world premiere

John Psathas View from Olympus   *23'*
world premiere of this version

Dame Evelyn Glennie *percussion*
Philip Smith *piano*

There will be no interval

Returning to the Proms for the first time since 2007, award-winning Scottish percussionist Evelyn Glennie celebrates her 50th birthday with a musical party. She performs alongside pianist Philip Smith, showcasing not only her expressive virtuosity and versatility in works by John Psathas and Keiko Abe, but also her skill as a composer, in *Orologeria aureola*, a joint composition for Halo (metallic 'handpan') and tape. The performance also features a world premiere for Aluphone – an instrument invented only in 2011 and introduced at the 2012 Olympics opening ceremony by Glennie herself. See 'New Music', pages 88–95.

RADIO *Live on BBC Radio 3*
ONLINE *Listen and catch up at bbc.co.uk/proms*

SPOTLIGHT ON...
Dame Evelyn Glennie • PCM 4

Dame Evelyn Glennie has spent her entire career pushing boundaries – and she's not about to stop now. A 50th birthday might seem like an opportune moment to take stock of what has been the most successful solo percussion career the world has ever seen – but instead, in her Prom, Glennie is looking forwards.

For a start, the programme features two new instruments. 'I already have my five-octave marimba, but that's still not the pinnacle of where the marimba can be. We don't yet have the Steinway marimba or the Stradivarius vibraphone.'

The first of the new instruments is a steel handpan called a Halo, the second is the Aluphone, an instrument – made of aluminium cones – that was developed with Glennie's help and on which she performed during the London 2012 Olympics opening ceremony.

In the new work for Aluphone by young composer Bertram Wee, Glennie has combined her passion for instrument development with her passion for commissioning. 'The career of solo percussionist did not exist when I started,' she says. 'There wasn't enough repertoire to sustain one. The important thing then was to commission as many pieces as possible.'

Thanks largely to Glennie's determination, it's now possible to be a solo percussionist. But, she says, 'it's important that every solo percussion player takes part in commissioning new works. It needs to carry on.'

MONDAY 10 AUGUST

PROM 34
7.30pm–c9.40pm • Royal Albert Hall

PRICE BAND Ⓐ *Seats £7.50 to £38 (plus booking fee*)*

Britten Four Sea Interludes from
'Peter Grimes'   *17'*

Korngold Violin Concerto   *26'*

INTERVAL

Prokofiev
Symphony No. 5 in B flat major   *42'*

Nicola Benedetti *violin*

Bournemouth Symphony Orchestra
Kirill Karabits *conductor*

A musical snapshot of 1945 – a world emerging from the haze of war into the neon glow of Hollywood and new-found hope. Three contrasting works sum up the spirit of this charged year: Britten's *Peter Grimes*, reinventing English opera; Prokofiev's Fifth Symphony, striving after the 'grandeur of the human spirit'; and Korngold's Violin Concerto. Hailed in his youth as a 'genius' and a 'miracle' by no lesser figures than Mahler and Puccini respectively, Korngold's reputation still rests mainly on his luscious film music. The Violin Concerto combines his instinct for melody (themes are borrowed from four of his finest film scores) with classical virtuosity and structural elegance. The soloist here is Proms regular Nicola Benedetti, a passionate champion of this unaccountably neglected work.

RADIO *Live on BBC Radio 3*
TV *Britten and Korngold recorded for broadcast on BBC Four on 13 August; Prokofiev recorded for broadcast on BBC Four on 30 August*
ONLINE *Complete Prom available to listen, watch and catch up at bbc.co.uk/proms*

PROMS EXTRA
5.30pm–6.30pm • Royal College of Music Join professional musicians for a family-friendly introduction to tonight's Prom. Bring your instrument and join in! See pages 98–103 for details

TUESDAY 11 AUGUST

PROM 35
7.30pm–c9.45pm • Royal Albert Hall

PRICE BAND Ⓐ *Seats £7.50 to £38 (plus booking fee*)*

CLARE TEAL

STORY OF SWING

Clare Teal *vocalist/presenter*

Guy Barker Big Band
Guy Barker *conductor*

Winston Rollins Big Band
Winston Rollins *conductor*

There will be one interval

After the success of last year's Battle of the Bands Prom, Clare Teal returns with a line-up of musicians to showcase the very best of the current UK jazz and big band scene. She's joined by Guy Barker and Winston Rollins to tell the story of the birth of swing, including tributes to 'King of Swing' Benny Goodman and the great trombonist and bandleader Tommy Dorsey. See 'The Proms Where You Are', *pages 106–109.*

RADIO *Live on BBC Radio 3 and recorded for future broadcast on BBC Radio 2*
TV *Recorded for broadcast on BBC Four on 28 August*
ONLINE *Listen, watch and catch up at bbc.co.uk/proms*

PROMS EXTRA
5.45pm–6.30pm • Royal College of Music Jazz historian and broadcaster Alyn Shipton explores the sounds of swing and its influences.
Edited version broadcast on BBC Radio 3 during tonight's interval

WEDNESDAY 12 AUGUST

PROM 36
6.30pm–c8.50pm • Royal Albert Hall

PRICE BAND Ⓐ *Seats £7.50 to £38 (plus booking fee*)*

MARC-ANDRÉ HAMELIN

Pierre Boulez
Figures – Doubles – Prismes   22'

INTERVAL

Ravel, arr. Boulez Frontispice   2'

Ravel
Piano Concerto for the Left Hand   19'

Stravinsky The Firebird   46'

Marc-André Hamelin *piano*

BBC Symphony Orchestra
François-Xavier Roth *conductor*

Textures and colours are to the fore in this concert with a French accent. Our triptych of Stravinsky ballets continues with The Firebird – the work that seized the ears of Paris's elite with its urgent rhythms and evocative Russian folk melodies. We celebrate Boulez's 90th-birthday year with his first work for full orchestra, a sophisticated experiment in colours and timbres. Marc-André Hamelin joins the BBC SO for Ravel's jazz-influenced Piano Concerto for the Left Hand, commissioned by the one-armed pianist Paul Wittgenstein. See 'Beautiful Logic', *pages 50–53.*

RADIO *Live on BBC Radio 3*
ONLINE *Listen and catch up at bbc.co.uk/proms*

PROMS EXTRA
4.45pm–5.30pm • Royal College of Music Marking the 90th-birthday year of the eminent composer and conductor Pierre Boulez, Julian Anderson surveys his life and career.
Edited version broadcast on BBC Radio 3 during tonight's interval

WEDNESDAY 12 AUGUST

PROM 37
10.15pm–c11.30pm • Royal Albert Hall

PRICE BAND Ⓔ *Seats £7.50 to £24 (plus booking fee*)*

WRETCH 32

LATE NIGHT WITH … BBC RADIO 1XTRA

Wretch 32 *rapper*
Stormzy *rapper*
Krept & Konan *rap duo*

MistaJam *presenter*
Sian Anderson *presenter*

Metropole Orkest
Jules Buckley *conductor*

There will be no interval

Following 2013's Urban Classic Prom, BBC Radio 1Xtra joins the BBC Proms in a high-octane Late Night celebration of the thriving urban music scene, from hip hop to grime. Rappers Wretch 32, Stormzy and Krept & Konan join presenters MistaJam and Sian Anderson on stage, to set the Royal Albert Hall dancing in new remixes blending classical and urban styles, with a little help from Jules Buckley and his Metropole Orkest. See 'The Proms Where You Are', *pages 106–109.*

RADIO *Live on BBC Radio 3 and BBC Radio 1Xtra*
ONLINE *Listen and catch up at bbc.co.uk/proms*

THURSDAY 13 AUGUST

PROM 38
7.30pm–c9.45pm • Royal Albert Hall

PRICE BAND A *Seats £7.50 to £38 (plus booking fee*)*

STEVEN OSBORNE

Foulds Three Mantras   26'

INTERVAL

Messiaen Turangalîla Symphony   75'

Steven Osborne *piano*
Cynthia Millar *ondes martenot*

London Symphony Chorus
(women's voices)
BBC Philharmonic
Juanjo Mena *conductor*

Hindu philosophy is the guiding thread through
this Prom of music by one of the 20th century's
undisputed masters and one of its neglected
mavericks. Messiaen's *Turangalîla Symphony*
translates the 'curious, exquisite, unexpected
melodic contours' of the Hindu tradition for
Western ears. John Foulds's music was heavily
influenced by his spiritual fascination with India; his
style shifts in his *Three Mantras* from the rhythmic
violence of Stravinsky to meditative loveliness and
the sleek modernism of Ravel.

RADIO *Live on BBC Radio 3*
ONLINE *Listen and catch up at bbc.co.uk/proms*

PROMS EXTRA
5.45pm–6.30pm • Royal College of Music Delve into
Messiaen's mammoth *Turangalîla Symphony* with guests
including Nigel Simeone.
Edited version broadcast on BBC Radio 3 during tonight's interval

c10.00pm–c11.00pm • Elgar Room, Royal Albert Hall
Informal late-night music and poetry, featuring young talent.
For details see bbc.co.uk/proms

FRIDAY 14 AUGUST

PROM 39
7.00pm–c10.25pm • Royal Albert Hall

PRICE BAND C *Seats £14 to £57 (plus booking fee*)*
WEEKEND PROMMING PASS *see page 164*

EDGARAS MONTVIDAS

Mozart The Abduction from the Seraglio
(semi-staged; sung and spoken in German)   140'

Edgaras Montvidas *Belmonte*
Sally Matthews *Konstanze*
Mari Eriksmoen *Blonde*
Brenden Patrick Gunnell *Pedrillo*
Tobias Kehrer *Osmin*
Franck Saurel *Pasha Selim*

Glyndebourne Festival Opera
Orchestra of the Age of Enlightenment
Robin Ticciati *conductor*

There will be two intervals

Energy and good humour meet musical exoticism in
Mozart's earliest operatic success – the storybook
fantasy *The Abduction from the Seraglio*. It's a
work born of the 18th-century fascination with
the Orient and there's no resisting the jangling
pulse of percussion that is the opera's heartbeat.
Glyndebourne Festival Opera returns for its annual
visit to the Proms under Music Director Robin
Ticciati, with an international cast led by British
soprano Sally Matthews and Lithuanian tenor
Edgaras Montvidas.

RADIO *Live on BBC Radio 3*
ONLINE *Listen and catch up at bbc.co.uk/proms*

PROMS EXTRA
5.15pm–6.00pm • Royal College of Music Sir Nicholas
Kenyon, former director of the Proms and author of
the *Faber Pocket Guide to Mozart*, introduces Mozart's
The Abduction from the Seraglio.
Edited version broadcast on BBC Radio 3 during tonight's first interval

---

SPOTLIGHT ON...

Sally Matthews • Prom 39

For soprano Sally Matthews, starting to
rehearse an opera is a lot of fun: 'When we
turn up, it's like we're children going out to
play. We're singing and laughing. We're so
lucky to do this job!' Right now Matthews
is preparing to sing Konstanze in Mozart's
The Abduction from the Seraglio, for
Glyndebourne's new production that is also
coming to the Proms. It's a notoriously
demanding role, 'extreme in range, incredibly
low and incredibly high,' says Matthews.
But it's a challenge which she relishes. 'I've
often sung the Mozart concert arias and
I love them, but I haven't always had the
opportunity to sing such difficult music in
opera,' she says, 'but this is what I started
out doing: I sang the Queen of the Night
at college. So I'm thrilled to do this.'

'The funny thing is I've never sung
Konstanze before, so I don't know what
she means to me yet,' says Matthews of her
character, 'but that's how I like to go into it.
Glyndebourne is ideal, in that you have time
to do all that character building.'

Sir David McVicar directs the production,
while Robin Ticciati conducts. Matthews
has worked with both before, memorably
bringing *The Marriage of Figaro* to the
Proms with Ticciati in 2012. 'Mozart seems
to click with Robin. He doesn't mess around
with it too much, which is exactly how I like
it. So we're going to have a ball!'

SATURDAY 15 AUGUST

PROMS SATURDAY MATINEE 3
3.00pm–c4.30pm • Cadogan Hall

Seats £10/£12 (plus booking fee*)

C. P. E. Bach Symphony in B minor,
Wq 182/5 'Hamburg'   10'

Vivaldi Violin Concerto in D major,
RV 234 'L'inquietudine'   7'

Telemann
Burlesque de Quixotte – excerpts   15'

J. S. Bach
Violin Concerto in F major, BWV 1042   17'

Brandenburg Concerto No. 5 in D major,
BWV 1050   22'

Alina Ibragimova *violin*

Apollo's Fire
Jeannette Sorrell *harpsichord/director*

There will be no interval

Apollo's Fire – otherwise known as the Cleveland
Baroque Orchestra – has been a lively force in
early music for over 20 years. Now, under director
Jeannette Sorrell, this quirky, energetic band makes
its BBC Proms debut in the second of this
season's early music Proms Saturday Matinees.
The ensemble is joined by violinist Alina Ibragimova,
soloist in much-loved concertos by Bach and Vivaldi.
Bach's Brandenburg Concerto No. 5, with its
brilliant writing for harpsichord and its bittersweet
slow movement, and music from Telemann's
vividly colourful suite following the adventures
of Cervantes's knight-errant Don Quixote,
complete the mix. See 'Me, Myself and Bach',
pages 78–81.

RADIO *Live on BBC Radio 3*
ONLINE *Listen and catch up at bbc.co.uk/proms*

SPOTLIGHT ON...

Jeannette Sorrell • PSM 3

When Apollo's Fire (the Cleveland Baroque
Orchestra) makes its Proms debut this summer,
there will be some fans from home in the
audience. 'Our audience in Cleveland is very
excited,' says Jeannette Sorrell, the group's
founder and director. 'The university has
organised a tour to coincide with our concert,
so a good 50 or 60 people will be coming from
the USA.'

Sorrell has taken inspiration for this Prom
from the concerts J. S. Bach put on in a coffee
house in Leipzig, bringing together music by
Bach's son Carl Philipp Emanuel, Vivaldi,
Telemann and J. S. himself. 'We know there
were sometimes 100 people at Zimmermann's
for these concerts,' she explains. 'Bach led the
Collegium Musicum, an orchestra of young
university students. They did his own music,
and pieces by his friends and colleagues,
who certainly included Telemann and Vivaldi.
It was a place where Bach had fun.'

Along with that spirit of fun, Apollo's Fire
is, says Sorrell, always thinking about the
music's mood: 'The role of the performer in
the Baroque period was to move the emotions
of the listener, the way great orators had done
in ancient Greece and Rome. So we try to be
very clear about the rhetorical expression.'
It's a quality that Sorrell also sees in their
Proms soloist, Alina Ibragimova. 'She's a
lovely, soulful player and very expressive –
she is a very good fit with Apollo's Fire.'

SATURDAY 15 AUGUST

PROM 40
7.30pm–c9.35pm • Royal Albert Hall

PRICE BAND Ⓐ *Seats £7.50 to £38 (plus booking fee*)*
WEEKEND PROMMING PASS *see page 164*

THOMAS DAUSGAARD

Sibelius
Finlandia   8'

Symphony No. 1 in E minor   39'

INTERVAL

Symphony No. 2 in D major   43'

BBC Scottish Symphony Orchestra
Thomas Dausgaard *conductor*

Celebrations for Sibelius's 150th anniversary
continue with a complete symphony cycle, launched
by the BBC Scottish Symphony Orchestra and
its new Chief Conductor Designate, Thomas
Dausgaard. The First Symphony is prefaced by the
nationalistic tone-poem *Finlandia*, its singing central
melody composed with an ear to mass appeal
as well as to political protest. The First Symphony
is no apprentice work; although drawing on the
legacy of Tchaikovsky and Brahms, Sibelius created
something distinctively and evocatively Nordic.
Still more sophisticated is the Second, often heard
as a musical shout of grief and rage at Russian
oppression. See 'A Force of Nature', pages 18–23.

RADIO *Live on BBC Radio 3*
ONLINE *Listen and catch up at bbc.co.uk/proms*

PROMS EXTRA

1.30pm–3.30pm • **Royal College of Music** Join professional
musicians and create your own music inspired by this
evening's Prom. Suitable for all the family (ages 7-plus).
See pages 98–103 for details

5.45pm–6.30pm • **Royal College of Music** As we launch our
complete symphonic cycle, explore Sibelius's symphonies
and their historical context with Charlotte Ashby.
Edited version broadcast on BBC Radio 3 during tonight's interval

SUNDAY 16 AUGUST

PROM 41
3.30pm–c5.30pm • Royal Albert Hall

PRICE BAND Ⓑ *Seats £9.50 to £46 (plus booking fee*)*
WEEKEND PROMMING PASS *see page 164*

CHRISTINE RICE

SHERLOCK HOLMES – A MUSICAL MIND

Music reflecting the personal tastes of Sherlock Holmes and drawn from TV and film scores associated with him – including works by Orlande de Lassus, Paganini, Tchaikovsky, Wagner, Miklós Rózsa and Patrick Gowers

Mark Gatiss *actor*
Christine Rice *mezzo-soprano*
Jack Liebeck *violin*
Matthew Sweet *presenter*

Stile Antico
BBC Concert Orchestra
Barry Wordsworth *conductor*

There will be one interval

The Proms salutes a crime-fighting violin virtuoso who wrote a pioneering study of Dutch sacred music, tussled with a contralto from the Warsaw Opera and used Offenbach to outwit a pair of jewel thieves. This Proms matinee celebrates music that conjures up the world of Sherlock Holmes: works by Paganini, Lassus and Wagner which Conan Doyle tells us Holmes loved, and the film and TV scores written for him – from Miklós Rózsa's *The Private Life of Sherlock Holmes* to David Arnold's music from the BBC's *Sherlock* series starring Benedict Cumberbatch. Special guests include *Sherlock* co-creator Mark Gatiss, as well as mezzo-soprano Christine Rice, who explores the repertoire of Holmes's nemesis, the opera singer Irene Adler.

RADIO *Live on BBC Radio 3*
ONLINE *Listen and catch up at bbc.co.uk/proms*

SUNDAY 16 AUGUST

PROM 42
7.30pm–c10.15pm • Royal Albert Hall

PRICE BAND Ⓐ *Seats £7.50 to £38 (plus booking fee*)*
WEEKEND PROMMING PASS *see page 164*

JULIAN RACHLIN

Sibelius
Symphony No. 3 in C major   30'
Violin Concerto in D minor   35'

INTERVAL

Michael Finnissy Janne   c15'
BBC commission: world premiere

Sibelius Symphony No. 4 in A minor   38'

Julian Rachlin *violin*

BBC Scottish Symphony Orchestra
Ilan Volkov *conductor*

The Proms' Sibelius symphony cycle continues with the concise, intricately wrought Third and the darker Fourth – once described by conductor Herbert Blomstedt as 'an essay in trying to be happy which fails – on purpose'. These are paired with the composer's popular Violin Concerto with Lithuanian soloist Julian Rachlin. Conductor Ilan Volkov is a passionate champion of contemporary music and here premieres a new Sibelius-inspired work by Michael Finnissy – a composer whose music, though fascinatingly complex, finds real connection with politics, society and culture. See 'A Force of Nature', pages 18–23; 'New Music', pages 88–95.

RADIO *Live on BBC Radio 3*
ONLINE *Listen and catch up at bbc.co.uk/proms*

PROMS EXTRA
5.45pm–6.30pm • Royal College of Music Michael Finnissy, in conversation with Andrew McGregor, discusses the world premiere of *Janne* and introduces performances of his chamber works. *Broadcast on BBC Radio 3 after tonight's Prom*

SPOTLIGHT ON...

Kitty Whately • PCM 5

Kitty Whately fell in love with the music of Stephen Sondheim when she was just 17. 'I was a member of Bedfordshire Youth Opera and I played Johanna in *Sweeney Todd*. After our first run-through, the whole cast sat around crying and talking about how amazing it was.'

Whately is far from alone in her admiration for Sondheim – who has continually reinvented himself over the course of a long and disinguished career. As she rightly points out, 'Anybody who is a connoisseur of musical theatre would agree that Sondheim is the king. He's almost a genre of his own.' Opera houses around the world stage his work and opera singers include his songs in recitals. As Whately says, 'I don't think anybody's ashamed to say they love Sondheim.'

That's not to say his music is easy – his famously inventive lyrics are, says Whately, challenging to memorise. What's more, Sondheim's work is not written for operatic voice types. 'Because I'm an essentially classical singer, Sondheim can be a bit high – if it goes above a certain note I have to be careful not to slip into the classical style of singing.'

But learning and performing Sondheim never feels like work, she says. 'I love the text, the poetry, his melodies. I don't see why they're not classed as operas, to be honest.'

MONDAY 17 AUGUST

PROMS CHAMBER MUSIC 5
1.00pm–c2.00pm • Cadogan Hall

Seats £10/£12 (plus booking fee*)

A SONDHEIM CABARET

Siân Phillips *vocalist*
Kitty Whately *mezzo-soprano*
Jamie Parker *vocalist*
Richard Sisson *piano*

There will be no interval

Stephen Sondheim is one of the greats of musical theatre – legendary for the sharp wit of his lyrics and his darkly distinctive scores for musicals including *Sweeney Todd*, *A Little Night Music*, *Into the Woods* and *Company*. We celebrate his 85th birthday with a musical trawl through the very best of Sondheim's back catalogue. Formerly the piano-playing half of cabaret duo Kit and the Widow, Richard Sisson joins Kitty Whately, Siân Phillips and Jamie Parker to bring a touch of Broadway to Cadogan Hall.

RADIO *Live on BBC Radio 3*
ONLINE *Listen and catch up at bbc.co.uk/proms*

MONDAY 17 AUGUST

PROM 43
7.30pm–c9.30pm • Royal Albert Hall

PRICE BAND Ⓐ *Seats £7.50 to £38 (plus booking fee*)*

OSMO VÄNSKÄ

Sibelius
Symphony No. 5 in E flat major   *32'*

INTERVAL

Symphony No. 6 in D minor   *27'*

Symphony No. 7 in C major   *22'*

BBC Symphony Orchestra
Osmo Vänskä *conductor*

Who better to bring this year's cycle of Sibelius symphonies to a close than Finnish conductor Osmo Vänskä, with one exceptional cycle already completed on disc and another currently under way. 'These symphonies of mine are more confessions of faith than are my other works,' wrote Sibelius, but the later symphonies were hard-won confessions in which the composer's creativity struggled with self-doubt and hostile critics. The results, however, are exceptional, from the soaring horn-led 'Swan Hymn' of the Fifth to the innocent beauty of the Sixth to the single-movement Seventh, with its total symphonic unity and an ending that has been called 'the grandest celebration of C major there ever was'. See 'A Force of Nature', pages 18–23.

RADIO *Live on BBC Radio 3*
ONLINE *Listen and catch up at bbc.co.uk/proms*

PROMS EXTRA
5.45pm–6.30pm • Royal College of Music In 1895, the year the Proms began, the National Trust was founded with the aim of preserving the nation's heritage and open spaces. Dame Helen Ghosh, Director-General of the Trust, discusses the history of the charity.
Edited version broadcast on BBC Radio 3 during tonight's interval

TUESDAY 18 AUGUST

PROM 44
7.30pm–c9.55pm • Royal Albert Hall

PRICE BAND Ⓓ *Seats £18 to £68 (plus booking fee*)*

KIAN SOLTANI

Schoenberg
Chamber Symphony No. 1   *22'*

Beethoven Concerto in C major for violin, cello and piano (Triple Concerto)   *35'*

INTERVAL

Tchaikovsky
Symphony No. 4 in F minor   *13'*

Guy Braunstein *violin*
Kian Soltani *cello*

West–Eastern Divan Orchestra
Daniel Barenboim *piano/conductor*

Daniel Barenboim returns to the Proms, this time as both conductor and soloist, taking the piano part in Beethoven's Triple Concerto. Schoenberg's Chamber Symphony startled audiences with its ruthless concision – a reaction against the excesses of the late-Romantics. But excess gets the last word, in Tchaikovsky's Fourth Symphony, the musical expression of some of its composer's most-troubled and heartfelt emotions.

RADIO *Live on BBC Radio 3*
TV *Recorded for broadcast on BBC Four on 21 August*
ONLINE *Listen, watch and catch up at bbc.co.uk/proms*

PROMS EXTRA
5.30pm–6.30pm • Royal College of Music Join professional musicians for a family-friendly introduction to tonight's Prom. Bring your instrument and join in! See pages 98–103 for details

WEDNESDAY 19 AUGUST

PROM 45
7.30pm–c9.50pm • Royal Albert Hall

PRICE BAND **B** *Seats £9.50 to £46 (plus booking fee*)*

ELISABETH LEONSKAJA

Debussy, orch. Büsser Petite suite   *13'*

Mozart Piano Concerto No. 22
in E flat major, K482   *36'*

INTERVAL

Shostakovich
Symphony No. 15 in A major   *44'*

Elisabeth Leonskaja *piano*

Royal Philharmonic Orchestra
Charles Dutoit *conductor*

It has been almost 30 years since the celebrated
Russian pianist Elisabeth Leonskaja last performed
at the Proms. She makes her return alongside
another international great, Charles Dutoit, in
Mozart's majestic E flat Piano Concerto. Written
concurrently with *The Marriage of Figaro*, the
concerto shares much of the opera's grace and
its abundance of tunes, as well as some strikingly
lovely woodwind textures. Shostakovich's 15th
Symphony is an altogether darker affair – intimate
and introspective. Musical memories haunt the
score as the composer searches for meaning in
what he surely knew would be his final symphony.

RADIO *Live on BBC Radio 3*
ONLINE *Listen and catch up at bbc.co.uk/proms*

PROMS EXTRA
5.45pm–6.30pm • Royal College of Music Tim Jones
explores the nature of the piano concerto in the context
of Mozart's own examples, with a focus on the
Piano Concerto No. 22.
Edited version broadcast on BBC Radio 3 during tonight's interval

THURSDAY 20 AUGUST

PROM 46
7.30pm–c10.30pm • Royal Albert Hall

PRICE BAND **B** *Seats £9.50 to £46 (plus booking fee*)*

Nielsen Overture 'Helios'   *13'*

Brahms Violin Concerto in D major   *40'*

INTERVAL

Nielsen
Three Motets   *15'*
Hymnus amoris   *21'*
Symphony No. 2,
'The Four Temperaments'   *35'*

Nikolaj Znaider *violin*
Anna Lucia Richter *soprano*
David Danholt *tenor*

Danish National Concert Choir
Danish National Symphony Orchestra
Fabio Luisi *conductor*

Continuing our celebration of Nielsen's 150th
anniversary, his Second Symphony is an exercise
in contrasting moods and textures – the
'Temperaments' of the subtitle are the Humours
of Greco-Roman medicine: Choleric, Phlegmatic,
Melancholic and Sanguine. Less familiar are Nielsen's
choral works – the swelling loveliness of *Hymnus
amoris*, inspired by a Titian painting, and the Three
Motets that pay homage to Renaissance polyphony.
Completing the programme is Brahms's warmly
Romantic Violin Concerto, with Danish-Israeli
Nikolaj Znaider. *See 'Nielsen and the Idea of
Danishness', pages 26–31.*

RADIO *Live on BBC Radio 3*
TV *Nielsen's Overture 'Helios' and Symphony No. 2
recorded for broadcast on BBC Four on 23 August*
ONLINE *Complete Prom available to listen, watch
and catch up at bbc.co.uk/proms*

PROMS EXTRA
5.45pm–6.30pm • Royal College of Music Prize-winning
writer Sally Gardner, whose novel *Tinder* was inspired by
a Hans Christian Andersen fairy tale discuss the work
and legacy of the Danish writer.
Edited version broadcast on BBC Radio 3 during tonight's interval

c10.45pm–c11.45pm • Elgar Room, Royal Albert Hall
Informal late-night music and poetry, featuring young talent.
For details see bbc.co.uk/proms

FRIDAY 21 AUGUST

PROM 47
7.00pm–c9.05pm • Royal Albert Hall

PRICE BAND **A** *Seats £7.50 to £38 (plus booking fee*)*
WEEKEND PROMMING PASS *see page 164*

SAKARI ORAMO

Sibelius Tapiola   *18'*

Leifs Organ Concerto   *20'*

INTERVAL

Anders Hillborg Beast Sampler   *11'*
UK premiere

Beethoven
Symphony No. 7 in A major   *36'*

Stephen Farr *organ*

BBC Symphony Orchestra
Sakari Oramo *conductor*

There's no denying the potent rhythmic urgency
of Beethoven's Seventh Symphony. Its giddying,
propulsive movement finds contrast in the
mysterious stillness of Sibelius's *Tapiola*, inspired by
the spirit of Finland's dusky forests, its wood-sprites
and magic secrets. Jón Leifs's Organ Concerto
harnesses the full power and scope of the Royal
Albert Hall's organ in its massive musical gestures,
while Anders Hillborg's *Beast Sampler* promises to
strip away all we know of the symphony orchestra,
transforming it into a 'sound animal'. *See 'A Force of
Nature', pages 18–23; 'New Music', pages 88–95.*

RADIO *Live on BBC Radio 3*
ONLINE *Listen and catch up at bbc.co.uk/proms*

PROMS EXTRA
5.00pm–6.00pm • Royal College of Music Join professional
musicians for a family-friendly introduction to tonight's Prom.
Bring your instrument and join in! See pages 103–108
for details

FRIDAY 21 AUGUST

PROM 48
10.15pm–c11.30pm • Royal Albert Hall

PRICE BAND **E** *Seats £7.50 to £24 (plus booking fee*)*
WEEKEND PROMMING PASS *see page 164*

SOPHIE BEVAN

J. S. Bach

Mass in G minor, BWV 235	*28'*
Brandenburg Concerto No. 2 in F major, BWV 1047	*12'*
Magnificat in D major, BWV 243	*26'*

Sophie Bevan *soprano*
Rebecca Evans *soprano*
Iestyn Davies *counter-tenor*
Nicky Spence *tenor*
Roderick Williams *baritone*

BBC Singers
Academy of Ancient Music
David Hill *conductor*

There will be no interval

Bach's much-loved *Magnificat*, bright with fanfares and lively with dance rhythms, is paired with the composer's Mass in G minor in this Late Night Prom by the BBC Singers and the Academy of Ancient Music. Though sometimes overlooked, Bach's Lutheran Masses are a treasure trove of melody, borrowing their themes from the best of Bach's own cantatas. Completing the programme is the Brandenburg Concerto No. 2, with its muscular textures and brilliant brass and wind colours.
See 'Me, Myself and Bach', pages 78–81.

RADIO *Live on BBC Radio 3*
ONLINE *Listen and catch up at bbc.co.uk/proms*

SATURDAY 22 AUGUST

PROM 49
6.30pm–c9.10pm • Royal Albert Hall

PRICE BAND **C** *Seats £14 to £57 (plus booking fee*)*
WEEKEND PROMMING PASS *see page 164*

HÅKAN HARDENBERGER

Brett Dean Dramatis personae   *28'*
INTERVAL

Mahler Symphony No. 6 in A minor   *83'*
Håkan Hardenberger *trumpet*

Boston Symphony Orchestra
Andris Nelsons *conductor*

Two contrasting heroes share the limelight in this evening of musical drama from the Boston Symphony Orchestra and its new Chief Conductor, Andris Nelsons. Brett Dean's trumpet concerto *Dramatis personae*, composed for tonight's Swedish virtuoso Håkan Hardenberger, assigns all roles to the trumpet, casting him by turns as fallen superhero and accidental revolutionary. Mahler's Sixth Symphony sees the composer himself as cursed hero – one, he explained, 'on whom fall three blows of fate, the last of which fells him as a tree is felled'. The conclusion may be a tragic one but there are also scenes of beauty and joy in a work that includes a glowing theme associated with Mahler's wife Alma.

RADIO *Live on BBC Radio 3*
ONLINE *Listen and catch up at bbc.co.uk/proms*

PROMS EXTRA
4.45pm–5.30pm • Royal College of Music In 1895, the year the Proms began, the pioneering Lumière Brothers developed their Cinématographe, the world's first motion-picture film camera. Film historian Ian Christie discusses how film became an art.
Edited version broadcast on BBC Radio 3 during tonight's interval

SATURDAY 22 AUGUST

PROM 50
10.15pm–c11.30pm • Royal Albert Hall

PRICE BAND **F** *Seats £10 to £30 (plus booking fee*)*
WEEKEND PROMMING PASS *see page 164*

SIR ANDRÁS SCHIFF

J. S. Bach 'Goldberg' Variations   *71'*
Sir András Schiff *piano*

There will be no interval

Grammy Award-winning pianist Sir András Schiff is a titan of the keyboard, bringing his distinctive blend of clarity and authority to repertoire from Bach to Bartók. Tonight he continues his long association with Bach's music in a performance of the composer's 'Goldberg' Variations – a monumental work composed, according to its title-page, 'for the refreshment of the spirits'. The resulting Aria and variations are a compositional wonder, a sequence of musical miniatures unequalled in all Bach's output.
See 'Me, Myself and Bach', pages 78–81.

RADIO *Live on BBC Radio 3*
TV *Recorded for broadcast on BBC Four on 3 September*
ONLINE *Listen, watch and catch up at bbc.co.uk/proms*

Susie Ahlburg (Bevan); Marco Borggreve (Hardenberger); Priska Ketterer, Lucerne (Schiff)

SUNDAY 23 AUGUST

PROM 51
3.00pm–c5.05pm • Royal Albert Hall

PRICE BAND C *Seats £14 to £57 (plus booking fee*)*
WEEKEND PROMMING PASS *see page 164*

ANDRIS NELSONS

Haydn Symphony No. 90 in C major   *24'*
Barber Essay No. 2   *11'*

INTERVAL

Shostakovich
Symphony No. 10 in E minor   *57'*

Boston Symphony Orchestra
Andris Nelsons *conductor*

Returning for a second appearance this summer,
Andris Nelsons and the Boston Symphony
Orchestra bring a piece of America with them in
Barber's Essay No. 2 – a symphony in miniature,
moving from lyrical loveliness through contrapuntal
conflict to end with a radiant chorale. They pair it
with Haydn's Symphony No. 90, where ebullient
mischief and dignity vie for supremacy in sunny
C major. Joy gives way to high drama, however, in
Shostakovich's Symphony No. 10 – a vivid portrait
of Stalinist Russia.

RADIO *Live on BBC Radio 3*
ONLINE *Listen and catch up at bbc.co.uk/proms*

PROMS EXTRA
1.00pm–2.00pm • Royal College of Music Join professional
musicians for a family-friendly introduction to this afternoon's
matinee Prom. Bring your instrument and join in! *See pages
98–103 for details*

SUNDAY 23 AUGUST

PROM 52
7.30pm–c9.30pm • Royal Albert Hall

PRICE BAND A *Seats £7.50 to £38 (plus booking fee*)*
WEEKEND PROMMING PASS *see page 164*

Programme to include:

J. S. Bach
Passacaglia and Fugue in C minor,
BWV 582   *12'*

Chorale Prelude 'In dir ist
Freude', BWV 615   *3'*

Chorale Prelude 'Aus tiefer Not
schrei ich zu dir', BWV 686   *6'*

J. S. Bach (attrib.)
Chorale 'Christ ist erstanden', BWV 746   *3'*

*and works by Brahms, Mendelssohn and Thierry
Escaich, plus improvisations on themes of Bach*

Thierry Escaich *organ*

There will be one interval

Bach and beyond – a fascinating musical journey
with Thierry Escaich, renowned organist of
the church of Saint-Étienne-du-Mont in Paris
(where he is a successor to Maurice Duruflé),
and an ambassador of the great French School
of improvisation. *See 'Me, Myself and Bach',
pages 78–81.*

RADIO *Live on BBC Radio 3*
ONLINE *Listen and catch up at bbc.co.uk/proms*

PROMS EXTRA
5.45pm–6.30pm • Royal College of Music Musicologist and
broadcaster Simon Heighes surveys J. S. Bach's organ works.
Edited version broadcast on BBC Radio 3 during tonight's interval

SPOTLIGHT ON...

Thierry Escaich • Prom 52

It's Thierry Escaich's third visit to the Proms,
so he's already forged a bond with the Royal
Albert Hall's organ. 'It took me a while to get
to know this organ; it was difficult at first to
understand how to achieve a balance in the
sound levels, but I've had a lot of fun
discovering its myriad colours and the
really orchestral dimension that are possible.'

His Proms solo recital programme is an
intriguing four-way conversation between
himself, Bach, Mendelssohn and Brahms,
featuring his own responses to chorale preludes
and other pieces by his illustrious predecessors.
'I wanted to build a dialogue between their
music and contemporary music, where themes
and forms find responses through the
centuries, to find a guiding thread that could
bring it all together. To me there is a real
continuity between these musical worlds, each
composer picking up an idea another has left.'

Although well-known for his imaginative
organ inventions, Escaich is increasingly
prominent as an orchestral and instrumental
composer. His Concerto for orchestra opened
the new Philharmonie de Paris earlier this year.
'I was very happy to represented by that work,
it was a great occasion,' he says. 'Architect
Jean Nouvel's new hall seems to me very
beautiful and opens the doors to new
programming, perhaps even new forms
of concert! It's essential that we musicians
and programmers know how to innovate.'

CONCERT LISTINGS

144

BOOK ONLINE AT BBC.CO.UK/PROMS • BY TELEPHONE 0845 401 5040† • IN PERSON AT THE ROYAL ALBERT HALL • BOOKING OPENS 9.00AM ON 16 MAY

MONDAY 24 AUGUST

PROMS CHAMBER MUSIC 6
1.00pm–c2.00pm • Cadogan Hall

Seats £10/£12 (plus booking fee)*

JEREMY DENK

Bartók Piano Sonata   13'

Scriabin
Piano Sonata No. 9, 'Black Mass'   10'

Beethoven
Piano Sonata No. 32 in C minor, Op. 111 25'

Jeremy Denk *piano*

There will be no interval

Jeremy Denk is one of America's foremost pianists – a musician the *New York Times* hails as someone 'you want to hear no matter what he performs'. He makes his BBC Proms debut in a recital that puts Beethoven's final piano sonata at its core. It's a work that blends extrovert passion with a depth that characterises all of the composer's late works, and is paired here with Bartók's Piano Sonata, a piece strongly coloured by Hungarian folk melodies and rhythmic attack. We mark the centenary of Scriabin's death with his most famous piano sonata, the 'Black Mass' – a disconcerting, phantasmagoric musical journey and a gleeful vision of horror. Jeremy Denk returns in Prom 60 to perform Henry Cowell's iconoclastic Piano Concerto.

RADIO *Live on BBC Radio 3*
ONLINE *Listen and catch up at bbc.co.uk/proms*

MONDAY 24 AUGUST

PROM 53
7.30pm–c9.50pm • Royal Albert Hall

PRICE BAND **B** *Seats £9.50 to £46 (plus booking fee*)*

Bartók The Miraculous Mandarin   32'

Mozart
Piano Concerto No. 24 in C minor, K491 29'

INTERVAL

Shostakovich, orch. G. McBurney
Orango – Prologue   32'
(semi-staged; sung in Russian)

David Fray *piano*
Natalia Pavlova *Susanna*
Natalia Yakimova *Renée*
Alexander Shagun *Armand Fleury*
Alexander Trofimov *Paul Mâche*
Vladimir Babokin *Foreigner 1*
Oleg Losev *Foreigner 2*
Dmitry Koleushko *Zoologist*
Ivan Novoselov *Orango*
Leo Elhardt *Voice from the Crowd*
Denis Beganski *Master of Ceremonies*
Yuri Yevchuk *Veselchak*

Philharmonia Voices
Philharmonia Orchestra
Esa-Pekka Salonen *conductor*

Shostakovich's *Orango* – an incomplete opera whose manuscript came to light only in 2004 – is a glossy fusion of wit and political venom. The 'Orango' of the title is half man, half ape – a symbol of the decadent West. It's a work matched for vivid colouring by Bartók's violent and sexually charged ballet-pantomime *The Miraculous Mandarin*. French pianist David Fray returns following his Proms debut in 2011 to play Mozart's Piano Concerto No. 24 – written at the height of the composer's fame in Vienna as a performer of his own works.

RADIO *Live on BBC Radio 3*
ONLINE *Listen and catch up at bbc.co.uk/proms*

PROMS EXTRA
5.45pm–6.30pm • Royal College of Music Gerard McBurney offers an introduction to Shostakovich's unfinished opera *Orango*, whose Prologue he has orchestrated.
Edited version broadcast on BBC Radio 3 during tonight's interval

TUESDAY 25 AUGUST

PROM 54
7.30pm–c9.45pm • Royal Albert Hall

PRICE BAND **A** *Seats £7.50 to £38 (plus booking fee*)*

Britten Sinfonia da Requiem   21'

Raymond Yiu Symphony   c24'
BBC commission: world premiere

INTERVAL

Nielsen Flute Concerto   18'

Janáček Sinfonietta   23'

Andrew Watts *counter-tenor*
Emily Beynon *flute*

BBC Symphony Orchestra
Edward Gardner *conductor*

Proms regular Edward Gardner continues this year's Nielsen anniversary celebrations with the Flute Concerto – a work that expresses what Nielsen perceived as the instrument's 'Arcadian' quality. This gentle, pastoral quality battles, however, with darker forces, characterfully symbolised by the bass trombone. Both Janáček's *Sinfonietta* and Britten's *Sinfonia da Requiem* are also vivid expressions of contrast – in mood, texture and colour. The five movements of the *Sinfonietta* are all scored for a different – and sometimes unlikely – combination of instruments, while the three episodes in Britten's elegiac *Sinfonia da Requiem* paint different stages of mourning, from grief, to anger and finally an uneasy acceptance. See 'Nielsen and the Idea of Danishness', pages 26–31; 'New Music', pages 88–95.

RADIO *Live on BBC Radio 3*
ONLINE *Listen and catch up at bbc.co.uk/proms*

PROMS EXTRA
5.45pm–6.30pm • Royal College of Music In the centenary of Nielsen's birth, Mikkel Zangenberg outlines the compositional styles in the composer's concertos.
Edited version broadcast on BBC Radio 3 during tonight's interval

Michael Wilson

WEDNESDAY 26 AUGUST

PROM 55
7.30pm–c9.40pm • Royal Albert Hall

PRICE BAND A *Seats £7.50 to £38 (plus booking fee*)*

FRANÇOIS-XAVIER ROTH

Pierre Boulez
'… explosante-fixe …'   34'

INTERVAL

Ligeti Lontano   14'

Bartók Concerto for Orchestra   38'

Sophie Cherrier *flute*

**SWR Symphony Orchestra
Baden-Baden and Freiburg
François-Xavier Roth** *conductor*

Bartók wasn't the first composer to write a
Concerto for Orchestra, but freewheeling virtuosity
and rhythmic energy set this one apart. Treating
individual instruments as soloists or partners in
exhilarating duets-to-the-death, Bartók reinvents
the orchestra itself. The whole classical canon
seems dissolved in Ligeti's *Lontano*, in which familiar
harmonies and styles are suspended in space and
time, and resolution continually hangs just out of
reach. Turning classical rules of development on
their head, Boulez's '… explosante-fixe …' works
backwards, moving from its most complex material
to its primary, original source *(see also PSM 4,
29 August)*. It's audacious and completely compelling.
See 'Beautiful Logic', pages 50–53.

RADIO *Live on BBC Radio 3*
ONLINE *Listen and catch up at bbc.co.uk/proms*

PROMS EXTRA
5.45pm–6.30pm • Royal College of Music Rachel Beckles
Willson offers an insight into Bartók's *Concerto for Orchestra*
and discusses the life and work of the Hungarian composer.
Edited version broadcast on BBC Radio 3 during tonight's interval

---

SPOTLIGHT ON…
Sophie Cherrier • Prom 55

In Boulez's fiendish '… explosante-fixe …'
Sophie Cherrier's flute is followed by a
computer. But, insists the French flautist,
'It will be like chamber music.' The work
has gone through several incarnations since
Boulez first planned it in 1971 as a memorial
to Igor Stravinsky. Now it involves three flutes,
the first with electronics. 'I have a microphone
on my flute and the computer knows every
note I'm meant to play. So, when I play an A,
a recording will start, for example, or reverb,'
explains Cherrier; 'And the three flutes are
far away from each other, so you don't know
where the sound comes from. It's like having
the light of the sun all around you.'

Cherrier has performed '… explosante-fixe
…' with conductor François-Xavier Roth
before and with the composer himself as a
member of his Ensemble Intercontemporain.
But it's still a tricky piece to put together.
'At first I practise alone with the computer
and that's a lot of fun. When there are three
flutes plus electronics, you don't know what's
going to happen. And, when you add the
orchestra, it's even harder, as there's so much
detail – Boulez has such a quick mind.'

It's an appetite for new music that inspires
Cherrier. 'With Boulez's *Répons*, we had
new music on our stands each day because
he wrote overnight. It was the most exciting
thing for a player who wants to perform
contemporary music.'

THURSDAY 27 AUGUST

PROM 56
7.30pm–c9.30pm • Royal Albert Hall

PRICE BAND B *Seats £9.50 to £46 (plus booking fee*)*

Ørjan Matre preSage   c12'
world premiere of this version

Mendelssohn
Violin Concerto in E minor   26'

INTERVAL

Alissa Firsova Bergen's Bonfire   c10'
world premiere

Stravinsky The Rite of Spring   33'

Alina Ibragimova *violin*

**Bergen Philharmonic Orchestra
Andrew Litton** *conductor*

Is there a better-known or better-loved violin
concerto than Mendelssohn's? Following her
two solo Late Night Proms, and Proms Saturday
Matinee appearance with Apollo's Fire, violinist
Alina Ibragimova returns to perform this inventive
and charming work, with the Bergen Philharmonic
Orchestra. They bring with them music by the
young Norwegian Ørjan Matre and a new work
by Russian-British composer Alissa Firsova inspired
by Norse mythology. This season's series of three
Stravinsky ballets written for the Ballets Russes
reaches its conclusion with *The Rite of Spring*, as
ferocious and exhilarating a musical assault now as
it was at its notorious Paris premiere over a century
ago. *See 'New Music', pages 88–95.*

RADIO *Live on BBC Radio 3*
ONLINE *Listen and catch up at bbc.co.uk/proms*

PROMS EXTRA
5.45pm–6.30pm • Royal College of Music Alissa Firsova, in
conversation with Andrew McGregor, discusses the world
premiere of *Bergen's Bonfire* and introduces performances
of her chamber works.
Broadcast on BBC Radio 3 after tonight's Prom

c9.45pm–c10.45pm • Elgar Room, Royal Albert Hall
Informal late-night music and poetry, featuring young talent.
For details see bbc.co.uk/proms

Marco Borggreve (Roth); Franck Ferville (Cherrier)

FRIDAY 28 AUGUST

PROM 57
7.30pm–c9.50pm • Royal Albert Hall

PRICE BAND **D** *Seats £18 to £68 (plus booking fee*)*
WEEKEND PROMMING PASS *see page 164*

MARIA JOÃO PIRES

Schubert
Overture in C major, 'In the Italian style'   *9'*

Mozart
Piano Concerto No. 23 in A major, K488   *26'*

INTERVAL

Schubert
Symphony No. 9 in C major, 'Great'   *51'*

Maria João Pires *piano*

Chamber Orchestra of Europe
Bernard Haitink *conductor*

Refined but also profoundly expressive, Maria João Pires is one of the great Mozart interpreters of her generation. She returns to the Proms to continue our series of late Mozart piano concertos. No. 23 in A major boasts quasi-operatic melodies and deft woodwind colouring. It took musicians and audiences a long time to come to terms with Schubert's 'unplayable' Ninth Symphony, but now – like that other great unplayable, Beethoven's Ninth – it has won an unquestioned place in the repertoire.

RADIO *Live on BBC Radio 3*
TV *Recorded for broadcast on BBC Four on 4 September*
ONLINE *Listen, watch and catch up at bbc.co.uk/proms*

PROMS EXTRA
5.00pm–6.30pm • Royal College of Music Nicholas Collon and the Aurora Orchestra perform the winning pieces of the 2015 BBC Proms Inspire Young Composers' Competition.

SATURDAY 29 AUGUST

PROMS SATURDAY MATINEE 4
3.00pm–c4.30pm • Cadogan Hall

Seats £10/£12 (plus booking fee*)

THIERRY FISCHER

Pierre Boulez Mémoriale
('… explosante-fixe …' Originel)   *7'*

Helen Grime A Cold Spring   *10'*

Pierre Boulez Domaines   *15'*

Christian Mason
Open to Infinity: a Grain of Sand   *9'*
BBC co-commission: UK premiere

Pierre Boulez Éclat/Multiples   *25'*

Michael Cox *flute*
Mark van de Wiel *clarinet*

London Sinfonietta
Thierry Fischer *conductor*

There will be no interval

Celebrations for Pierre Boulez's 90th-birthday year reach a climax in this matinee performance, in which contemporary music specialists the London Sinfonietta pair Boulez's own music with that of young British composers Helen Grime and Christian Mason. Pierre Boulez's *Mémoriale* puts the flute in the spotlight, showcasing minutiae of texture and articulation, while in *Domaines* it's a solo clarinet that gives out a sustained soliloquy. The two contrasting parts of *Éclat/Multiples* (1970) are theoretically part of a larger work, as yet unfinished by the composer. They make for a striking contrast: the brilliant, glittering colours of *Éclat* set against the nervy perpetual motion of *Multiples*. See 'Beautiful Logic', pages 50–53; 'New Music', pages 88–95.

RADIO *Live on BBC Radio 3*
ONLINE *Listen and catch up at bbc.co.uk/proms*

SATURDAY 29 AUGUST

PROM 58
7.30pm–c9.40pm • Royal Albert Hall

PRICE BAND **A** *Seats £7.50 to £38 (plus booking fee*)*
WEEKEND PROMMING PASS *see page 164*

JOHANNA RUSANEN-KARTANO

Sibelius
En saga   *20'*

INTERVAL

Kullervo   *75'*

Johanna Rusanen-Kartano *soprano*
Waltteri Torikka *baritone*

Polytech Choir
BBC Symphony Chorus (men's voices)
BBC Symphony Orchestra
Sakari Oramo *conductor*

Finnish conductor Sakari Oramo pairs two of Sibelius's most engagingly descriptive works as we continue our 150th-anniversary celebrations of the composer. The folk hero Kullervo was the inspiration behind a powerful national statement for a country struggling to overthrow Russian rule. This massive musical hybrid – part cantata, part symphony, part suite – is a vivid work, richly melodic but looking ahead to modernism in some striking musical gestures. *En saga* is a fairy tale without a plot, whose contrasting movements suggest many possible stories, but never commit to just one. See 'A Force of Nature', pages 18–23; 'With One Voice', pages 44–47.

RADIO *Live on BBC Radio 3*
ONLINE *Listen and catch up at bbc.co.uk/proms*

PROMS EXTRA
5.45pm–6.30pm • Royal College of Music Daniel M. Grimley explores Sibelius's choral symphony *Kullervo* and its influences.
Edited version broadcast on BBC Radio 3 during tonight's interval

SUNDAY 30 AUGUST

PROM 59
3.30pm–c5.30pm • Royal Albert Hall

PRICE BAND B Seats £9.50 to £46 (plus booking fee*)
WEEKEND PROMMING PASS see page 164

SIR DAVID ATTENBOROUGH

LIFE STORY PROM

Excerpts from the original score by Murray Gold and footage from the recent BBC One series

Sir David Attenborough presenter

BBC Concert Orchestra
Jeremy Holland-Smith conductor

There will be one interval

Distinguished naturalist and broadcaster Sir David Attenborough presents a concert inspired by his recent BBC Television series, *Life Story*. The soundtrack, composed by Murray Gold (who has written the music for *Doctor Who* since 2005), takes centre-stage, performed by the BBC Concert Orchestra. Sir David introduces sequences from the series played on big screens and is joined by members of the production team, who offer insights into the making of this stunning natural history series. See 'Natural Sounds', pages 70–71.

RADIO Live on BBC Radio 3
ONLINE Listen and catch up at bbc.co.uk/proms

PROMS EXTRA
1.45pm–2.30pm • Royal College of Music Michael Gunton, Executive Producer of *Life Story*, talks about the acclaimed BBC series and about working with Sir David Attenborough.
Edited version broadcast on BBC Radio 3 during this afternoon's interval

---

SUNDAY 30 AUGUST

PROM 60
7.30pm–c9.45pm • Royal Albert Hall

PRICE BAND C Seats £14 to £57 (plus booking fee*)
WEEKEND PROMMING PASS see page 164

MICHAEL TILSON THOMAS

Schoenberg
Theme and Variations, Op. 43b   13'

Cowell Piano Concerto   15'

INTERVAL

Mahler Symphony No. 1 in D major   56'

Jeremy Denk piano

San Francisco Symphony
Michael Tilson Thomas conductor

It has been almost a decade since the San Francisco Symphony visited the Proms. The orchestra is joined by its Music Director of more than 20 years, Michael Tilson Thomas, and by American pianist Jeremy Denk in the latter's second concert of the season. Here Denk tackles an American rarity – Henry Cowell's extraordinary Piano Concerto, whose primitive textures require the soloist to pound the piano with fists and forearms. It is paired with Mahler's First Symphony, an ebullient youthful work filled with hints of the mature composer to come, and Schoenberg's imaginative Theme and Variations, heard in the composer's own orchestral arrangement.

RADIO Live on BBC Radio 3
ONLINE Listen and catch up at bbc.co.uk/proms

PROMS EXTRA
5.45pm–6.30pm • Royal College of Music An insight into the work of the San Francisco Symphony, with guests including the orchestra's Director of Artistic Planning, Nicholas Winter.
Edited version broadcast on BBC Radio 3 during tonight's interval

---

SPOTLIGHT ON...

Jeremy Denk • Prom 60

'It's hard to make your elbows sing, but I've had to find a way – sometimes requiring duct tape – to stop my sleeve catching other notes!' laughs American pianist Jeremy Denk, an expert performer of Henry Cowell's outlandish 1928 Piano Concerto.

Cowell's piano clusters were his most bizarre and marketable innovation in the 1910s, but Denk is keen to point out that it's not simply about noise. 'He was one of the first to use the piano as a purely percussive instrument, but his clusters are largely melodic, not rhythmic: you have to "voice" your arm and the top note of the cluster is by no means random. After Cowell, the piano became the subject of all manner of "abuses" – Cage was fascinated, for example – but I think of his armfuls of notes as ecstatic, not violent, in the manner of Messiaen.'

In some ways the concerto does have a conventional 'heroic' appeal and a neo-Classical clarity. 'Cowell was the original hippy kid, a child-like figure who lived in the moment and retained his optimism, even when he was imprisoned on a morals charge. He had that very American blend of naivety and modernist sophistication.' It was Bartók, no less, who asked Cowell's permission to adopt tone-clusters, and whose bracing Piano Sonata opens Denk's Cadogan Hall recital (24 August), a fascinating programme of symmetries, where Bartók and Scriabin mirror the stark contrast in Beethoven's own two-movement Sonata No. 32.

MONDAY 31 AUGUST

PROMS CHAMBER MUSIC 7
1.00pm–c2.00pm • Cadogan Hall

Seats £10/£12 (plus booking fee*)

EMERSON STRING QUARTET

Barber String Quartet, Op. 11 –
Molto adagio   8'

Debussy
Préludes, Book 2 – Feux d'artifice   7'

Shostakovich Piano Quintet   35'

Elisabeth Leonskaja *piano*
Emerson String Quartet

There will be no interval

Eminent Russian pianist Elisabeth Leonskaja returns for her second Prom this season, joining the Emerson String Quartet for its Proms debut in a programme of great chamber works of the 20th century. From France, there's Debussy's 'Feux d'artifice' – a display of technical and aural fireworks for solo piano. From the Emerson's native America there's the original string quartet version of Barber's hauntingly beautiful *Adagio for strings*, and Russia is represented by Shostakovich's popular Quintet, with its darkly comic Scherzo and meditative, delicately melancholy Intermezzo.

RADIO *Live on BBC Radio 3*
ONLINE *Listen and catch up at bbc.co.uk/proms*

SPOTLIGHT ON...
Elisabeth Leonskaja • PCM 7

'Shostakovich's music is like a mirror held up to the life of Russia in the 20th century,' says Elisabeth Leonskaja, who performs in his Piano Quintet. 'His music is so charismatic and so tragic.'

Leonskaja – who celebrates her 70th birthday later this year and made her Proms debut more than 30 years ago – has been playing the quintet for many years but she vividly remembers her first encounter of it, with the Borodin Quartet. 'My first experience was probably the most important for me. At the time, I was playing a lot of music by Chopin and at the first rehearsal, after we'd played the quintet through for a short time, cellist Valentin Berlinsky said to the others, "She's playing it Romantically," and that opened up possibilities for our performance.'

At this year's Proms, Leonskaja will be performing with the Emerson String Quartet. 'All four musicians are so involved,' she says, 'but at the same time they are so independent. I'm looking forward to building this music together with them.'

Leonskaja is a true legend of the piano and still has a busy schedule of work, including chamber music and solo recitals. 'If you are playing solo, you can be very free with time,' she explains. 'If you're playing with an orchestra or a quartet, it is a different discipline. I enjoy it very much.'

MONDAY 31 AUGUST

PROM 61
7.30pm–c9.50pm • Royal Albert Hall

PRICE BAND C Seats £14 to £57 (plus booking fee*)
WEEKEND PROMMING PASS *see page 164*

YUJA WANG

Ives A Symphony: New England Holidays
– Decoration Day   10'

Bartók Piano Concerto No. 2   28'

INTERVAL

Beethoven
Symphony No. 3 in E flat major, 'Eroica'   52'

Yuja Wang *piano*

San Francisco Symphony
Michael Tilson Thomas *conductor*

Chinese virtuoso Yuja Wang is the soloist in Bartók's Second Piano Concerto – a work the composer intended to pose 'fewer difficulties for the orchestra' and to be 'more pleasing in its thematic material' than his First. Beethoven's emotionally charged 'Eroica' Symphony forms the second half – the groundbreaking symphony that would pave the way for the mighty Romantic works of Mahler and Bruckner. The concert opens with Charles Ives's atmospheric *Decoration Day*, inspired by his father's marching band.

RADIO *Live on BBC Radio 3*
ONLINE *Listen and catch up at bbc.co.uk/proms*

PROMS EXTRA

2.00pm–4.30pm • Royal College of Music/Royal Albert Hall
Your chance to perform on the stage of the Royal Albert Hall. Join professional musicians to create a celebration of 20th-century American music. Suitable for all the family (ages 7-plus). *See pages 103–108 for details*

5.45pm–6.30pm • Royal College of Music Willa Cather's *The Song of the Lark* was first published 100 years ago. Cather's biographer Dame Hermione Lee discusses the novel. *Edited version broadcast on BBC Radio 3 during tonight's interval*

TUESDAY 1 SEPTEMBER

PROM 62
7.30pm–c9.45pm • Royal Albert Hall

PRICE BAND **B** *Seats £9.50 to £46 (plus booking fee*)*

Brahms

Academic Festival Overture	*11'*
Alto Rhapsody	*13'*
Triumphlied	*25'*

INTERVAL

Symphony No. 1 in C minor	*45'*

Jamie Barton *mezzo-soprano*
Benjamin Appl *baritone*

Choir of the Enlightenment
Orchestra of the Age of Enlightenment
Marin Alsop *conductor*

Proms favourite Marin Alsop returns prior to her second Last Night appearance for an all-Brahms evening. The *Academic Festival Overture* is an ebullient work the composer himself described as 'a very boisterous potpourri of student songs', and there's also a rare opportunity to hear the epic *Triumphlied* – celebrating German victories in the Franco-Prussian War in choral settings of striking power and vividness. American mezzo-soprano Jamie Barton, winner of the 2013 BBC Cardiff Singer of the World, is the soloist in Brahms's glorious *Alto Rhapsody*, and completing the concert is Brahms's First Symphony – a work nicknamed 'Beethoven's 10th' for its obvious debt to the elder composer. See 'With One Voice', pages 44–47.

RADIO *Live on BBC Radio 3*
ONLINE *Listen and catch up at bbc.co.uk/proms*

PROMS EXTRA
5.45pm–6.30pm • Royal College of Music Nicholas Baragwanath explores the musical styles of Brahms's era and how they affect present-day performances of the composer's works.
Edited version broadcast on BBC Radio 3 during tonight's interval

---

SPOTLIGHT ON...
Jamie Barton • Prom 62

Many will recall American mezzo-soprano Jamie Barton's darkly lustrous performance of Brahms songs in her winning recital at the BBC Cardiff Singer of the World competition in 2013. 'I first fell in love with Brahms with his "Von ewiger Liebe". I understand his language and love his musical stories.' The *Alto Rhapsody*, which she'll sing at this year's Proms 'is very special to me. I was chosen to sing the solo part with the chorale at my undergraduate school: what a gift! It's almost like Brahms's mini-opera – starting off quite dark, but blooming into a gorgeous chorus of light and prayer.'

Since winning in Cardiff, Barton has sung at the Met and as Fricka in *Das Rheingold* at Houston Grand Opera. Is it unusual for her to be working with a period-instrument orchestra? 'It's a particular delight: I actually sang a lot of Baroque opera during my training; it was through Purcell, Bach, Handel that I discovered different aspects of my voice. I'm both fascinated and happily challenged to find a way to meld my voice with the style and timbre of the Orchestra of the Age of Enlightenment.'

This will be her Proms debut. 'I used to be under an old-fashioned impression of the Proms – imagining the whole audience to be in black tie, everyone listening to Elgar – but I know now that it encompasses a huge range of music!' What's the secret of maintaining her voice while travelling? 'Hydration. You'll see me with a contraption called a "HumidiFlyer"!'

WEDNESDAY 2 SEPTEMBER

PROM 63
7.30pm–c10.05pm • Royal Albert Hall

PRICE BAND **A** *Seats £7.50 to £38 (plus booking fee*)*

IGOR LEVIT

Messiaen Hymne	*12'*
Mozart Piano Concerto No. 27 in B flat major, K595	*32'*

INTERVAL

Bruckner Symphony No. 7 in E major	*65'*

Igor Levit *piano*

Royal Scottish National Orchestra
Peter Oundjian *conductor*

Former BBC Radio 3 New Generation Artist Igor Levit made his Proms debut at a Cadogan Hall chamber music recital in 2012. Now he makes his Proms concerto debut in Mozart's poignantly delicate No. 27, completing this year's series of late great Mozart piano concertos. Delicacy gives way to orchestral weight and heft in Bruckner's popular Seventh Symphony, its beautiful Adagio a tribute to Wagner, and a finale that, according to composer Robert Simpson, 'blends solemnity and humour in festive grandeur'.

RADIO *Live on BBC Radio 3*
ONLINE *Listen and catch up at bbc.co.uk/proms*

PROMS EXTRA
5.45pm–6.30pm • Royal College of Music Founded in 1895, the London School of Economics shares its 120th anniversary with the Proms. Professor Michael Cox explores the key events in the history of the university founded by the Fabians to promote greater equality.
Edited version broadcast on BBC Radio 3 during tonight's interval

THURSDAY 3 SEPTEMBER

PROM 64
6.30pm–c8.40pm • Royal Albert Hall

PRICE BAND **A** *Seats £7.50 to £38 (plus booking fee*)*

Nielsen Aladdin – excerpts   *17'*

B Tommy Andersson Pan   *c20'*
BBC commission: world premiere

INTERVAL

Mahler Symphony No. 4 in G major   *54'*

David Goode *organ*
Klara Ek *soprano*

BBC National Orchestra of Wales
Thomas Søndergård *conductor*

Thomas Søndergård and the BBC NOW return for their fourth concert, opening with a suite from Nielsen's music for Oehlenschläger's play *Aladdin*. It's one of the composer's best-loved works, one that avoids musical clichés of the exotic Orient, conjuring scenes altogether more subtle and vivid. A major premiere by the orchestra's Composer-in-Association, B Tommy Andersson, puts organist David Goode in the spotlight and the concert concludes with the sunniest and most intimate of Mahler's symphonies – the concise No. 4, a work filled with birdsong and pastoral landscapes that features a child's-eye view of Heaven in its final movement. See 'Nielsen and the Idea of Danishness', pages 26–31; 'New Music', pages 88–95.

RADIO *Live on BBC Radio 3*
ONLINE *Listen and catch up at bbc.co.uk/proms*

THURSDAY 3 SEPTEMBER

PROM 65
10.15pm–c11.30pm • Royal Albert Hall

PRICE BAND **E** *Seats £7.50 to £24 (plus booking fee*)*

ALICE COOTE

A programme of arias from Handel's operas, oratorios and cantatas – including Giulio Cesare, Semele, Hercules, Theodora, Messiah and Tra le fiamme – as a window on 'being both': the dilemmas and turbulent emotions experienced by both male and female characters

Alice Coote *mezzo-soprano*

The English Concert
Harry Bicket *conductor*
There will be no interval

Few composers express emotion as directly or with greater psychological truth than Handel. British mezzo-soprano Alice Coote explores the full gamut of these emotions in a Late Night Prom featuring some of Handel's greatest arias. Taking on both male and female roles, she delves into what it means to be a man, or a woman, in Handel's world of sorceresses and knights, kings and queens. She is joined in her theatrical journey by regular collaborators and period-performance specialists Harry Bicket and The English Concert.

RADIO *Live on BBC Radio 3*
ONLINE *Listen and catch up at bbc.co.uk/proms*

FRIDAY 4 SEPTEMBER

PROM 66
7.30pm–c9.45pm • Royal Albert Hall

PRICE BAND **B** *Seats £9.50 to £46 (plus booking fee*)*
WEEKEND PROMMING PASS *see page 164*

MITSUKO UCHIDA

Beethoven Fidelio – overture   *7'*

Schoenberg Piano Concerto   *20'*

INTERVAL

Shostakovich
Symphony No. 8 in C minor   *64'*

Mitsuko Uchida *piano*

London Philharmonic Orchestra
Vladimir Jurowski *conductor*

Mitsuko Uchida makes a welcome return to the Proms for Schoenberg's rarely heard Piano Concerto. It's a work whose 12-tone abstraction is tempered by intriguing autobiographical suggestions – 'Life was so easy', 'Suddenly hatred broke out' – scribbled on the original manuscript. Autobiography is also at the fore in Shostakovich's Eighth Symphony. Composed in 1943, at a particularly dark moment for Russia in the war, the work is a fragile statement of hope that the composer himself summarised as: 'All that is dark and oppressive will disappear; all that is beautiful will triumph.'

RADIO *Live on BBC Radio 3*
ONLINE *Listen and catch up at bbc.co.uk/proms*

SATURDAY 5 SEPTEMBER

PROM 67
5.30pm–c7.45pm • Royal Albert Hall

PRICE BAND **D** *Seats £18 to £68 (plus booking fee*)*
WEEKEND PROMMING PASS *see page 164*

BERNSTEIN – STAGE AND SCREEN

Music from Bernstein's Broadway musicals, including 'Candide', 'On the Town', '1600 Pennsylvania Avenue', 'Wonderful Town' and 'West Side Story', plus the suite from his only film score, 'On the Waterfront'

Cast to include:

Louise Dearman *vocalist*
Julian Ovenden *vocalist*

Maida Vale Singers
John Wilson Orchestra
John Wilson *conductor*

There will be one interval

John Wilson and his orchestra are an annual Proms highlight, bringing the glitz and glamour of old-time stage and screen to the Royal Albert Hall. The second of their two performances this year is all about Leonard Bernstein – America's multitalented conductor, pianist and composer. He reinvented the musical with the anger, energy and feral beauty of *West Side Story*, his updated take on *Romeo and Juliet*. A starry cast of soloists including Proms favourite Julian Ovenden and the West End's Louise Dearman join the John Wilson Orchestra and Maida Vale Singers for a tribute to the composer that includes Bernstein's biggest hits as well as a selection of rarities. See 'Popular Idols', pages 66–67.

RADIO *Live on BBC Radio 3*
TV *Recorded for broadcast on BBC Four on 11 September*
ONLINE *Listen, watch and catch up at bbc.co.uk/proms*

PROMS EXTRA
11.00am–1.00pm • Royal College of Music Join Rebecca Lodge and other members of the BBC Singers to explore the choral works of Bernstein. Suitable for all abilities. *See pages 103–108 for details*

3.45pm–4.30pm • Royal College of Music Examine the stage and screen music of Leonard Bernstein, with guests including Nigel Simeone. *Edited version broadcast on BBC Radio 3 during tonight's interval*

SATURDAY 5 SEPTEMBER

PROM 68
9.00pm–c11.40pm • Royal Albert Hall

PRICE BAND **B** *Seats £9.50 to £46 (plus booking fee*)*
WEEKEND PROMMING PASS *see page 164*

YO-YO MA

J. S. Bach
Suites for solo cello:

No. 1 in G major, BWV 1007	*19'*
No. 2 in D minor, BWV 1008	*21'*
No. 3 in C major, BWV 1009	*21'*
No. 4 in E flat major, BWV 1010	*27'*
No. 5 in C minor, BWV 1011	*26'*
No. 6 in D major, BWV 1012	*30'*

Yo-Yo Ma *cello*

There will be no interval

American cellist Yo-Yo Ma has been a regular Proms soloist for almost 40 years, and now tackles perhaps his boldest performance to date. He performs the complete Bach solo cello suites – over two hours of music – in a single concert: a feat as challenging intellectually as it is physically. Though neglected until the 20th century, the suites represent some of Bach's greatest musical achivements – music at its purest and most profound. Ma's relationship with them extends back over many decades and multiple recordings, generating expressive performances distinguished by their depth of emotion. See 'Me, Myself and Bach', pages 78–81.

RADIO *Live on BBC Radio 3*
TV *Recorded for broadcast on BBC Four on 10 September*
ONLINE *Listen, watch and catch up at bbc.co.uk/proms*

SUNDAY 6 SEPTEMBER

PROM 69
7.30pm–c10.00pm • Royal Albert Hall

FREE PROM: tickets available from 3 July

Saint-Saëns Danse macabre	*8'*
Guy Barker The Lanterne of Light	*c30'*

BBC commission: world premiere

INTERVAL

Orff Carmina burana	*65'*

Charles Mutter *violin*
Alison Balsom *trumpet*
Olena Tokar *soprano*
Thomas Walker *tenor*
Benjamin Appl *baritone*

Southend Boys' Choir
Southend Girls' Choir
BBC Symphony Chorus
London Philharmonic Choir
BBC Concert Orchestra
Keith Lockhart *conductor*

This year's free Prom is an ideal opportunity to introduce family and friends to classical music. *Carmina burana* is as musically inventive as it is irreverent – a choral cantata based on a medieval text charting the joys, fickleness and excesses of human life. The BBC Concert Orchestra's Composer-in-Association Guy Barker provides a new concerto for trumpet virtuoso Alison Balsom and the orchestra's own Charles Mutter is the soloist in Saint-Saëns's devilish *Danse macabre*. See 'With One Voice', pages 44–47; 'New Music', pages 88–95.

RADIO *Live on BBC Radio 3*
ONLINE *Listen and catch up at bbc.co.uk/proms*

PROMS EXTRA
2.30pm–5.30pm • Royal Albert Hall Join Mary King, members of the BBC Singers and the BBC Concert Orchestra to sing excerpts from Carl Orff's *Carmina burana*. Experience in sight-reading or a knowledge of the piece is an advantage but not essential. *See pages 98–103 for details*

5.45pm–6.30pm • Royal College of Music Erik Levi introduces Carl Orff's *Carmina burana*. *Edited version broadcast on BBC Radio 3 during tonight's interval*

MONDAY 7 SEPTEMBER

PROMS CHAMBER MUSIC 8
1.00pm–c2.00pm • Cadogan Hall

Seats £10/£12 (plus booking fee*)

BENEDETTI ELSCHENBROICH GRYNYUK TRIO

Brahms
Piano Trio No. 1 in B major, Op. 8   39'

Arlene Sierra
Butterflies Remember a Mountain   11'

Benedetti Elschenbroich Grynyuk Trio

There will be no interval

When not performing as a soloist, violinist
Nicola Benedetti appears frequently as a chamber
musician – most often with the trio she co-founded
with pianist Alexei Grynyuk and cellist Leonard
Elschenbroich. Here the three musicians pair
Brahms's first and stormiest piano trio – its darkness
belying the work's major key – with music by
American-born composer Arlene Sierra. Inspired
by the migration patterns of butterflies, her
Butterflies Remember a Mountain is a work of
pointillist detail and shimmering harmonies,
painted in a sequence of delicate textural gestures.

RADIO *Live on BBC Radio 3*
ONLINE *Listen and catch up at bbc.co.uk/proms*

MONDAY 7 SEPTEMBER

PROM 70
7.30pm–c9.55pm • Royal Albert Hall

PRICE BAND **C** *Seats £14 to £57 (plus booking fee*)*

YURI TEMIRKANOV

Tchaikovsky Francesca da Rimini   18'

Rachmaninov
Piano Concerto No. 2 in C minor   35'

INTERVAL

Rimsky-Korsakov Scheherazade   42'

Nikolai Lugansky *piano*

St Petersburg Philharmonic Orchestra
Yuri Temirkanov *conductor*

Just over a decade since their most recent visit,
the St Petersburg Philharmonic and its renowned
Artistic Director and Chief Conductor, Yuri
Temirkanov, return to the Proms with a home-
grown programme of Russian greats. Pianist
Nikolai Lugansky is the soloist in Rachmaninov's
most famous work, the Second Piano Concerto,
with its lyrical slow movement and brilliant, virtuosic
finale. Rimsky-Korsakov's *Scheherazade* dissolves the
magic and colour of the tales of the *Thousand and
One Nights* into a glittering musical tapestry that
the composer himself described as 'an oriental
narrative of fairy-tale wonders'. Tchaikovsky's
swirling tone-poem of doomed lovers opens
the programme.

RADIO *Live on BBC Radio 3*
ONLINE *Listen and catch up at bbc.co.uk/proms*

PROMS EXTRA
5.45pm–6.30pm • Royal College of Music Shahidha Bari
traces the history of the *One Thousand and One Nights*,
the collection of stories and folk tales compiled during the
Islamic Golden Age.
Edited version broadcast on BBC Radio 3 during tonight's interval

SPOTLIGHT ON...

Nikolai Lugansky • Prom 70

'With some very good musicians, you can
explain what they do. With Yuri Temirkanov
you cannot,' says Nikolai Lugansky. 'There
is something inexplicable. Music starts to live
under his hands and it is impossible to
understand how.'

At this year's Proms, Lugansky will be
tackling Rachmaninov's much-loved
Second Piano Concerto. 'There are lots of
compositional tricks in this concerto – such
as recurring and evolving themes – but the
main thing is Rachmaninov's genius with
melody and the emotional force of the piece.'

Few pianists know Rachmaninov like
Lugansky: he has recorded and performed
his music throughout his career. 'I love
everything that he wrote. I think it's the
combination of his introvert character and
very strong emotional features in his music,'
he says. 'But if you're in love you don't try
to explain – you are just in love.'

Both Temirkanov and Lugansky are
regular visitors to the Proms but this is the
first time they've performed here together.
There's one specific reason Lugansky is
looking forward to it. 'The worst thing the
media says about classical music is that it's
an elite art. The Proms is an ideal scenario,
where people of all ages and groups come
to these high-level concerts and enjoy
them. The music is for anybody with
an open mind and soul.'

TUESDAY 8 SEPTEMBER

PROM 71
7.30pm–c9.35pm • Royal Albert Hall

PRICE BAND C *Seats £14 to £57 (plus booking fee*)*

JULIA FISCHER

Rimsky-Korsakov
The Legend of the Invisible City of Kitezh –
symphonic pictures   *13'*

Tchaikovsky Violin Concerto   *33'*

INTERVAL

Elgar 'Enigma' Variations   *29'*

Julia Fischer *violin*

St Petersburg Philharmonic Orchestra
Yuri Temirkanov *conductor*

German violinist Julia Fischer joins the St Petersburg
Philharmonic Orchestra for its second concert, as
soloist in Tchaikovsky's much-loved Violin Concerto
– a work in which concert-hall sophistication
balances rustic folk-simplicity, overflowing with tunes
and climaxing in a dazzling rondo finale. Big tunes
– or, at least, one big tune – also dominate Elgar's
'Enigma' Variations, his affectionate musical portrait
of friends and acquaintances. The concert opens
with one of Rimsky-Korsakov's finest scores, the
'three symphonic pictures' adapted from his 1907
opera *The Legend of the Invisible City of Kitezh* – a
work sometimes nicknamed 'the Russian *Parsifal*'.

RADIO *Live on BBC Radio 3*
ONLINE *Listen and catch up at bbc.co.uk/proms*

PROMS EXTRA
5.45pm–6.30pm • Royal College of Music BBC Radio 3
presenter Ian McMillan and poet Kate Clanchy introduce the
winning entries in this year's BBC Proms Poetry Competition
– and welcome some of the winners on stage to read them.
In association with the Poetry Society.
Edited version broadcast on BBC Radio 3 after tonight's Prom

WEDNESDAY 9 SEPTEMBER

PROM 72
7.30pm–c9.55pm • Royal Albert Hall

PRICE BAND A *Seats £7.50 to £38 (plus booking fee*)*

Nielsen Springtime on Funen   *19'*
Violin Concerto   *35'*

INTERVAL

Webster In the Sweet By and By   *3'*
Zeuner Ye Christian Heralds   *2'*
Marsh Jesus, Lover of My Soul   *3'*
Mason Nearer, My God, to Thee   *4'*
Ives Symphony No. 4   *34'*

Henning Kraggerud *violin*
Malin Christensson *soprano*
Ben Johnson *tenor*
Neal Davies *bass-baritone*
William Wolfram *piano*

Tiffin Boys' Choir
Tiffin Girls' Choir
BBC Singers
Crouch End Festival Chorus
BBC Symphony Orchestra
Andrew Litton *conductor*

Ives's Fourth Symphony demands massive orchestral
forces and quotes from his own earlier works as well
as from traditional American hymns. Completing this
year's Nielsen concerto cycle is the Violin Concerto
– a work that wears its technical demands with
great delicacy. Nielsen also provides the concert-
opener, the folk-inspired choral cantata *Springtime
on Funen*. See 'Nielsen and the Idea of Danishness',
pages 26–31; 'With One Voice', pages 44–47.

RADIO *Live on BBC Radio 3*
ONLINE *Listen and catch up at bbc.co.uk/proms*

PROMS EXTRA
5.45pm–6.30pm • Royal College of Music Investigate Charles
Ives's Symphony No. 4 in the context of his life, with guests
including Richard Bernas.
Edited version broadcast on BBC Radio 3 during tonight's interval

c10.15pm–c11.15pm • Elgar Room, Royal Albert Hall
Informal late-night music and poetry, featuring young talent.
For details see bbc.co.uk/proms

SPOTLIGHT ON...

Henning Kraggerud • Prom 72

Carl Nielsen's Violin Concerto finds a
passionate advocate in Norwegian violinist
and composer Henning Kraggerud. 'When I
was 12, I vividly remember reading Nielsen's
book *Living Music* and his way of thinking
influenced me a great deal. He composed the
first part of this concerto in Grieg's hut near
Bergen and I think this can be felt in the
music. Nielsen described how he was
determined not to go down well-trodden
paths but to deliberately make the concerto
unidiomatic: he succeeded in creating a work
unlike any other. His powerful ideas of
expressivity and seriousness speak from the
very first bar, dragging you into his universe.
His humour is ever-present, especially in the
last movement. He manages to make
wonderful colours and takes unexpected
turns; it's truly one of the great concertos.'

Those fortunate to have been at
Kraggerud's performance of Tchaikovsky's
Violin Concerto at the Proms in 2010 will
remember his own fabulous encore, *Fantasy
on a Theme by Ole Bull*. What's next on
his slate? 'I've just recorded my new piece
Equinox: 24 Postludes for violin and
orchestra, written to texts by Jostein
Gaarder, author of *Sophie's World*.
The music travels round the circle of fifths
before returning to C major. There's also
a romance involved ...'

THURSDAY 10 SEPTEMBER

PROM 73
7.00pm–c9.10pm • Royal Albert Hall

PRICE BAND **C** *Seats £14 to £57 (plus booking fee*)*

SEMYON BYCHKOV

Brahms Symphony No. 3 in F major   39'

INTERVAL

Schmidt
Symphony No. 2 in E flat major   53'

Vienna Philharmonic
Semyon Bychkov *conductor*

The first of two consecutive nights with the Vienna Philharmonic under two different conductors. Here, Semyon Bychkov showcases Franz Schmidt's neglected Second Symphony – a work he has passionately championed. A bold piece of Brucknerian ambition, it has more than a hint of Richard Strauss about it. It's paired with Brahms's Third Symphony – the work that saw the composer finding his true musical identity, stepping out from behind his influences to create something lyrical yet strangely unresolved.

RADIO *Live on BBC Radio 3*
ONLINE *Listen and catch up at bbc.co.uk/proms*

THURSDAY 10 SEPTEMBER

PROM 74
10.15pm–c11.30pm • Royal Albert Hall

PRICE BAND **F** *Seats £10 to £30 (plus booking fee*)*

JARVIS COCKER

WIRELESS NIGHTS PROM WITH JARVIS COCKER

Jarvis Cocker *presenter*

BBC Philharmonic
Maxime Tortelier *conductor*

There will be no interval

In the last of this year's Proms collaborations with six of the BBC national radio stations and BBC Music, popular Radio 4 show *Wireless Nights* becomes a live concert experience, pairing music and spoken word inspired by the night. Singer-songwriter Jarvis Cocker presents an evening he describes as 'a nocturnal investigation of the human condition', with Maxime Tortelier conducting the BBC Philharmonic. Badgers, stars, elves and lambs may or may not be involved. See 'The Proms Where You Are', pages 106–109.

RADIO *Live on BBC Radio 3 and recorded for future broadcast on BBC Radio 4*
ONLINE *Listen and catch up at bbc.co.uk/proms*

FRIDAY 11 SEPTEMBER

PROM 75
7.30pm–c9.40pm • Royal Albert Hall

PRICE BAND **D** *Seats £18 to £68 (plus booking fee*)*

SIR SIMON RATTLE

Elgar The Dream of Gerontius   96'

Magdalena Kožená *mezzo-soprano*
Toby Spence *tenor*
Roderick Williams *baritone*

BBC Proms Youth Choir
Vienna Philharmonic
Sir Simon Rattle *conductor*

There will be one interval

Sir Simon Rattle conducts the second of two performances by the Vienna Philharmonic, completing a Proms triptych of Elgar's great oratorios, spread across recent seasons, with arguably the greatest of them all: *The Dream of Gerontius*. This is spiritual inquiry at its most musically intoxicating and ecstatic – a work that reaches after the same mystic transcendence as Wagner's *Parsifal*. The BBC Proms Youth Choir returns for its fourth festival appearance, joining soloists Toby Spence and Roderick Williams, with Czech mezzo-soprano Magdalena Kožená as the Angel. See 'With One Voice', pages 44–47.

RADIO *Live on BBC Radio 3*
ONLINE *Listen and catch up at bbc.co.uk/proms*

PROMS EXTRA
5.15pm–6.00pm • Royal College of Music Gavin Plumley discusses the life and work of Austrian composer Franz Schmidt, including his Symphony No. 2.
Edited version broadcast on BBC Radio 3 during tonight's interval

PROMS EXTRA
5.45pm–6.30pm • Royal College of Music Join Proms Director, Edward Blakeman, and Chris Cotton, Chief Executive of the Royal Albert Hall, as they look back over the 2015 BBC Proms season.

SATURDAY 12 SEPTEMBER

PROM 76

7.15pm–c10.30pm • Royal Albert Hall

PRICE BAND G *Seats £27 to £95 (plus booking fee*)*

Eleanor Alberga Arise, Athena!   *c3'*
BBC commission: world premiere

Shostakovich
Piano Concerto No. 2 in F major   *20'*

Arvo Pärt Credo   *12'*

R. Strauss Till Eulenspiegels
lustige Streiche   *16'*

Puccini Opera arias   *15'*

INTERVAL

Johnson Victory Stride   *4'*

Copland Old American Songs –
'I bought me a cat'   *3'*

Grieg Peer Gynt – Morning   *4'*

Gershwin, arr. Grainger
Love walked in   *4'*

M. Gould Boogie Woogie Étude   *2'*

Lehár The Land of Smiles – 'Dein ist
mein ganzes Herz'   *4'*

Rodgers, arr. C. Hazell
The Sound of Music – medley   *6'*

Wood Fantasia on British Sea-Songs – Jack's
the Lad (Hornpipe); Home, Sweet Home   *6'*

Arne, arr. Sargent Rule, Britannia!   *5'*

Elgar
Pomp and Circumstance March No. 1
in D major ('Land of Hope and Glory')   *8'*

Parry, orch. Elgar Jerusalem   *3'*

The National Anthem (arr. Britten)   *3'*

Trad., arr. Thorpe Davie
Auld Lang Syne   *2'*

Benjamin Grosvenor *piano*
Danielle de Niese *soprano*
Jonas Kaufmann *tenor*

BBC Singers
BBC Symphony Chorus
BBC Symphony Orchestra
Marin Alsop *conductor*

Marin Alsop, who triumphed at 2013's Last Night,
presides over a finale that opens with the new and
ends with the Last Night favourites. See 'With One
Voice', pages 44–47; 'New Music', pages 88–95.

RADIO *Live on BBC Radio 3*
TV *First half live on BBC Two, second half live on BBC One*
ONLINE *Listen, watch and catch up at bbc.co.uk/proms*

MARIN ALSOP

"I am truly honoured to be returning
to conduct the Last Night of the Proms
and to work again with the BBC Symphony
Orchestra. I have wonderful memories of
the Last Night in 2013 and it's a dream
come true to return again so soon to share
my love of classical music with audiences
across the UK and around the world.
Here's to another great celebration –
it's certainly like no other!"

PROMS EXTRA
5.00pm–5.45pm • Royal College of Music Prepare for the
Last Night of the Proms singalong with Mary King and
members of the BBC Singers. Suitable for all abilities
(ages 7-plus). See pages 103–108 for details

Chris Christodoulou/BBC (Last Night of the Proms); Grant Leighton (Alsop)

SATURDAY 12 SEPTEMBER

PROMS IN THE PARK, LONDON
Gates open 3.00pm • Entertainment from 5.15pm • Hyde Park

THE
ROYAL
PARKS

Tickets £39 (plus booking fee*)

DANIELLE DE NIESE

Danielle de Niese *soprano*

Royal Choral Society
BBC Concert Orchestra
Richard Balcombe *conductor*
Sir Terry Wogan *presenter*

Join in the Last Night of the Proms celebrations in Hyde Park, hosted by Proms in the Park stalwart Sir Terry Wogan. The open-air concert features a host of musical stars, including Proms in the Park favourites the BBC Concert Orchestra under the baton of Richard Balcombe, and special guest Danielle de Niese, who will also appear across the road at the Royal Albert Hall.

Presenter Tony Blackburn joins us again, introducing a range of artists to get this year's party under way.

Listen to BBC Radio 2 from Monday 11 May for announcements of further special guests.

RADIO *Live on BBC Radio 2*
TV *Highlights from all of the Proms in the Park concerts live on the red button*
ONLINE *Listen, watch and catch up at bbc.co.uk/proms*

BOOKING TICKETS

Tickets will be available from 11.00am on Friday 15 May from the Royal Albert Hall. Ticket requests may also be included in the Proms Planner submitted from 9.00am on Saturday 16 May. See below for details of how to book.

ONLINE bbc.co.uk/promsinthepark

BY PHONE
from the **Royal Albert Hall** on **0845 401 5040** †
(a booking fee of 2% of the total value plus £1.50 per ticket up to a maximum of £20.00 applies for telephone bookings)

IN PERSON at the Royal Albert Hall Box Office
(no fees apply to tickets bought in person)

BY POST see page 161

For details of how to order a picnic hamper for collection on the day, or to find out about VIP packages and corporate hospitality, visit bbc.co.uk/promsinthepark

PLEASE NOTE In the interest of safety, please do not bring glass items (including bottles), barbeques or flaming torches to the event.

† *Calls cost up to 5p/min from most landlines (an additional connection fee may also apply). Calls from mobiles may be considerably more. (All calls to the Royal Albert Hall Box Office will be recorded and may be monitored for quality-control purposes.)*

EXPERIENCE THE LAST NIGHT MAGIC AROUND THE UK!

HYDE PARK, LONDON
NORTHERN IRELAND
SCOTLAND
WALES

The BBC Proms in the Park events offer live concerts featuring high-profile artists, well-loved presenters and BBC Big Screen link-ups to the Royal Albert Hall, when you can join in song with audiences across the nations. So gather your friends and your Last Night spirit for an unforgettable evening.

Keep checking bbc.co.uk/promsinthepark for announcements of artists and venue and booking information.

Highlights of the Last Night celebrations around the UK will feature as part of the live television coverage of the Last Night and you can watch more at bbc.co.uk/proms.

You can also access Proms in the Park content via the red button.

BELFAST, NORTHERN IRELAND

GLASGOW, SCOTLAND

SWANSEA, WALES

BBC RADIO **2**

BBC Radio 2 Live in Hyde Park

A festival in a day

Sunday 13th September 2015

Tickets on sale Friday 12th June
£39 plus booking fee / Child tickets £10
For information or to book tickets visit:
bbc.co.uk/radio2

Press: Eye/BBC Northern Ireland (N. Ireland); AP/BBC (Scotland)

THE LAST NIGHT OF THE PROMS

Owing to high demand, the majority of tickets for the Last Night of the Proms are allocated by ballot to customers who have bought tickets to at least five other Proms concerts at the Royal Albert Hall. A further 200 tickets will be allocated by the Open Ballot (see far right).

The Five-Concert Ballot

Customers who purchase tickets for at least five other concerts are eligible to enter the Five-Concert Ballot. (The Free Prom [Prom 69], concerts at Cadogan Hall and Proms in the Park do not count towards the Five-Concert Ballot.) You can apply to buy a maximum of two tickets for the Last Night. If you are successful in the Ballot, you will not be obliged to buy Last Night tickets should your preferred seating area not be available.

Please note: you must tick the Ballot opt in box when booking online, or inform the Box Office that you wish to enter this Ballot when booking by telephone, in person or by post.

If you require a wheelchair space for the Last Night of the Proms, you will still need to book for five other concerts but you must phone the Access Information Line (020 7070 4410) by Thursday 28 May and ask to be entered into the separate Ballot for wheelchair spaces. This Ballot cannot be entered online.

The Five-Concert Ballot closes on Thursday 28 May. Successful applicants will be informed by Friday 5 June. If you are successful, **please note that your Last Night Tickets will not be issued until Friday 4 September.** We regret that, if you are unsuccessful in the Five-Concert Ballot, no refunds for other tickets purchased will be payable.

GENERAL AVAILABILITY FOR THE LAST NIGHT

Any remaining tickets will go on sale on Friday 10 July at 9.00am. There is exceptionally high demand for Last Night tickets, but returns occasionally become available, so it is always worth checking with the Box Office.

Please note: for all Last Night bookings, only one application (for a maximum of two tickets) can be made per household.

PROMMING AT THE LAST NIGHT

Whole Season Tickets include admission to the Last Night.

A limited allocation of Last Night tickets (priced £5.00) is also reserved for Prommers who have attended five or more concerts (in either the Arena or the Gallery). They are eligible to purchase one ticket each for the Last Night (priced £5.00) on presentation of their used tickets (which will be retained) at the Box Office. Tickets will be available to buy from the Box Office from the following dates:

- Tuesday 21 July for First Half Season Ticket-holders and Day Prommers and Weekend Pass-holders with five used tickets.

- Tuesday 18 August for Second Half Season Ticket-holders and Day Prommers and Weekend Pass-holders with five used tickets.

- Friday 4 September for both First and Second Half Season Ticket-holders and Day Prommers and Weekend Pass-holders with five used tickets.

On the Night A limited number of Promming tickets will be available on the Last Night itself (priced £5.00, one per person). No previous ticket purchases are necessary.

Queuing Please note that queuing locations for the Last Night of the Proms may differ from other Proms, but stewards will be on hand to assist you.

Whole Season Ticket-holders are guaranteed entrance until 20 minutes before the concert.

Sleeping Out Please note that it is not necessary for Prommers with Last Night tickets to camp out overnight to secure their preferred standing place inside the Hall. Ticket-holders may add their name to a list which will be held at the Stage Door at the Royal Albert Hall from 4.00pm on Friday 11 September. They then need to return to the queue in list order by 10.00am on Saturday 12 September.

LAST NIGHT OF THE PROMS
2015 Open Ballot Form

One hundred Centre Stalls seats (priced £87.50* each) and 100 Front Circle seats (priced £57.00* each) for the Last Night of the Proms at the Royal Albert Hall will be allocated by Open Ballot. No other ticket purchases are necessary. Only one application (for a maximum of two tickets) may be made per household.
**Booking fees apply (see page 162)*

If you would like to apply for tickets by Open Ballot, please complete the official Open Ballot Form on the back of this slip and send it by post only – to arrive no later than Thursday 2 July – to:

BBC Proms Open Ballot
Box Office
Royal Albert Hall
London SW7 2AP

Note that the Open Ballot application is completely separate from other Proms booking procedures. Envelopes should be clearly addressed to 'BBC Proms Open Ballot' and should contain only this official Open Ballot Form. The Open Ballot takes place on Friday 3 July and successful applicants will be contacted by Thursday 9 July.

This form is also available to download from bbc.co.uk/proms; or call 020 7765 2044 to receive a copy by post.

Please note: if you are successful in the Five-Concert Ballot, you will not be eligible for Last Night tickets via the Open Ballot.

LAST NIGHT OF THE PROMS
2015 Open Ballot Form

Title _____ Initial(s) _____

Surname _____

Address _____

_____

_____

_____

Postcode _____

Country _____

Daytime tel. _____

Evening tel. _____

Mobile tel. _____

Email _____

_____

Please indicate your preferred seating option[‡] (Booking fees apply, see page 162)

☐ I wish to apply for one Centre Stalls ticket (£87.50)

☐ I wish to apply for two Centre Stalls tickets (£175.00)

☐ I wish to apply for one Front Circle ticket (£57.00)

☐ I wish to apply for two Front Circle tickets (£114.00)

[‡] We cannot guarantee that you will be offered tickets in your preferred seating section. You will not be obliged to buy tickets outside your preference, but we regret we cannot offer alternatives.

The personal information given on this form will not be used for any purpose by the BBC or the Royal Albert Hall other than this Ballot.

HOW TO BOOK

General booking opens on Saturday 16 May at 9.00am

Online at bbc.co.uk/proms or www.royalalberthall.com

By telephone on 0845 401 5040[†] (open 9.00am–9.00pm daily). From outside the UK, please call +44 20 7589 8212.

In person at the Royal Albert Hall Box Office

Tickets may also be requested **by post.**

Promming Season Tickets and Weekend Promming Passes are available to purchase online, by phone and in person from 9.00am on Friday 15 May.

Promming: for standing tickets in the Arena and Gallery, priced £5.00, see page 164.

Last Night of the Proms: owing to high demand, special booking arrangements apply to tickets: see page 159.

Proms in the Park: for tickets, see page 157.

Free Prom tickets (Prom 69) are available from Friday 3 July. Please note that there is a limit of four tickets per booking.

ONLINE

Thursday 23 April (2.00pm) to Friday 15 May (midnight)

Use the **Proms Planner**, accessible via bbc.co.uk/proms to create your personal Proms Plan. Once completed, this is ready for you to submit as soon as general booking opens at 9.00am on Saturday 16 May. Submitting your Proms Plan as soon as booking opens speeds up the booking process and means that you may be more successful in securing your preferred tickets for concerts in high demand.

You must submit your Proms Plan in order to make a booking.

If you have any queries about how to use the Proms Planner, call the Royal Albert Hall Box Office on **0845 401 5040**[†].

Should you not wish to use the Proms Planner, you can visit www.royalalberthall.com from 9.00am on Saturday 16 May to book your tickets online.

Please note: it is not possible to book entire boxes online. If you would like to book a full box, call the Box Office on 0845 401 5040[†] from 9.00am on Saturday 16 May.

The 'Select Your Own Seat' option is not available via the Proms Planner or during the first few days that Proms tickets are on sale. You will be allocated the best available places within your chosen seating area. This is to allow as many customers as possible to book as efficiently as possible and to speed up the queue during the period of high demand.

From 9.00am on Saturday 16 May

From 9.00am on Saturday 16 May you can book online at **www.royalalberthall.com**.

Please note that the website will experience very high demand for tickets that day, so you will be placed in a queue. **Please use a secure connection to maintain your place in the queue.**

If you already have a Proms Plan, you can redeem your plan and process your booking. If you do not have a Proms Plan, you can just book online. You will not be able to create a Proms Plan at this time.

A booking fee of 2% of the total value (plus £1.50 per ticket up to a maximum of £20.00 per booking) applies.

BY TELEPHONE

From 9.00am on Saturday 16 May, call the Royal Albert Hall Box Office on **0845 401 5040**[†] (open 9.00am–9.00pm daily). From outside the UK, please call +44 20 7589 8212.

A booking fee of 2% of the total value (plus £1.50 per ticket up to a maximum of £20.00 per booking) applies.

IN PERSON

From 9.00am on Saturday 16 May, visit the Royal Albert Hall Box Office at Door 12. (The Box Office is open 9.00am–9.00pm daily.)

No fees apply to tickets bought in person.

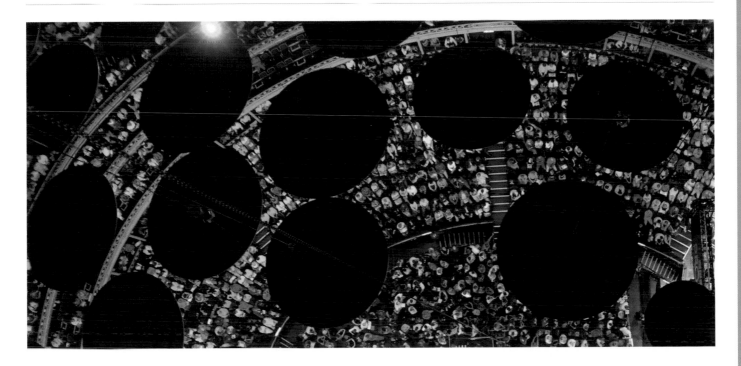

Chris Christodoulou/BBC

BY POST

Please write to BBC Proms, Box Office, Royal Albert Hall, London SW7 2AP with the following details:

- your name, address, telephone number(s) and email address (if applicable)
- the concerts you wish to attend
- number of tickets required
- preferred seating section, preferably with alternatives (see ticket prices and seating plan on page 162)
- applicable discounts (see page 163)
- a cheque, payable to 'Royal Albert Hall' and made out for the maximum amount (including booking fees); or your credit card details, including type of card, name on the card, card number, issue number (Maestro only), start date, expiry date and security code (last three digits on back of Visa/Mastercard or last four digits on front of American Express).

Your details will be held securely. General postal bookings will start to be processed from 9.00am on Saturday 16 May, when booking opens.

Postal bookings for Season Tickets and Weekend Promming Passes must be made separately to other booking requests. Please mark your envelope 'Proms Season Ticket' or 'Weekend Pass' as appropriate. These bookings will be processed from 9.00am on Friday 15 May.

Please note: following the start of booking, all postal applications are processed in random order; not the order in which they are received.

A booking fee of 2% of the total value (plus £1.50 per ticket up to a maximum of £20.00 per booking) applies.

[1] Calls cost up to 5p/min from most landlines (an additional connection fee may also apply). Calls from mobiles may cost considerably more. All calls will be recorded and may be monitored for training and quality-control purposes.

TICKETS SOLD OUT? DON'T GIVE UP!

If you are unable to get tickets for a popular Prom, **keep trying** at bbc.co.uk/proms or the Royal Albert Hall Box Office, as returns often become available. In addition, many boxes and some seats at the Royal Albert Hall are privately owned, and these seats may be returned for general sale in the period leading up to the concert. The Royal Albert Hall does not operate a waiting list.

If you can't sit, stand
Up to 1,350 Promming (standing) places are available in the Arena and Gallery on the day for every Prom at the Royal Albert Hall. If you arrive early enough on the day of the concert, you have a very good chance of getting in. For more details, see page 164.

TICKET PRICES

ROYAL ALBERT HALL

A wide variety of seated tickets is available for all BBC Proms concerts at the Royal Albert Hall, as well as hundreds of Promming (standing) places in the Arena and Gallery. Concerts fall into one of eight price bands, indicated below each concert listing on pages 119–156.

PROMMING

Standing places are available in the Arena and Gallery on the day for £5.00 *(see page 164).* Save by buying a Weekend Promming Pass, or a Whole- or Half-Season Ticket, available from 9.00am on Friday 15 May *(see page 164 for details).*

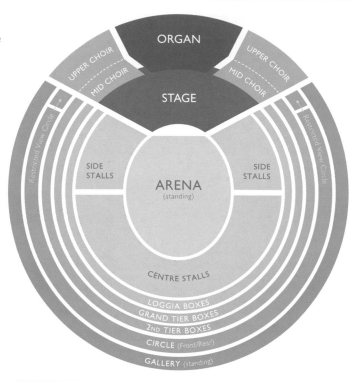

	A	B	C	D	E	F	G	H
Grand Tier Boxes 12 seats, price per seat	£38.00	£46.00	£57.00	£68.00	£24.00	£30.00	£95.00	
	(As most grand tier boxes are privately owned, availability is limited)							
Loggia Boxes 8 seats, price per seat	£34.00	£42.00	£52.00	£62.00	£24.00	£30.00	£90.00	
2nd Tier Boxes 5 seats, price per seat	£30.00	£38.00	£48.00	£58.00	£24.00	£30.00	£86.00	
Centre Stalls	£30.00	£38.00	£48.00	£58.00	£20.00	£25.00	£87.50	
Side Stalls	£26.00	£34.00	£44.00	£54.00	£20.00	£25.00	£85.00	
Mid Choir	£19.00	£23.00	£32.00	£42.00	£20.00	£25.00	£65.00	
Upper Choir	£17.00	£21.00	£27.00	£35.00	£15.00	£20.00	£62.00	
Front Circle	£16.00	£20.00	£23.00	£27.00	£15.00	£20.00	£57.00	
Rear Circle	£12.00	£15.00	£19.00	£24.00	£15.00	£20.00	£47.00	
Restricted View Circle	£7.50	£9.50	£14.00	£18.00	£7.50	£10.00	£27.00	

ALL SEATS £12.00 (UNDER-18s £6.00)

Please note: a booking fee of 2% of the total value (plus £1.50 per ticket up to a maximum of £20.00) applies to all bookings (including Season Tickets and Weekend Promming Passes), other than those made in person at the Royal Albert Hall.

BOOKING INFORMATION

162

BOOK ONLINE AT BBC.CO.UK/PROMS • BY TELEPHONE 0845 401 5040† • IN PERSON AT THE ROYAL ALBERT HALL • BOOKING OPENS 9.00AM ON 16 MAY

TICKET PRICES

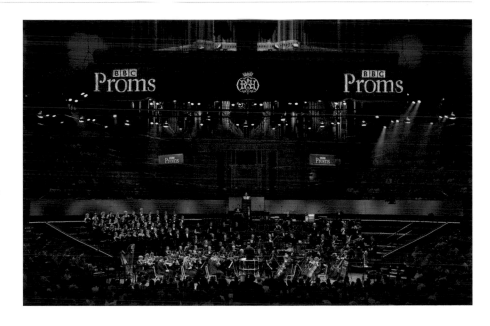

UNDER-18s GO HALF-PRICE

The Proms are a great way to discover live music and we encourage anyone over 5 years old to attend. Tickets for persons aged 18 and under can be purchased at half price in any seating area for all Proms except the Last Night (Prom 76). This discount is available through all booking methods.

GREAT SAVINGS FOR GROUPS

Groups of 10 or more can claim a 10% discount (5% for C-band and D-band concerts) on the price of Centre/Side Stalls or Front/Rear Circle tickets (excluding the Last Night), subject to availability.

Please note: group bookings can only be made by phone or in person at the Royal Albert Hall. To make a group booking, or for more information, call the Group Booking Information Line on 020 7070 4408 (from 9.00am on Saturday 16 May).

TICKETS AND DISCOUNTS FOR DISABLED CONCERT-GOERS

All disabled concert-goers (and one companion) receive a 50% discount on all ticket prices (except Arena and Gallery areas) for concerts at the Royal Albert Hall and Cadogan Hall. To claim this discount, call the **Access Information Line 020 7070 4410** (from Saturday 16 May) if booking by phone. Note that discounts for disabled concert-goers cannot be combined with other ticket offers.

Tickets can also be purchased in person from 9.00am on Saturday 16 May at the Royal Albert Hall. The Box Office has ramped access, an induction loop and drop-down counters.

Ambulant disabled concert-goers (disabled concert-goers who do not use a wheelchair) can also book tickets online from 9.00am on Saturday 16 May and use the online Proms Planner from 2.00pm on Thursday 23 April (see page 160).

Please note that wheelchair spaces cannot be booked online or via the Proms Planner.

CADOGAN HALL (PROMS CHAMBER MUSIC AND PROMS SATURDAY MATINEES)

Stalls: £12.00, Centre Gallery: £10.00, Day Seats: £5.00 (Booking fees apply)

Cadogan Hall tickets are available to book from 9.00am on Saturday 16 May and may be included in the Proms Planner (see page 160).

From Saturday 23 May Cadogan Hall tickets can also be bought from Cadogan Hall (020 7730 4500) as well as from the Royal Albert Hall Box Office. All online and telephone bookings made through the Cadogan Hall Box Office are subject to a fee of £2.50 per transaction.

On the day of the concert, tickets can be bought at Cadogan Hall only – from 10.00am. At least 150 Day Seats (Side Gallery bench seats) are available from 10.00am on the day of the concert. They must be purchased in person, with cash only, and are limited to two tickets per transaction. Save by buying a Proms Chamber Music Series Pass, available from 9.00am on Friday 15 May (see page 165 for details).

Unwanted tickets for all Royal Albert Hall and Cadogan Hall Proms may be exchanged for tickets to other Proms concerts (subject to availability). A fee of £1.00 per ticket will be charged for this service. Call the Royal Albert Hall Box Office (0845 401 5040†) for further details.

BBC PROMS IN THE PARK, HYDE PARK, LONDON SATURDAY 12 SEPTEMBER

All tickets £39.00 (under-3s free)

A booking fee of 2% of the total value (plus £1.50 per ticket up to a maximum of £20.00) applies, unless booking in person at the Royal Albert Hall. See page 157 for details on how to book

HOW TO PROM

WHAT IS PROMMING?

The popular tradition of Promming (standing in the Arena or Gallery areas of the Royal Albert Hall) is central to the unique and informal atmosphere of the BBC Proms.

There are two standing areas: the **Arena**, the large space in the centre of the auditorium directly in front of the stage, which gives you the opportunity to get up close to the performers, and the **Gallery**, running round the top of the Hall, which has an incredible acoustic and a spectacular bird's-eye view of the stage. All spaces are unreserved.

HOW TO PROM

Up to 1,350 standing places are available for each Proms concert at the Royal Albert Hall, although the capacity may vary for each Prom.

Just turn up and, if you are in doubt about where to go, Royal Albert Hall stewards will point you in the right direction. The traditionally low prices allow you to enjoy world-class performances for just £5.00 each (or even less with a Season Ticket or Weekend Promming Pass).

PROMMING SEASON TICKETS AND WEEKEND PROMMING PASSES

Frequent Prommers can save money by purchasing a Season Ticket covering the whole Proms season (including the Last Night), or only the first or second half (ie Proms 1–38 or Proms 39–75, excluding the Last Night), or a Weekend Promming Pass. These allow access to either the Arena or Gallery.

Season Ticket- and Promming Pass-holders benefit from:
- guaranteed entrance (until 20 minutes before each concert)
- great savings – prices can work out at less than £2.65 per concert

Please note: Season Ticket- and Promming Pass-holders arriving at the Hall less than 20 minutes before a concert are not guaranteed entry and should join the back of the Day Queue.

All Promming Season Tickets and Weekend Promming Passes are subject to availability.

Promming Season Tickets and Weekend Promming Passes can be purchased from 9.00am on Friday 15 May. These tickets cannot be planned online via the Proms Planner.

Season Tickets are non-transferable and two passport-sized photographs must be provided before tickets can be issued. ID may be requested upon entry.

Whole-Season Tickets include admission to the Last Night and Half-Season Ticket-holders have special access to a reserved allocation of Last Night Tickets *(see page 159)*.

Weekend Promming Passes must be purchased a minimum of two hours before the start of the first concert covered. Prices vary for each weekend depending on the number of concerts covered – see box below.

Please note: you may purchase a maximum of four passes per weekend.

There is no Weekend Promming Pass covering Proms 75 and 76. Weekend Promming Passes are not valid for concerts at Cadogan Hall.

Pass	Concerts	Price*
Whole Season 17 July – 12 September	Proms 1–76	£200.00
First Half 17 July – 13 August	Proms 1–38	£120.00
Second Half 14 August – 11 September	Proms 39–75	£120.00
Weekend 1	Proms 1–4 *(excluding Proms 2 & 3)*	£9.00
Weekend 2	Proms 10–12	£13.50
Weekend 3	Proms 18–23	£27.00
Weekend 4	Proms 29–33	£22.50
Weekend 5	Proms 39–42	£18.00
Weekend 6	Proms 47–52	£27.00
Weekend 7 *(including Bank Holiday Monday)*	Proms 57–61	£22.50
Weekend 8	Proms 66–68	£13.50

*Booking fees apply (see page 162)

†SEE PAGE 161 FOR CALL-COST INFORMATION

HOW TO PROM

DAY PROMMERS

All remaining Arena and Gallery Promming tickets (priced £5.00) are available on the day and cannot be booked in advance. You must buy your ticket in person and must pay by cash.

The number of Promming tickets available is dependent on capacity and the number of Pass-holders in attendance; however, over 500 Arena and Gallery tickets are usually available, so you always have a good chance of getting in (although early queuing is advisable for the more popular concerts). Please see map (right) for queue locations. Ticket purchases are made as you enter, in queue order, through the relevant doors.

A limited number of Arena tickets will usually be sold to the Day Queue from two and a half hours before each performance (one and a quarter hours before Prom 3). The remaining Day Promming tickets will then be sold from Door 11 (Arena) and Door 10 (Gallery) from 45 minutes before the performance to those queuing.

Tickets for Late Night Proms are available only on the doors, from 30 minutes before the performance. Arena and Gallery tickets are available only at Door 11 and Door 10, not at the Box Office.

QUEUING

Prommers should join the relevant Arena or Gallery Day or Season queue, as shown on the map above. Stewards will be on hand to assist Prommers from 9.00am, for anyone wishing to make an early start.

PROMMING TICKETS FOR WHEELCHAIR-USERS

The Gallery can accomodate up to four wheelchair users. On arrival at the Royal Albert Hall, ask a steward for assistance. Wheelchair-users will be issued a queue number and can leave and return in time for doors opening, at which point all Prommers will enter in queue order. Please note that the Arena is not accessible to wheelchair-users.

PROMMING TICKETS FOR AMBULANT DISABLED CONCERT-GOERS

Up to 25 seats in the Arena and up to 36 seats in the Gallery will be available for

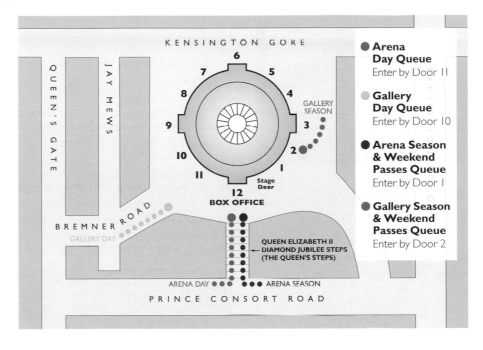

reservation each day by ambulant disabled concert-goers (disabled concert-goers who do not use a wheelchair) who wish to Prom.

On arrival at the Royal Albert Hall, Day Prommers should ask a steward (on duty from 9.00am) for a **Seat Reservation Card**, along with a queue number. You can then leave the queue, returning in time for doors opening (see page 166), at which point all Prommers will enter in queue order. If you secure entry with a Seat Reservation Card, a seat will have been reserved for you.

Please note: a Seat Reservation Card does not guarantee entry.

Season Ticket- and Weekend Promming Pass-holders can also make reservations for an allocation of seats in either the Arena or Gallery. Reservations can be made between 9.00am and 12.00pm on the day of each Prom by telephone only. Please call 020 7070 4410 to request a Seat Reservation Card, which you will need to collect from the Box Office before joining the queue for that day's Prom.

After 12.00pm reservations may be made in person only – please ask a steward for a Seat Reservation Card along with a queue number. You must be in the queue, having collected your seat reservation card, no less than 20 minutes before the concert to guarantee entry, and a seat will have been reserved for you.

PROMS CHAMBER MUSIC SERIES PASS (CADOGAN HALL)

Hear all eight Monday-lunchtime Proms Chamber Music concerts for just £30.00 (plus booking fee, see page 162), with guaranteed entrance to the Side Gallery until 12.50pm (after which Proms Chamber Music Series Pass-holders may be asked to join the Day Queue). Passes can be purchased from 9.00am on Friday 15 May online, by phone or in person at the Royal Albert Hall. Two passport-sized photographs must be provided.

Please note: Proms Chamber Music Series Passes cannot be purchased from Cadogan Hall. Proms Chamber Music Series Passes are not valid for Proms Saturday Matinee concerts at Cadogan Hall and are subject to availability.

ROYAL ALBERT HALL

Kensington Gore, London SW7 2AP *(see map opposite)* www.royalalberthall.com

Royal Albert Hall

FOOD AND DRINK
AT THE ROYAL ALBERT HALL

With a number of restaurants and bars, as well as box catering, there is a wide range of food and drink to enjoy at the Royal Albert Hall, from two and a half hours before each concert.

Booking in advance is recommended. Visit www.royalalberthall.com or call the Box Office on 0845 401 5040† to make your reservation.

BARS are located throughout the building, and open two hours before each concert.

INTERVAL DRINKS are available from any bar and, to beat the queues, you can order before the concert.

RESTAURANTS

Verdi – Italian Kitchen offers casual dining and authentic Italian dishes. (First Floor, Door 12)

Elgar Bar & Grill is relaxed and stylish, offering fantastic flavours from the Josper Grill. Set menu available. (Circle level, Door 9).

The Elgar Room will stay open late on 23 & 30 July, 6, 13, 20 & 27 August and 4 & 9 September for the informal Proms Extra Late events – see bbc.co.uk/proms for more information.

Coda Restaurant offers a two-course set menu, or French-influenced à la carte dishes. (Circle level, Door 3)

Cloudy Bay and Seafood Bar – enjoy light seafood and fish dishes alongside complementary wines. (Second Tier, Door 3)

Berry Bros. & Rudd No. 3 Bar offers a selection of seasonal British dishes, sharing plates and salad bar. (Basement level, Door 1)

Café Bar serves food and drink all day, including cakes, pastries, salads and sandwiches. The bar is open until 11.00pm. (Ground Floor, Door 12)

GRAND TIER, SECOND TIER
AND LOGGIA BOX SEATS

If you have seats in one of the Royal Albert Hall's boxes, you can pre-order food and drinks to be served upon arrival or at the interval. The selection ranges from sandwiches and smoked salmon blinis to hot pies. Visit boxcatering. royalalberthall.com and please order at least 48 hours before the concert that you are attending.

Please note: the consumption of your own food and drink in the Hall is not permitted. Glasses and bottles are permitted in boxes, as part of box catering ordered through "rhubarb".

DOORS OPEN 45 minutes before the start of each concert (two and a half hours for restaurant and bar access) and 30 minutes before each late-night concert. Tickets and passes will be

scanned upon entry. Please have them ready, one per person.

LATECOMERS will not be admitted into the auditorium unless or until there is a suitable break in the performance.

BAGS AND COATS may be left in the cloakrooms at Door 9 (ground level) and at basement level beneath Door 6. A charge of £1.00 per item applies (cloakroom season tickets priced £20.40, including a 40p payment-handling fee, are also available).

Conditions apply – see www.royalalberthall.com. For reasons of safety and comfort, only small bags are permitted in the Arena. If you bring multiple bags, you may only be allowed to take one bag into the Arena for busy concerts.

SECURITY In the interests of safety, bags may be searched upon entry.

CHILDREN UNDER 5 are not allowed in the auditorium out of consideration for both audience and artists, with the exception of the Ten Pieces Proms (Proms 2 & 3).

DRESS CODE Come as you are: there is no dress code at the Proms.

MOBILE PHONES and other electronic devices are distracting to other audience members. Please ensure they are switched off.

THE USE OF CAMERAS, video cameras and recording equipment is strictly forbidden.

STORY OF THE PROMS TOURS
OF THE ROYAL ALBERT HALL

To learn more about the fascinating history of the Proms at the Royal Albert Hall, join this seasonal tour. For bookings and further information, including the Royal Albert Hall's regular Grand Tours, call 0845 401 5045† or visit www.royalalberthall.com. For group bookings of 15 people or more, call 020 7959 0558.

PROMS AND ROYAL ALBERT HALL
GIFTS AND MERCHANDISE

Available inside the porches at Doors 6 and 12 and on the Circle level at Doors 4 and 8.

Chris Christodoulou/BBC (RAH)

GETTING THERE Royal Albert Hall & Royal College of Music

The nearest Tube stations are High Street Kensington (Circle & District Lines) and South Kensington (Piccadilly, Circle & District Lines). These are all a 10- to 15-minute walk from the Hall.

The following buses serve the Royal Albert Hall and Royal College of Music (via Kensington Gore, Queen's Gate, Palace Gate and/or Prince Consort Road): 9/N9, 10 (24-hour service), 49, 52/N52, 70, 360 & 452. Coaches 701 and 702 also serve this area.

Bicycle racks are near Door 11 of the Royal Albert Hall. (Neither the Hall nor the BBC can accept responsibility for items lost or stolen from these racks.) The Royal Albert Hall has limited cloakroom space and may not be able to accept folding bicycles. Santander Cycles hire racks are positioned outside the Royal College of Art, the Royal College of Music and in Cadogan Place.

CAR PARKING

A limited number of parking spaces, priced £10.20 each (including a 20p payment-handling fee), are available from 6.00pm (or two hours before weekend matinée concerts) in the Imperial College car park. Entrances are located on Prince Consort Road (open daily until 7.00pm) and Exhibition Road. Vouchers are only valid until 45 minutes after the end of the concert. These can be booked online, by phone or in person at the Royal Albert Hall from 9.00am on Saturday 16 May, and planned online via the Proms Planner from 2.00pm on Thursday 23 April. Please note that, if you are attending both early-evening and late-night concerts on the same day, only one parking fee is payable.

Please note: the Royal Albert Hall is not within the Congestion Charge zone.

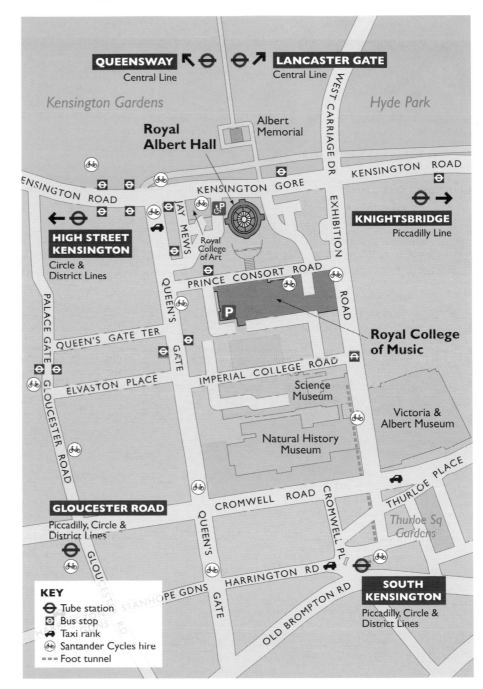

KEY
- Tube station
- Bus stop
- Taxi rank
- Santander Cycles hire
- Foot tunnel

CADOGAN HALL

5 Sloane Terrace, London SW1X 9DQ
www.cadoganhall.com

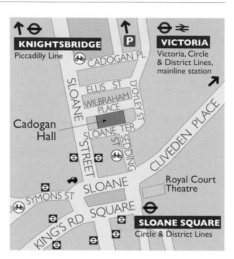

ROYAL COLLEGE OF MUSIC

Prince Consort Road, London SW7 2BS
(see map, page 167) www.rcm.ac.uk

FOOD AND DRINK AT CADOGAN HALL

A selection of savouries, sandwiches and cakes is available from the Oakley Bar and Café. The café and bar will be open at 11.00am for Proms Chamber Music Concerts and at 1.00pm for Proms Saturday Matinees.

Cadogan Hall's bars offer a large selection of champagne, wines, spirits, beer, soft drinks and tea and coffee.

DOORS OPEN at 11.00am for Proms Chamber Music concerts (entrance to the auditorium from 12.30pm) and at 1.00pm for Proms Saturday Matinees (entrance to the auditorium from 2.30pm).

LATECOMERS will not be admitted unless or until there is a suitable break in the music.

BAGS AND COATS may be left in the cloakroom on the lower ground level.

CHILDREN UNDER 5 are not admitted to Cadogan Hall out of consideration for both audience and artists.

DRESS CODE Come as you are: there is no dress code at the Proms.

MOBILE PHONES and other electronic devices are distracting to other audience members. Please ensure they are switched off.

THE USE OF CAMERAS, video cameras and recording equipment is strictly forbidden.

GETTING THERE

The following buses serve Cadogan Hall (via Sloane Street and/or Sloane Square): 11, 19, 22, 137, 170, 211, 319, 360, 452 & C1.

CAR PARKING

Please check street signs for details. Discounted car parking for Cadogan Hall performers and customers is available at the NCP Car Park, Cadogan Place, just 10 minutes' walk from Cadogan Hall. Parking vouchers are available on request from the Box Office.

PROMS EXTRA

Proms Extra pre-concert events will be held in the Amaryllis Fleming Concert Hall at the Royal College of Music.

Proms Extra events are free of charge and unticketed (seating is unreserved), with the exception of the First Night live *In Tune* event on Friday 17 July, for which free tickets will be available from BBC Studio Audiences (bbc.co.uk/tickets or 0370 901 1227[†]). Places must be reserved in advance for all Proms Extra Family Orchestra & Chorus events and most Proms Extra Sing events (visit bbc.co.uk/proms or call 020 7765 0557).

Please note: all Proms Extra events are subject to capacity and we advise arriving early for the more popular events. Latecomers will be admitted but, as many of these events are being recorded for broadcast, you may have to wait until a suitable break. The event stewards will guide you.

Prommers who join the Royal Albert Hall queue before the Proms Extra event should make sure they take a numbered slip from one of the Royal Albert Hall stewards to secure their place back in the queue.

If you have special access requirements, see the Royal College of Music information opposite.

[†] *Standard geographic charges from landlines and mobiles will apply.*

ACCESS AT THE PROMS

ACCESSIBLE PRINT MATERIALS

- Audio CD and Braille versions of this Guide are available in two parts, 'Articles' and 'Concert Listings/Booking Information', priced £3.00 each. For more information and to order, call the RNIB Helpline on 0303 123 9999.

- A text-only large-print version of the Proms Guide is available, priced £6.50.

- Large-print concert programmes can be made available on the night (at the same price as the standard programme) if ordered not less than five working days in advance.

- Complimentary large-print texts and opera librettos (where applicable) can also be made available on the night if ordered in advance.

To order any large-print BBC Proms Guide, programmes or texts, please call 020 7765 3246. The programmes and texts will be left for collection at the Door 6 Information Desk 45 minutes before the start of the concert.

ROYAL ALBERT HALL

The Royal Albert Hall has a silver-level award from the Attitude is Everything Charter of Best Practice. Full information on the facilities offered to disabled concert-goers (including car parking) is available online at www.royalalberthall.com. Information is also available through the Access Information Line, **020 7070 4410** (9.00am–9.00pm daily).

Provision for disabled concert-goers includes:

- 20 spaces bookable for wheelchair-users with adjacent companion spaces. For more details and to book call the Access Information Line.

- Six additional Side Stalls wheelchair spaces available for Proms 58–76.

- Up to 20 seats available in the Arena and Gallery for reservation each day by ambulant disabled Prommers. For details see page 165.

- Ramped access, located at Doors 1, 3, 8, 9 and 12. For arrival by car, taxi, minibus or Dial-a-Ride, the most convenient set-down point is at Door 1, which is at the rear of the building and has ramped access.

- A small car park for disabled concert-goers adjacent to the Royal Albert Hall.

- Public lifts located at Doors 1 and 8 with automatic doors, Braille and tactile numbering and voice announcements.

- Accessibility for wheelchair-users to all bars and restaurants.

Wheelchair spaces and car parking can be booked by calling the Access Information Line or in person at the Royal Albert Hall Box Office. For information on wheelchair spaces available for the Last Night of the Proms via the Five-Concert Ballot, see page 159.

Other services available on request are as follows:

- The Royal Albert Hall auditorium has an infra-red system with a number of personal headsets for use with or without hearing aids. Headsets can be collected on arrival from the Information Desk at Door 6.

- If you have a guide or hearing dog, the best place to sit in the Royal Albert Hall is in a box, where your dog may stay with you. If you prefer to sit elsewhere, stewards will happy to look after your dog while you enjoy the concert.

- Transfer wheelchairs are available for customer use.

- A Royal Albert Hall steward will be happy to read your concert programme to you.

To request any of the above services, please call the Box Office Access line or complete an accessibility request form online at www.royalalberthall.com 48 hours before you attend. Alternatively you can make a request upon arrival at the Information Desk at Door 6 on the Ground Floor, subject to availability.

Following the success of the signed Proms in the past five years, a sign language interpreter will guide you through the Ten Pieces Prom (Prom 3) on Sunday 19 July. Tickets cost £12; disabled concert-goers (plus one companion) receive a 50% discount. Please book your tickets online in the usual way (see page 160). If you require good visibilty of the signer, please choose the 'Stall Signer Area' online when selecting your tickets, or call the Access Information Line and request this area.

CADOGAN HALL

Cadogan Hall has a range of services to assist disabled customers, including:

- Three wheelchair spaces in the Stalls available for advance booking and one space reserved for sale as a day ticket from 10.00am on the day of the concert. Please note: there is no lift access to the Gallery.

- Box Office counter fitted with a loop system.

- An infra-red amplification system in the auditorium. This is not the same as a loop system, so switching your hearing aid to 'T' is not sufficient. You will need to use an amplification aid.

Guide dogs are welcome to access the Hall and auditorium but please contact Cadogan Hall prior to arrival, so that any special arrangements can be made if necessary.

For further information, call 020 7730 4500.

ROYAL COLLEGE OF MUSIC

The Royal College of Music has a range of services to assist disabled customers, including:

- Six spaces for wheelchair-users in the Amaryllis Fleming Concert Hall.

- An induction loop installed in the Amaryllis Fleming Concert Hall.

- Step-free access from Prince Consort Road, located to the left of the main entrance.

If you require further assistance for your visit, contact the Facilities Team on 020 7591 4322 or email facilitiesstaff@rcm.ac.uk.

For further information, call the Royal College of Music on 020 7591 4314.

INDEX OF ARTISTS

Bold italic figures refer to Prom numbers
PCM indicates Proms Chamber Music concerts at Cadogan Hall
PSM indicates Proms Saturday Matinee concerts at Cadogan Hall
*first appearance at a BBC Henry Wood Promenade Concert
†current / ‡former member of BBC Radio 3's New Generation Artists scheme

INDEX OF WORKS

Bold italic figures refer to Prom numbers
PCM *indicates Proms Chamber Music concerts at Cadogan Hall*
PSM *indicates Proms Saturday Matinee concerts at Cadogan Hall*
*first performance at a BBC Henry Wood Promenade Concert

INDEX OF WORKS

MISCELLANEOUS

BBC Proms 2015

Director, BBC Proms 2015 Edward Blakeman
Controller, BBC Radio 3 Alan Davey
Personal Assistant Yvette Pusey

Editor, BBC Radio 3 Emma Bloxham

Proms & Live Events Manager Helen Heslop
Proms & Live Events Producers Alys Jones, Helen White
Proms & Live Events Co-ordinators Lucy Barrie, Julia Vivian

Head of Marketing, Publications and Learning Kate Finch

Communications Manager Maddie Castell
Assistant Publicist David Hopkins
Publicity Assistant Caitlin Benedict

Marketing Manager Emily Caket
Marketing Assistant Lydia Smith

Senior Learning Manager Ellara Wakely
Learning Managers Melanie Fryer, Garth McArthur
Learning Co-ordinators Rebecca Burns, Lauren Creed, Naomi Selwyn
Learning Administrator Catherine Humphrey

Business Co-ordinator Tricia Twigg

BBC Music Library Natalie Dewar (Senior Media Manager), David Vivian Russell (Team Leader), Tim Auvache, Anne Butcher, Rachel Davis, Deborah Fether, Emily Field, Raymond Howden, Alison John, Michael Jones, Emma McDonald, Richard Malton, Claire Martin, Liam Taylor West, Paul Turner

Head of Music Television (London) Mark Cooper
Executive Producer, Music Television Francesca Kemp
Series Production Manager Michael Ledger

Business Affairs Executives Karl Batterbee, Sarah Bredl-Jones, Penelope Davies, Sue Dickson, Hilary Dodds, Annie Kelly, Simon Launchbury, Pamela Wise

Editor, BBC Proms, Performing Groups and Radio 3 Multiplatform Steve Bowbrick
Editorial Lead, BBC Proms Multiplatform Andrew Downs

BBC PROMS GUIDE 2015

Publications Editor Laura Davis
Editor Edward Bhesania
Sub-Editor Úna-Frances Clarke
Publications Designer Joanna Robbins
Junior Publications Designer Niamh Richardson
Publications Assistant Francesca Geach

Published by BBC Proms Publications
Room 1045, Broadcasting House, London W1A 1AA

Cover illustration Justin Krietermeyer/Premm Design/Red Bee Media
RAH photography by Simon Keats

Distributed by BBC Books, an imprint of Ebury Publishing, a Random House Group Company, 20 Vauxhall Bridge Road, London SW1V 2SA
Advertising John Good Ltd, Oxford (01869 332150)
Printed by APS Group. APS Group holds ISO 14001 environmental management, FSC and PEFC accreditations

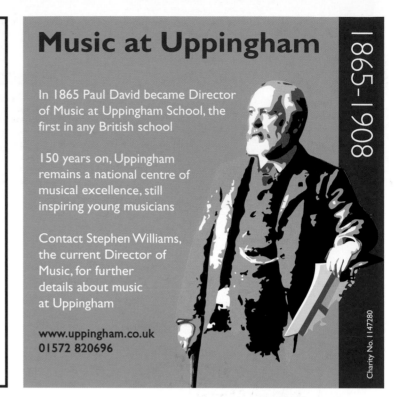